# *How deep is th*

-An autobiography about navig
them. The metaphor is apt for livir̠ ̠ ̠ ̠.

Ian Clarke is self-deprecating about himself, his ambitions and achievements. The stories which illustrate his themes are on an epic scale, though they mostly concern very ordinary people. They endure conditions, which prompt 'Docta' to reflect on the world into which he pitched himself, his wife and children, more than twenty years ago, and the purpose he found in responding to the needs and the scarcities he found all around.

Each time he sensed he was getting into a rut – another metaphor from the roads – he determined to get himself out of it (though he described the ruts, bizarrely, as comfort zones) and set about a new challenge. He finds his meaning and his hope not in a suburban United Kingdom, but in Uganda. He sank all he had into developing his chosen country.

The achievements of the doctor who taught himself building in order to establish his first rural clinic are truly staggering. But physical buildings are only part of it. Building, or re-building people, and developing young people were what he did most.

Why is it that we hear so little from Africans about their own contemporary societies, and have so few insights from them ? This is memoir which tells us so much, in plain terms, about how things are. *How deep is this pothole?* is a resource for our times: less than literature, more than journalism, and candid. Ian Clarke has naturally much to say about how to develop things, but highlights the limitations of aid. Ian is frank about the problems he encounters in trying to make things work better – a poor work ethic, corruption, nepotism, superstition. But he is more critical of western official aid for its incompetence of approach and for its relative failure to make the difference which, on the scale of its investment, it should have.

When the Millennium Development Goals are under such scrutiny, the private enterprise approach commands attention for its effectiveness, its scalability, its sustainability and its transparency.

Some of Ian Clarke's reflections on politics and policy will attract criticism. But they go further in rigour and candour than most contemporary writing in Uganda. Why is that? Why is much African writing on such matters so diminished by deference? This book is rendered even more valuable by its being outstanding in a field which is under-populated.

*How deep is this pothole?* is a compendium of case studies of a country's suffering, its resurgence, and of a foreigner's affinity with people who have an immense capacity for putting up with abuse of every kind and coming back. At independence, observers thought Uganda, its talented people and developed education system would make them the stars of Africa. Its rulers wrecked the country's renowned university and removed many of its most able heads. Now it is resurgent. I served in both Kenya and Uganda, and used to feel that if I needed surgery, I'd prefer to be in Nairobi but if I wanted counselling, I'd go to Kampala. Now, I think Kampala offers medical expertise for which it was famous long ago; while Ugandans still provide solace, style and comfort for those far less afflicted than themselves.

Ian Clarke has helped make a difference and contributed to that process of resurgence and restoration. His book tells the story without bombast or complaint.

*Sir Edward Clay*
*(High Commissioner in Uganda, 1993 – 7; non-resident Ambassador to Rwanda and Burundi during part of that period. High Commissioner in Kenya, 2001 – 5)*
*29 September 2010*

2

# How deep is this pothole?

### An Irish Doctor seeks to establish an alternative model for the development of healthcare in Uganda

### Dr Ian Clarke

Published 2010

Printed in the United Kingdom


ISBN 978-1-905991-61-7


*PO Box 8177*
*Kampala, Uganda*

*To the young people of Uganda -*
*the hope for its future*

# Contents

## Acknowledgements

Since this book is the story of my life there are so many people to whom I owe a debt of gratitude for the role they have played-but that would be a book in itself. However, the first on my list is my wife, Robbie, who is not only the person who has been prepared to follow me half way round the world, but she has encouraged and cheered me on because of her own vision and commitment. As an added bonus, her skills as an English teacher were also put to good use in editing this book.

I also wish to thank my children Sean, Michael and Lauren who have put up with the many changes that have been thrust upon them throughout their lives, without complaint – well not much.

To my extended family, especially Rose: you have made us so proud and brought us much joy throughout the years.

To the nurses and doctors of Belfast City Hospital Oncology department: you gave me my life back.

To both my mother and Robbie's mum who loved and supported us until their death.

To my brother, Ken, for his generosity, and my sisters, Margaret and Jenny, who have lent their support throughout the years.

To Pastor Livingstone Bataganya who was the person who welcomed us to Luweero and worked tirelessly to bring health and healing to his flock.

To all the staff of Kiwoko Hospital and CMSI who made Kiwoko Hospital come into being and have continued to grow and develop it years after my departure.

To the government of Uganda who first accepted me as a guest in Uganda and then naturalised me as a citizen.

To all the Ugandans who have not only worked with me in IMG to make the dream a reality, but have become my dear friends.

Finally, to Uganda itself which has given me more than I could ever give in return.

# Prologue

I was in the operating theatre watching open heart surgery take place. Open Heart surgery is now commonplace in the developed world, but this was the first time in Uganda. As I surveyed the theatre crawling with activity, I had a sense of nervousness that everything would go according to plan and pride that the first open heart surgery to take place in Uganda was being carried out in the hospital which I had founded.

Not only was the surgery the culmination of months of preparation, it was the culmination of many years of work to reach the point where all the necessary elements for such a high level procedure were in place. Apart from the cardiac surgeon and the perfusion technician, the rest of the team were Ugandan – my own hospital staff. This was no large visiting team of experts who had jetted in from America, but these were our own people.

I thought back to twenty years earlier, when I originally came to Uganda and held my first clinic – under a tree in Luweero. From there we progressed to the village church, which smelled strongly of bats, where I sat on a three-legged stool and examined patients on a mat on the floor. Then there was the building of a maternity centre, which became a health-centre, which became a mission hospital. Then my move to Kampala to start all over again with a small private clinic, the recurrence of cancer as I tried to renovate a dilapidated building into a hospital, the birth of the first thirty bed International Hospital and our Health Management Organisation, IAA Healthcare. Then the vision to build a new purpose built hospital, which entailed finding a suitable piece of land and negotiating a bank loan.

I could see myself looking over the four and a half acre green field site and hiring a bulldozer to level the plot. There were trips to South Africa to meet the architects, the hiring of masons and porters to start the project. I remembered talking to the first group of masons, telling them that they would look back and take pride in this project, then watching as the foundations were dug and the concrete poured, going to the site every day, as the building rose out of the ground.

There were visits from various doctors whom I showed round, pointing out the shell for theatre, ICU or the wards. Then there was the opening of the first phase and the struggle to get equipment and complete the building. There was also scrutiny and criticism if someone was not satisfied with the service we were providing. There was the struggle for staff to buy into the vision of attaining international standards. Then the satisfaction of seeing an ICU (intensive care unit) come into being and the theatre staff gain a high level of proficiency.

As I walked into the theatre and saw everything working like a well oiled machine, I knew personally all that it had taken to reach this point. As I watched the operation progress, I looked at the theatre lights and remembered exactly where I had bought them, I knew each staff member, where they had come from and how we had trained and prepared them for this day. I even knew how much the flooring had cost per square metre and how it had been laid. And in that moment of watching the inside of an open heart – staring into the hole which was about to be repaired, I felt that perhaps the struggle might be finally paying off.

I did not set foot on the African continent until I was in my thirties. At that stage in life I was an established GP in Northern Ireland, the classic settled middle-class doctor, with three children at prep schools, a mortgage and a wife – though not necessarily in that particular order. I also had a deep seated restlessness. Perhaps it was the beginnings of a midlife crisis, but the question at the back of my mind was – is this it? Is this all that life has for me? The process of wrestling with this question ultimately led me to resign my job as a GP and relocate with the wife and kids to a village in Uganda.

When it comes to Africa and how we can help, there is often a stereotype in people's minds, fed by images of brave self-sacrificing aid workers, who have left home comforts to toil in the heart of the African bush. These are the images which make people send donations to Oxfam and other aid agencies; it all seems somewhat heroic and worthy of support. When I came to Uganda I probably fitted the stereotype; I was the Irish missionary doctor working in the bush. For the first time in my life I was a 'hero' and people pulled out their cheque books to support the work we were doing. There was nothing wrong with this perception; I had made sacrifices to come to Africa – though not nearly as many as my wife. We had given up the middle class lifestyle in the suburbs, we were living and working in the bush in very basic conditions, and we did save lives.

But was that the only way to develop Africa? And besides, I was the one who had gained most from my endeavours; I could have lived the rest of my life as a mediocre, grumpy GP, but I was able to break the mould and do something which I believed in and enjoyed. But was development work all about aid agencies, non-governmental organization, civil society organizations, bi-lateral aid, multi-lateral donors or mission hospitals? Everyone wanted to know how we could rid the world of poverty, how we would cleanse our television screens of the unending scenes of people dying in poor countries and particularly on the African continent.

I don't claim to have the answers, but perhaps I have a different perspective, drawn from years of living and working in Uganda. I am no longer a missionary, I am not even an aid worker and I have never worked for a diplomatic mission. I don't receive a salary from any outside organization, though I pay hundreds of salaries; I generally don't receive grants or donations and I don't represent anyone except myself. I am just a private citizen, living in Uganda, trying to make a living and make a difference. Africa can no longer exist on aid and hand-outs, and much of the money which comes into developing countries does not produce results, while some of it makes the situation worse by increasing the opportunities for corruption. I believe that long term sustainable development will come through the growth of a healthy private sector which will produce measurable results in a competitive marketplace.

When I hear diplomats or foreign policy experts expound on the evils of African governments or corruption, I often feel that they are pigeonholing and categorizing Africans according to their own perspective which is never a complete picture. I may not have the whole picture either; I am just an Irishman living in Uganda, but I have chosen to settle in this country and to risk my own money and future. This does not make me blind to the evils which I see around me or to the risks of living in an African country – far from it – but this is my adopted country, and I want to find solutions, not just point out what ails it.

This story of an Irishman in Uganda may give you a window into the development of Uganda over the past two decades and our experiences along the journey we have taken.

*In some cases names have been changed to protect the identity of the person.*

14

# An exploratory trip

Born in South Armagh, an area well known for the activities of the Irish Republican Army, our family moved to the more peaceful and fertile County Antrim when I was eight, but no sooner had we settled on a farm than my father died. I was the oldest boy in the family and was thus expected to shoulder my share of work, which was mainly to do with raising chickens; hence, there were days when I missed school due to the intense pressures of being one of Ireland's youngest chicken farmers.

It was not that I lacked commitment to my school work, but one must realise that there are other priorities in a chicken farmer's life

'Where is Ian today?' the science teacher asked.

'He is off, catching chickens,' one of my schoolmates helpfully replied. This was not the usual reason for her students failing to attend class and the teacher, being from the city, had not previously given any consideration to the duties which a chicken farm-boy might have to shoulder. On any occasion, thereafter, when I was not seen in her class, she would remark,

'I suppose he is catching chickens.'

When the chickens reached maturity, they were sent to become 'layers', meaning that they laid eggs for the rest of their lives, and since they were not in cages but roamed in chicken houses on what was termed 'deep litter' (loosely meaning chicken shit mixed with sawdust), we had to round them up for the next season of their lives. The chickens were not very keen on this turn of events and made valiant efforts to escape their destiny, so my early childhood memories are interwoven with images of chasing chickens, though I am sure that I did other worthwhile activities. Perhaps it was this Northern Irish work ethic which instilled a sense of responsibility in me at a very young age, but I realised that there must be more to life than chickens and I set my sights on wider horizons.

'What do you want to do when you grow up?' was a question which was frequently put to me as a boy who had more important things to think about at that moment.

'I dunno,' I would reply, like every other well focused child. But these weighty career decisions were being pushed upon me, and on studying the options, I decided that I had only a limited number of choices. I was hopeless at science, except for biology. I could continue to be a farmer, but I was already finding this a bit limiting. What could I do using biology and which would give me a portable profession? I decided I wanted to be a doctor since I was good at human anatomy, and I saw medicine as my escape from farming.

I may not have wanted to be tied down to the land, but before I had even graduated from medical school, I had tied the knot in marriage with a beautiful dark haired, green eyed teacher. Robbie was not only beautiful, but had that faraway wistful look in her eyes which I found enchanting. I met her on several occasions over a period of years and fell in love with the girl with the wistful look. I later discovered that the faraway look was because she was short-sighted!

After graduating in medicine, we got swallowed up in middleclass life – not through any conscious decision; rather it was life that happens to people automatically. I was working as a junior hospital doctor when I got a call from a senior general practitioner who was running a successful practice.

'My practice is getting too large for one person, would you like to join me as a partner?'

I was flattered that he would even consider me, since I was barely out of medical school, but despite this he made me an excellent offer, so I found myself working as a GP, and it looked like the pattern of my life was set for the next thirty years. However, within a few years, my restless spirit started questioning the inevitability of it all. Fortunately, or perhaps

16

unfortunately for her, since the upheaval may have been slightly more than she bargained for, Robbie was also asking the same questions.

As a doctor I wanted to be engaged in work where I felt useful, and I was not particularly satisfied with the challenges I faced as a GP in Northern Ireland, even though we were financially comfortable. At the time, stories of the AIDS epidemic in Africa were beginning to emerge and, of course, there were the usual pictures of wars and famines which had become our staple diet on TV and formed one's perceptions of that continent. Neither of us had ever been to any part of Africa, but we thought that it was a place where we could put our professional skills to work and practise our Christian faith in a tangible way.

'Why don't I make a short exploratory trip to Africa to ascertain the needs for the services of a doctor and a teacher?' I suggested. But where exactly to go? We might have been ill informed, but at least we knew that Africa was not one country; it was a vast diverse continent, and we had to choose which country we would like to work in.

Our desire to go to Africa was possibly naïve. One doesn't just up and leave all one's commitments and go to Africa to help out, and realistically do-gooders can sometimes do more harm than good. I don't know if we were classic do-gooders; I was, after all, a doctor and could make a difference professionally, but at that point we had to admit that we barely knew any black people since Northern Ireland was not exactly a favourite destination for immigrants, and we knew little about the African continent. When we hinted to friends and acquaintances that we were thinking of shifting to Africa, people's reactions were varied. One of my colleagues told me categorically, 'You cannot just go to Africa, you have responsibilities here; you have children and a mortgage to think of.'

17

It was true that indeed we did have progeny by this time – three children, ages eight, nine and eleven – and a mortgage. But despite this well meaning advice, I thought that the best way to explore our desire to use our skills was not just to talk about it, but to do something. I was of that well known school of philosophy – act first, and if all else fails, read the instructions. This rather simple and considered philosophy of life has stood me in good stead over the years and explains many of the subsequent situations I found myself in.

At this time we were heavily involved in the local church and, unexpectedly, there was an opportunity to fulfil my wish to travel to Africa through tagging along with a group of pastors who were visiting a church in Uganda. It was not the ideal medical trip, but at least I would be with some familiar faces. Uganda was famous for several things: Idi Amin, the expulsion of the Asians and, to those of us in the medical community, it was the first African country which had reported cases of AIDS. It was not the most popular tourist destination, since even after Amin was ousted there had been continued civil war. Then just a few months previously, Yoweri Museveni and his National Resistance Army had marched into Kampala, with their motley crew of youngsters and seasoned veterans, and taken power. It appeared that I had an opportunity to travel to Africa and at this point I did not really have a strong preference as to which country, since I was equally ignorant about them all. Not knowing a great deal of the history of Uganda, I got a quick briefing of recent events: Idi Amin had been ousted in the late seventies, but after Amin, Uganda had another civil war, which eventually finished with the rebels taking power in 1986. When I arrived in 1987 the country was largely at peace under the rule of the National Resistance Movement.

Driving from Entebbe to Kampala, there were soldiers and checkpoints along the roads, but being from Belfast this was no big deal, since we were used to Saracen army cars on the streets. I had a classic moment when I was riding on a *matatu* (a minibus used as a taxi). The person beside me was reading the book *Trinity* by Leon Uris, which is set in Ireland. I introduced myself and told him I was from Ireland.

'Oh,' he said, 'you have come to escape the bombs?'

Well, I hadn't quite thought of it like that and there appeared to be more gunfire in Kampala than in Belfast, but I suppose he had a point. As we were stopped by the soldiers at the various check-points, they would rummage through our belongings and remark, 'Have you anything good for me?'

They were not threatening, apart from having AK 47s slung over their shoulders, and if one just joked with them, there was no serious coercion; they were simply trying their luck. This was in sharp contrast to previous regimes where soldiers had demanded payment to cross every checkpoint and many had paid with their lives.

I was invited to join a Ugandan doctor who was working at a mission hospital, and I think it was that experience which really touched and impacted me. There was a shortage of everything, particularly rubber gloves, so they were re-sterilising the gloves by boiling them. This is practically impossible because if you boil rubber it softens and becomes sticky. Stephen would spend as much time getting into the sticky re-sterilised rubber gloves as he would in carrying out the surgical procedure. I could not imagine, coming from working in the National Health Service, anyone having to re-use rubber gloves. One of the procedures which he carried out in the outpatient department was a supra-pubic tap, where he punctured a hole in the bladder through the abdomen and inserted a catheter to relieve acute retention of urine. I had never seen this done before, as when my patients had acute retention, I could simply pass a catheter through the correct route. However, these patients had bad strictures of the urethra from repeated gonorrhoea, such that it was impossible to pass the tube through the usual route and more innovative exits had to be found.

The waiting area in the outpatient department was full of patients and I had to elbow my way through the crowd in order to get through to the consultation room. (I was back at that same hospital years later and not much had changed in terms of the structure and buildings, except that the crowds had gone because there were more medical facilities.)

Twenty years ago it was mainly the mission hospitals which kept the medical services of the county working. The British professors who had been running Mulago, the main government hospital, left during the Amin era and many of the top Ugandan doctors also fled when random acts of brutality became commonplace, such as Amin's men entering theatre and dragging off a doctor during surgery. Those doctors who remained survived as best they could as medical supplies ran out and as their pay progressively shrank. Many doctors adopted the habit of running small private clinics downtown in order to make ends meet.

This fragmentation of the medical profession meant that the country fell behind in modern medical practices compared to its neighbour, Kenya, which did not suffer such civil disruption. Many of the gaps were filled by mission hospitals, often 'manned', so to speak, by Sisters who had been in Uganda for thirty or forty years. I knew one sister who was a skilled surgeon, while her colleague was an excellent paediatrician and sonographer. They ran one of the best hospitals in Kampala and were heavily involved in caring for the victims of the AIDS epidemic, though it was a pity that they were not allowed to advocate condoms or marriage planning since they were Catholic. They were doing such a great job in caring for people with AIDS that it was rather a jarring contradiction that they could not advocate an effective method of prevention.

'Would you like to visit the Luweero Triangle?' I was asked by my host.

'What is the Luweero Triangle?' was my natural reply. I had never heard of such a place, and as far as I was concerned, it could be Lake Victoria's equivalent of the Bermuda Triangle.

'It is known as "the killing fields of Africa," I was informed. 'It is a triangular region, north of Kampala where the last civil war was fought between Museveni and the Obote regime and they reckon around 300 - 500,000 people were killed in that conflict.'

It might not have had the drawing power of the normal type of tourist attraction, like visiting the mountain gorillas, but I had a natural curiosity, so we were off to the Luweero Triangle. This region lay only fifty kilometres from Kampala, but the vegetation, swamps and tall elephant grass had made it an ideal territory for the guerrilla war which raged from 1981 to 1986. We bumped along a very potholed road in a small Suzuki jeep for about two and a half hours, like biscuits rattling round a tin, until we reached a partially destroyed farmhouse deep in the bush. This area had been ravaged by the war and had largely been a no-go area to civilians, so that even those living in Kampala had not appreciated the scale of the killing. I found myself examining hundreds of skulls and bones which were the remains of those who had been massacred and not yet buried. Those who had survived desperately needed medical help, and if I was serious in my desire to be useful as a doctor, I had come to the right place since there was absolutely no other medical expertise in the whole area.

The local people told me many stories of atrocities that had been carried out during the war. Milton Obote was Uganda's first Prime Minister after independence, but during his tenure there was a power struggle between him and the King of Buganda who was forced to flee the country, while Obote abrogated the position of President for himself. However, when

21

he was out of the country at a conference, the tables were turned and he was deposed by his own army commander, Idi Amin, who took over in a bloodless coup. Initially, the population was delighted to be rid of Obote because of the repression for which he was responsible, but the euphoria did not last long, as killings and disappearances soon became the order of the day. Amin eliminated anyone whom he felt was a threat and it was commonplace to see bodies floating down the Nile, or find they had been disposed of in Mabira Forest. He also killed many prominent people, including Archbishop Janani Luwum and the Attorney General, who had dared to reverse one of his decisions.

Amin managed to hold on to power for seven years, gradually impoverishing the country, until he made the miscalculation of seizing a disputed area of land between Uganda and Tanzania. The Tanzanians invaded, and Amin promptly fled north, eventually ending up in exile in Saudi Arabia, where he lived happily ever after until he died of old age in 2003. After the ousting of Amin there was an interim government, and elections which resulted in Obote's party being re-elected, but the results were widely disputed and Yoweri Museveni, who was the Minister of Defence in the interim government, refused to accept the results. He retreated to the bush with twenty-seven men, raided a military barracks to obtain a supply of arms and thus commenced another bloody civil war, during which tens of thousands more people were killed.

By the time we arrived in 1987, this war was over, but it had left behind deep seated tribal animosity. Obote was from the Langi tribe and government troops had been made up of Acholi and Langi soldiers – both tribes from the north. When people of Luweero told us how their friends and relatives had been tortured and murdered, they would not say that a soldier had killed them, they would tell us that an Acholi had murdered them. This deep seated animosity would continue to dog

Uganda's history for many years. After Museveni took power, the remnants of Obote's regime fled north, causing continued instability, and eventually some of these disillusioned elements joined another rebel movement known as the Lord's Resistance Army (LRA), led by a quasi-religious leader, Joseph Kony. The LRA caused endless suffering in the north of Uganda over the next twenty years, and the enmity between the northern and southern tribes led to the feeling that the northerners were being deliberately punished for what had happened in Luweero. There was probably some truth behind this sentiment, though one could not say that it was an institutionalized policy.

In 1987 it was difficult to say which previous government had been the worst. Amin was a bloodthirsty killer who personally tortured and killed hundreds of people, mainly to eliminate any threat to his power base either within the army or politically. During this time he maintained an affable, avuncular exterior and entertained the world with his quirky remarks and opinions. Meanwhile, behind the jocular exterior, he was cold-bloodedly eliminating anyone perceived as a threat. The subsequent period, when Milton Obote was again in power, was not much better, when thousands more Ugandans perished. This war had ended just before my visit, and peace reigned, at least in the south, even though gunshots were commonplace at night.

Despite Uganda's troubled history, there was something about the place which drew me to it. I wandered down the unpaved red dirt roads, with children calling after me, *'Mzungu, mzungu'* (white Man). There were not many whites in Uganda at that time, so the sight of one provoked curiosity and interest, but I felt at home and did not mind the children chanting, 'How are you *mzungu*? How are you *mzungu*?'

It was a strange experience to be the only white face among a sea of black, but people were welcoming, and despite the fact that a war had just ended, I felt completely safe – I was

23

probably safer than in South Armagh. People were curious, but were neither hostile nor unfriendly, and there seemed to be a ready acceptance of this particular white man.

# Luweero

A year later I arrived back in Luweero, this time complete with wife and three children, Sean, Michael and Lauren. We may have been thought of as naïve by those who had told me that my place was in middleclass suburbia, but we just showed up and started work – I as a doctor and Robbie teaching our children and managing the family. We did happen to be living and working in the middle of the African bush, which was pretty far removed from our experience in Bangor, but we were still the same people with that Northern Irish work ethic, and we simply got on with life in a different environment. Of course life was not easy, particularly for Robbie, since our circumstances were so basic and far removed from what we had known, but the children didn't bat an eyelid about the change and, personally, I felt completely at home. Robbie was in culture shock, and the first night she cuddled up to me in the African pitch-darkness and whispered, 'Two years Ian, two years, I will never manage this for two years.'

Little did she know it, but we were destined to spend much more than two years in this foreign land.

Our feelings at that point were diametrically opposite: I felt that I had come home, while she felt that she was in an alien environment far from any familiar social network or any home comforts. But over the years Robbie's feelings changed, and she also came to love Uganda and wondered how she would live anywhere else.

Since we were the first *bazungu* (white people) to come to this post-war area, the word quickly went round the jungle drums that a white doctor had taken up residence, and patients started arriving every day before dawn. I had completed a diploma in tropical medicine at the Liverpool School of Hygiene and Tropical Medicine, so I knew about primary healthcare and like all good development workers I had also read the book *The Barefoot Doctor,* and wished to train village health workers to work in the community. I set about recruiting and training a dozen villagers, but quickly realised that, although these health workers could sensitise the community about good health and hygiene practices, I was the only professionally trained medical person who could treat the sick. Since this was obviously a bit of an imbalance of labour, and I felt that the basics of medicine were not that difficult, I trained some of the health workers to administer rudimentary treatments.

Within a few weeks we were doing clinics with three hundred people attending – so the waiting times were even longer than in the UK National Health Service. The clinics were very basic, but the people waited anyway. Some of them waited because they were sick and some waited just in case they might get sick when I was not around – they were definitely the most difficult to treat.

I had arrived in Luweero with a tin trunk of donated drugs – mostly multivitamins and de-worming pills – my doctor's bag and little else, and I suppose one could legitimately question what I thought I would accomplish with such limited resources. I was not part of some well funded aid agency which was going to pour in resources to rebuild this war-torn area. But I reasoned that since no-one else was doing anything, whatever we did should be better than nothing. I had no plan, except the rather esoteric theories I had picked up at the Liverpool School of Tropical Medicine.

One of the people who came to my aid was a girl called Janet Kalungi who had been placed in our parish as a development worker by World Vision. Janet became my guide and translator. We would both sit on three-legged stools as I took the history of the patient and then I would ask the patient to lie down on a straw mat on the ground and examine him. If medication was needed, I would dispense it from my tin box of drugs. Years later, Janet was conducting a seminar for World

26

Vision; the people she was addressing wished to start a hospital in their area and they hung on Janet's every word since she had first-hand experience of getting such a project going.

'How do we get started?' they asked

'All you need to start a hospital,' she told them, 'are two three-legged stools and a mat.' They looked at her as if she was mad, but she went on to explain: 'When Dr Clarke came to Luweero we had very little, but we did what we could with what we had, and from those small beginnings we went on to build a hospital.'

I don't think that particular group was very impressed by Janet's ideas for a start-up medical project – they had expected something more substantive. It was my innate tendency to optimism which got me through such situations since I did not over-analyse the possible of the futility of what I was doing and simply concerned myself with the immediate needs around me.

Within a few months I had a team of health workers, including some professional nurses from both Uganda and abroad, and we were carrying out regular clinics and outreaches in the surrounding villages, providing health education and immunisations. But our main problem was that we had no referral centre. It was all very well to train health workers to pick up risk factors, but if there was no local hospital to intervene, one was not going to change the outcome. We found ourselves making emergency trips to Kampala hospitals, ferrying very sick patients and mothers in obstructed labour to have caesarean sections. These excursions, sometimes in the dead of night, were through an area where random killings and torture had been the order of the day no more than two years previously, but we travelled in blissful ignorance and, thankfully, were left unmolested.

It soon became obvious that we needed to build a basic health facility to treat patients and carry out deliveries. It was also evident that there was a serious problem with TB and that

27

the underlying factor for this resurgence was HIV. In the early eighties Uganda had identified a disease known as 'slim' where people just wasted away; then 'slim' was shown to be AIDS, which had first been diagnosed in the gay community in California. The decrease in the person's immunity through HIV allowed the reactivation of dormant TB, which was often the disease that actually killed them. The epidemic of HIV was causing another epidemic of TB.

We had been sponsored by C.M.S.I., Church Mission Society Ireland, an Anglican mission, but they did not have a budget for programme costs, and their mandate was simply to sponsor people to support grassroots initiatives associated with the Church. But we needed resources, we needed a clinic; we needed drugs and money to run a programme. This prompted us to write letters to friends and churches back home recounting our experiences, which became the focus for fundraising efforts. Tragically, the main seed money came through the death of a close friend, Barbara Kelly, the wife of Dr John Kelly, a medical doctor turned pastor of the church to which we belonged in Northern Ireland. Within six months of arriving in Luweero, John and Barbara came to visit – a great morale boost for us – but ten days after their return home, Barbara died suddenly from a ruptured aneurysm. Since her visit to Luweero was the last thing she had done before she died, John and the family asked friends to donate money to the building of a clinic in Luweero. This clinic was initially to cater for the needs of TB patients, but within a few months it became a health centre, treating a myriad of conditions.

Living in Luweero was a fairly intense experience for both Robbie and me – in her case because it was far removed from the kind of suburban existence with which she was familiar. She had moved from a large family house, situated on the seafront, to a small part of a Ugandan farmhouse in the middle of a banana plantation. We lived upstairs in this partially rehabilitated house, which also had a number of other occupants, in particular rats and bats. The bats screeched and scraped in the walls and the rats made midnight forays in search of food. We did have a WC, which functioned by recycling: we flushed by pouring used dishwater down the toilet – so we were way ahead in terms of eco-solutions. In these water scarce situations there was also the maxim, 'If it is yellow let it mellow; if it is brown flush it down.'

We also had a fridge, which ran on paraffin and a gas cooker. All in all, we had our home comforts, though mice tended to take up residence in the insulation of the cooker and rats had midnight swims in the toilet. I was awakened one evening by splashing noises from the toilet and went to explore, to find a rat swimming round the bowl. Not knowing how to help it out of there, I just put the seat down and put a brick on it until I could get some help in the morning.

For the following five years we worked in Luweero, and although our first clinic was held under a tree, we rapidly progressed to holding clinics in the church vestibule, then to a one roomed clinic and subsequently to the health-centre, built from the Barbara Kelly Memorial Fund. Over the next several years the health centre developed into a hospital; all of this was driven by the immense medical needs which we found around us. During this time we continued to train community health-workers and run outreach clinics in the surrounding villages. The funding for the work came from various sources: friends and churches, aid agencies and philanthropists, and part of our role involved writing letters and drumming up support (we did not have the ubiquitous e-mail at that time).

We did not come with a grand plan or grand design; we were witnessing avoidable death, and our response was to do something by developing a facility and programmes to meet the needs. And although we did put long hours into this work, this was not the most critical aspect; it was that we lived among the people and were able to assess the needs on the

29

ground. We then set out to meet those needs and sensitise others as to how they could help in the most appropriate way.

# Cultural values

My work at Kiwoko involved general oversight of the hospital, running clinics, training local health workers and conducting health education in the local community. As part of the community health programme, we encouraged family planning since many of the village women had eight to twelve children. During this process I encountered many cultural traditions and values which made family planning unpopular, even though Uganda has one of the highest birth rates in the world. This situation was further exacerbated by some dim-witted politicians who encouraged their constituents to have more children, with the logic: 'It is a big land, there is enough space.'

Such advice was driven by the belief that more children meant more honour, more family members to look after you in your old age, and a larger population would make the nation stronger. This view was fine if one was breeding rabbits, but with human-beings there were other factors to take into account, such as resources available for education, the availability of employment, and the leadership and systems in place which would produce responsible citizens. The alternative was to produce more children who had no real opportunities in life and with little to do but watch the grass grow.

Interestingly, family planning was usually opposed by the men, not the women. Husbands did not want their wives to stop having children, even if they had already gone through numerous pregnancies.

'How many children do you have?' was a regular question I asked the mothers. And when they told me they had eight or more, I would ask if they would like to stop and tell them that we could carry out a small operation to ensure that they did not have any more. Normally, they would reply that they would love to stop, but the line of authority demanded they first consult their husbands. Almost invariably the husband would refuse, usually because he had fathered only two or three children by that particular wife and felt they should have some more together. The men did not seem to take into account the children their wives had through other relationships, nor indeed the children they also had by other wives.

Another reason for the lack of popularity of family planning among men arose from the cultural throwback to the days of the tribal kings when status was measured by the number of children borne. The tribal King, Katchiba, from the north of Uganda, boasted of one hundred and sixteen children and was known as a clever ruler who had sown his seed wisely since he had a son to rule each of his villages. But while the family planning practices of one hundred and fifty years ago may have achieved an inclusive political dynasty, large numbers of children brought altogether different challenges in the modern Uganda.

In the world today there are many marriage practices, and there is probably no perfect formula, but traditionally Uganda practiced polygamy along with most other African countries. This was the norm until the missionaries arrived with their preaching on monogamy, so polygamy was to some extent suppressed. But Africans are inclusive in their beliefs, so rather than abolish their traditional marriage practices, they just grafted on the Christian ways. This meant that there were now two ways to get married – the traditional way and the religious way. If the couple could afford it, they could go through both ceremonies, but it was the high cost of going through these ceremonies which hastened the breakdown of formal marriage practices. In Luweero I found that there were many forms of relationship, depending on whether the couple was simply living together, whether a bride-price had been negotiated but not actually paid, or whether the bride price had been fully paid, or the couple had attended a church or mosque wedding.

The pattern of the relationships also varied, with many of the women practicing serial monogamy, with only one partner at a time, but moving from one partner to the next. The men often continued traditional polygamist practice informally, with an official wife and several girlfriends, or unofficial wives (on the side). These were usually referred to as side-wives or side-dishes. The wives had more than one partner consecutively, while the husbands had more than one partner at the same time, which was probably the worst combination in terms of risky sexual networking in facilitating the rapid spread of HIV.

Traditional marriage involved the payment of bride-price, with the men having to come up with an agreed price for the bride which was payable to the bride's parents. This was in the form of cattle, goods or cash, but most couples in Luweero who were living together had not actually completed the payment, due to their impoverished economic circumstances. Therefore, although everyone referred to their partner as their 'wife' or 'husband', many were not formally married, either traditionally or in a religious ceremony. The result was that there was no real commitment, and if a better offer came along, the wife would be tempted to take it. The better offer could consist of a new dress, a pair of shoes or the promise of better economic circumstances. Life was hard, and the incentive to change partners did not need to be large.

Even though Uganda had one of the fastest growing populations in the world, the issue of the population explosion did not seem to rank high on the political agenda. And although Uganda began to have a healthy economic growth rate after the National Resistance Movement came to power, the effects of the spiralling population were not taken into account.

Several years later when the Minister of Finance, (who also happened to be the MP for Luweero), read her budget speech,

33

there was still no mention of Uganda's high population growth rate. At the post-budget breakfast, the IMF representative waxed lyrical about the country's healthy economic growth and sound macroeconomic policy, while the opposition parties then rubbished the economic progress. But the reality lay somewhere between these two perspectives. It was true that Uganda was making sound economic progress, but much of the economic gains were cancelled out by a population that was doubling and tripling every few years. The country sustained a 6-7 % economic growth rate per year for many years, but this growth rate, minus an inflation rate of 6 - 12%, plus a population growth rate of 3.5% practically cancelled themselves out, particularly in rural areas. This meant that Uganda was running fast just to stand still.

What did change over the years was those people who began to earn higher incomes also recognised the cost of bringing up children and were the first to practise family planning. Hence, the Kampala elite had only two or three children, but their peasant counterparts in Luweero continued to have a fertility rate of approximately seven per woman. Thus children were begotten to the poorer members of society who were the least able to feed, educate, and bring them up to be good citizens. Unlike cattle or wild flowers, and contrary to the advice of the MPs, children needed individual attention from the parents plus an adequate infrastructure in terms of education and health. Uganda had one of the youngest populations in the world, and while many western countries might have envied its population demographics, it was in danger of producing a generation which had no skills.

To be fair to the government, Uganda was also one of the first African countries to develop a programme of Universal Primary Education, in which every child was offered schooling at primary level, but the resources to cope with the programme were inadequate and the standards achieved were relatively low. The issue of the high population growth rate deserved

34

attention, planning, and input from the politicians and experts as the economic growth, but it was rarely mentioned.

While we were living in Luweero it was commonplace to hear stories of marital violence, a phenomenon which many of the women took as a normal part of life. Domestic violence was another issue which did not generate much attention and there were widely contrasting views on the subject. Differing views were expressed by men and women and by various social groups. The polarization existed between those who were influenced by western values and those who held traditional cultural views. There were men who were implacably opposed to lifting a hand against the fairer sex, while there were women who felt that a good beating once in a while demonstrated that their husband had not lost interest in them and still cared enough to take the trouble. There were other women who reasoned that if their husband was only guilty of the occasional violent outburst in the marriage, it was worthwhile accepting this, if he was a good husband in other ways.

Most of the village wives expected to get beaten from time to time and saw it as part of the package. They viewed the relationship with their husbands like that of a child to a father, where discipline of the children was a sign that the father was still engaged in the upbringing. The law in Uganda was no different than in Britain, in that if a husband beat his wife he could be charged, but most village wives appeared to be ignorant of this fact, or else they put the authority of their husbands above the law. Many beatings were by husbands who were insecure because their wives were more successful than they, and they felt driven to demonstrate that they had the physical authority. The husbands often justified beatings, saying that their wives had become 'proud', which usually implied that she had gained some degree of financial independence. But one wondered when such men, in that

35

cultural context, would ever be secure enough to handle wives who were achieving more than they.

Some years later, the issue of wife beating did come into the public domain when the Vice-President of Uganda took the unusual step of divorcing her husband, citing marital violence. While many people from western cultures felt that this was a step forwards for an African female leader to recognize the problem of domestic violence, there were many Ugandan women who were scandalized by her actions. Such issues were not for the public domain. In their view, an African wife should deal with a husband's bad behaviour – whether it be philandering or domestic violence – behind closed doors, and the last thing she should do was go public or, God forbid, divorce. This was bringing shame on the whole family. I found that the influence of cultural values was far more significant than was commonly recognised. Superficially, much of modern Africa appeared the same as any modern western culture, but one just had to scratch below the surface to find that there were fundamental differences. Women in Kampala were able to assert their rights to a large degree – there were a mandated number of women Members of Parliament, many management positions were held by women, and many Kampala women were well educated and articulate. But even in emancipated Kampala, it was still a man's world.

As Robbie built up her social network she was invited along as a *senga* (aunt) to the *okubulilira* (get-together of the bride and the aunties to give a prospective bride advice about sex and marriage). Robbie was not supposed to tell me what went on, but she did drop a few juicy bits of information which I found very interesting. Some of the advice was regarding how to hold on to your man, since it seemed to be accepted that the man would inevitably stray. While the *sengas* were probably being realistic, I wondered how this presupposition would have gone down in a western context. According to American culture, if the man even thought about straying, the woman

36

would be looking for a top class divorce lawyer so that she could relieve him of all his worldly possessions. But the cultural norm in Uganda focused on how the woman could learn the tricks to keep her man happy, and she was generally blamed if she failed in this, even when the fault obviously lay with the husband.

Living in Uganda, I found that it was important not to make assumptions just because the culture seemed westernised or the person I was dealing with had received a western education. The underlying norms and paradigms might still be very different. I found this applied particularly to the messages being promoted by the American aid organisations regarding HIV, where much work went into the anthropological research, but, in my view, they still got it wrong. In the HIV epidemic, older men were having sex with young girls, with the result that the prevalence of HIV was five times higher among girls than boys of the equivalent age.

Much of the reason for this behaviour lay in the 'sugar daddy' phenomenon, where older guys plied girls with gifts or provided cash for the necessities of life. A USAID organisation devised an advertising campaign to alert young women of the dangers of such relationships, with the slogan 'Stop transgenerational sex'. While this message translated perfectly well in a western society, which is generally stratified by age, this is not the case in African society, where older men frequently marry much younger girls. So the message was confused because many Ugandans could not see the problem, even though everyone knew that sugar daddies were dangerous. The message got lost in translation.

As the aids epidemic progressed it became clear that there was also high transmission among married couples. This required a more complex health education message, in that it concerned the sexual networking which was influencing the rapid spread of aids – essentially men were having more than one partner, which resulted in HIV being spread rapidly among those in stable married relationships. The message which needed to go out was, 'know your status, know your partner's status', but instead, a message was put out saying, 'get off the sexual network', which was meaningless to the normal person on the street. A person was either on the 'sexual network' because he did not see anything wrong with having more than one partner, or, in the case of his wife, she probably did not know she was riding the sexual network in the first place. Another agency put out the message: 'Take regular HIV tests together, test together, know together', which was more to the point because people could take action.

# The Spread of AIDS

At the height of the AIDS epidemic the lifespan of Ugandans was reported as thirty-nine years. This was an incredibly short life since life expectancy in most developed countries has risen to the eighties. The very low life expectancy was caused by high infant mortality from malaria, respiratory and diarrhoeal diseases, and a high mortality among young adults from HIV. This meant that during my time in Uganda I quickly exceeded my allotted years and was living on borrowed time – a sobering thought.

As far as untimely death in Uganda was concerned, we had more than our share, yet the paradox was that since Ugandans experienced it so frequently, people hardly seemed to notice. Babies died every day of malaria, dehydration or malnutrition, but no-one raised an eyebrow. Mothers died in childbirth – on average one for every two hundred and forty births – but such a horrifying statistic was accepted as normal. Young people died of AIDS, and when they were buried, no-one mentioned the condition from which they died. And people, young and old, died in their scores every day on the roads, but it was not called a national scandal. The government just paid lip-service to improving standards of road safety, but over the years nothing really changed.

While many of the deaths from HIV were preventable, this had certainly not been the case in the initial stages of the epidemic. For example, in the mid eighties those who graduated from Makerere University (the main university in Kampala) lost at least 30% of their classmates to AIDS because they did not know how the disease was being spread. Of the classmates who graduated with me, only a few have since died, and I cannot imagine the impact of losing 30% of my fellow doctors within five years. There is now hope as far as AIDS is concerned, but many people continue to be infected, even when the knowledge of how to prevent and treat the disease is readily available.

By the early nineties everyone in Uganda knew that HIV was spread through unprotected sex, but relatively few used this knowledge appropriately, to a large extent because cultural norms were slow to change. One method of prevention was the use of condoms, but people said that using a condom was like eating a banana without peeling the skin, or eating a sweet in the wrapper and that they needed the 'feel' of a woman. And within marriage many men would not even think of using a condom. In Uganda traditional cultural pressures often had a stronger influence than scientific facts, and this was also the case with AIDS. I knew men from Kiwoko who were aware that they were infected, but went ahead and married because in the culture it seemed strange that a man should live alone without a woman (even if he knew that he was infected with HIV), and consequently these men infected their new wives.

In the early stages of the epidemic, patients with AIDS presented with diarrhoea and weight loss and wasted away over a period of months, and because of this the disease became known as 'slim'. It was soon deduced that 'slim' was in fact AIDS, and Uganda was the epicentre of a serious epidemic, but unlike the cases that had been reported in America among the gay community, AIDS in Uganda was transmitted through heterosexual sex and was rampant in the general population. The disease had spread from Congo and southwest Uganda, along the main trade routes into neighbouring Kenya, Tanzania, and southwards to Malawi and South Africa. Sentinel surveys carried out in the major population centres and in antenatal clinics showed that up to thirty-five percent of people were infected, though the average prevalence in the adult population was 14%. This prevalence varied in different population groups, with 25 - 35% of expectant mothers being found to be HIV positive.

40

We were working in pretty basic conditions at Kiwoko in these early stages and we did not have a properly equipped laboratory where we could carry out AIDS tests. Rapid HIV tests were still being developed at the time and when a visiting doctor brought out a batch of new tests Gudrun, our German nurse, decided to get tested. None of us were worried about the outcome since she was not at risk, but the test result was positive. This appeared to call into question whether I was exposing my staff to significant medical risks, and if this was the case, it might be best to pack up and leave. We sent a confirmatory test and spent several more days anxiously awaiting the results, but, fortunately, the results showed that the first test was a false positive. The rapid tests and Eliza tests, which were developed later, were much more sensitive and specific, and when we began testing widely, we found that, not only were a large percentage of our patients positive, a significant number of our staff were also infected.

Over the years we lost many close friends to AIDS. These were dark times for everyone as there was not a glimmer of hope on the horizon. When a person was given the diagnosis that he was infected with HIV, no matter what reassuring or supportive words were used, it was a death sentence. Many local people preferred not to know their sero-status since they reasoned that there was nothing they could do about it, and the pressure of living with the knowledge was worse than ignorance. The diagnosis itself also had the effect of making a number of those who were positive try to live in a way that 'proved' they were healthy by having normal partnerships and unprotected sex. The strata of society which was being decimated were the parents, who left behind countless orphans. The grandparents buried the children and were left to bring up the grandchildren.

When we found someone was HIV positive, we counselled him about his lifestyle and explained how the virus was passed on, but most patients did not appear to understand or wish to

41

grasp the risk of transmission to others. One must appreciate that we were not dealing with an ordinary terminal disease such as cancer which went through certain defined stages until the person died. HIV had a relapsing pattern which could continue for years. Normally, if a person has a terminal illness, he becomes progressively more ill until he dies, and as this process unfolds he has time to go through the accepted stages of grieving and come to terms with his impending death. However, the patient with HIV would usually first present at the hospital because he had an opportunistic infection, which would then improve. A common opportunistic infection which was usually the first sign of HIV was Herpes Zoster, or shingles, but when the shingles cleared, the patient thought he was cured. When I told the patients their underlying diagnosis, they usually appeared to understand, but their understanding only lasted as long as they had signs and symptoms and once they were feeling better they carried on with their previous lives.

President Museveni was the first African President to acknowledge that his country had a serious problem with HIV, and the government launched an extensive health education programme. The general public was informed that AIDS was spread through sex, and the way to avoid it was to be faithful, practise safe sex, or abstain – ABCs: Abstinence, Be faithful, or use a Condom. The natural result of this campaign was that when a person was told he was infected, he made the assumption that his spouse was also infected. Therefore, when husbands were urged to bring their wives for testing, they did not see the point. In the mind of the villager it was a question of: which is it? Is it spread through sex or not? Because if it is spread through sex, I have been having regular sex with this woman and she must already be infected, so why do I need to upset her now?'

The man simply went home, told no one, got on with life and gradually put all the information about having HIV out of his mind. I followed up a number of patients whom I had personally diagnosed with HIV, all of whom eventually died. I tested them and gave them their HIV results, yet each later denied that he was infected. They gave various rationales, but the most compelling was that, as long as they were not actually sick, they would not accept they had AIDS. Some took new partners during this time, who, in turn, died.

The public health message was that HIV was spread through sex, but what did this mean? If a person had sex with an infected partner once, was he bound to get AIDS? Surprisingly, the chances of transmission were much less than one percent per encounter and many couples were in a relationship for years, where one partner was positive, yet the virus was not passed on. These were discordant couples, and the rate of discordancy in Uganda was at least fifty percent. It was difficult for people to understand how they could then have sex without their partner becoming infected. The reason lay in the natural history of the disease: the HIV virus, having infected its victim, went into a quiescent phase and retreated to the lymphatic tissues. During this time there was a battle between the body's immune system and the virus, with the body slaying millions of viruses, but HIV not being annihilated completely. Very little virus was shed in the body fluids during this phase, making it less likely that the person would transmit the disease, but eventually HIV would overwhelm the body's defences, and increasing amounts of virus would be shed in the secretions. It was at this time that transmission was more likely to occur.

One of my patients became ill with septicaemia, and in the course of carrying out investigations, I found she was HIV positive. She was treated successfully, but I had to tell her husband she was infected.

'I had an AIDS test carried out only a year ago which was negative,' he reminded me.

We repeated his test but during the year he had converted from negative to positive. They had been together for eight years, and for seven years she had failed to transmit. It was not surprising that many people were confused about the transmission of HIV, since we were telling them they got it through sex, but they could also have sex with an infected partner for years and still remain negative.

There were other factors associated with the transmission of HIV. If the skin of the penis and the lining of the vagina were intact, there was less chance that the virus would be transmitted, but if these defences were broken down by inflammation, abrasions or ulcers, the virus could penetrate more easily. The practice of 'dry sex' was common in the village because the men wanted more sensation, so Ugandan women, being very accommodating, obliged by putting herbs into the vagina to produce more friction. In the process, there was excoriation of the vagina, and the virus was more likely to be transmitted. Men were also keen to find a young girl because they reasoned that she was less likely to be infected. They would woo the girl with small presents like shoes, a handkerchief or underwear, and unfortunately, if the girl was a virgin and the sex was rough, she had a high chance of becoming infected in the first sexual encounter. In a rural community, where there was very little cash for the purchase of small luxuries, it was not hard for a man with some money to persuade a girl to have sex with him and younger girls were five times more likely to be infected than boys of the same age. Many girls died for the price of a pair of knickers, or a pack of sanitary towels.

Surveys also showed that men who were circumcised were 30% less likely to become infected, because the moist area under the foreskin was prone to inflammation and thus allowed easier transmission, while the harder skin of the glans in the circumcised man, acted as a natural barrier. This led to many African countries promoting circumcision as a measure to reduce the transmission of HIV.

Anti-retroviral drugs (ARVs) only began to emerge in the mid-nineties. They were not able to wipe out the virus completely, but as long as the person kept taking the drugs, they kept the multiplication of the virus under control, and the person's immunity recovered. At first, there was only one anti-viral drug, known as AZT, and it was shown that this drug did not work because the virus simply mutated and became resistant within a few weeks. Subsequently, another anti-viral drug came on to the market, which when used in combination with AZT, had a more significant effect on slowing the progress of the disease. I found dual therapy could help patients clinically for up to a year, but eventually the virus became resistant to this combination and the patients relapsed. Finally another anti-viral drug was manufactured, which worked on a different site of the virus. Thus three different drugs were used in combination to prevent the virus mutating, with each of the drugs working in a different way to impede replication. Triple therapy had finally succeeded in controlling the multiplication of HIV.

The advent of triple therapy brought hope for those suffering from AIDS, but this hope was mainly confined to the first world as the cost was prohibitive, running to at least a thousand dollars a month per patient. Needless to say, very few patients in poor countries could afford such treatment. One of my patients happened to be travelling in the USA when she became ill and was diagnosed with AIDS. Fortunately, she met a sympathetic social worker who was able to get her on a programme for free anti-retroviral drugs in the USA, but when she returned to Uganda, she was no longer eligible to receive these drugs. Despite this, ways were found, and every month her supply of drugs arrived at my office. She was one of the first Ugandan patients who had access to dual and then triple therapy. When she started treatment, her CD4 count was only 64, which meant that without treatment she would have died within a couple of years, but thanks to the sympathetic social worker in the USA, she is still very much alive today.

Some other patients were not so fortunate, even if they could afford to pay. One had discovered he was HIV positive when his girlfriend had contracted meningitis and died. He travelled to London for treatment just before the advent of triple therapy, but despite the best medication which money could buy, his condition deteriorated rapidly, and he came home to die. It was heartrending to watch a thirty year old wither away and die in the space of a few months, and within a year of his death, drugs were available which could have saved his life. His father did not want his son's life to go unmarked and gave me a significant amount of money which I was later able to use to save the lives of many children from AIDS.

The availability of highly priced drugs for the treatment of AIDS left me with difficult decisions to make: in essence who would live and who would die, and essentially, it came down to who could pay. I had access to the drugs, but they were expensive and I could not give them out free, so I was often in the position of telling a patient that he had AIDS and would need treatment, but he would have to find several hundred dollars a month for the medication. Ugandans are resourceful, and a black market for anti-AIDS drugs sprang up, with the drugs originating mainly from Sweden and the UK though some found their way from the States. These were bona-fide anti-retroviral drugs, but they were sold in small Ugandan pharmacies at much cheaper prices than in Europe or America. I was not concerned where the drugs came from, only that they were available to my patients, and there were many Ugandans who managed to scrape the money together to access the treatment. The problem arose when patients bought the drugs for a few months but then ran out of money and stopped taking the medication, thus allowing the virus to develop resistance. I had mixed feelings about some people starting treatment as I suspected that they could not sustain it, but I felt that if a person was about to die and had managed to get the money for a few months, I could not deny him hope. A number of these patients led a hand to mouth existence, but those months of life which they gain often proved critical in buying time until the prices of anti-AIDS drugs reduced. These were the dilemmas I faced as a doctor working in a third world country, but even though there were huge ethical and practical problems, at least there was hope. It may only have been hope for the few, but it was the harbinger of hope for many.

The price of antiretroviral drugs progressively reduced over the years to a dollar a day, and the government of Uganda promised to develop a programme to make the drugs available free. This would give hope to the masses but bring with it enormous logistical problems in ensuring that patients took their drugs on a regular basis. There were those who were genuinely worried about the spread of another HIV bug that would be resistant to all drugs because patients would take the drugs erratically. This was a legitimate concern, but the answer was not to deny treatment to millions of people with AIDS just in case they might forget to take their medicine.

Unlike the rest of sub-Saharan Africa, in Sudan the overall prevalence of HIV was only two to three percent. The reason was that large parts of Sudan were cut off due to the war between north and south Sudan. AIDS was one killer, but there were other more immediate killers such as people with AK 47s, which prevented movement of the population and thus the spread of infection. On the other hand, when armies themselves became infected, they then infected the local population through sexual relations and mass rape, as has been the case in Congo. The virus spread along the truck routes from Rwanda to Uganda, Kenya and Tanzania, while the war in South Sudan cut the Sudanese off. But war also brought about the breakdown of social structures and traditional values which eventually facilitated the rapid spread of HIV.

It was one of the few Sudanese whom I treated in Uganda who faced me with a dilemma. She sat in my office and told me calmly that she knew she had AIDS but had no money to pay for the treatment. I carried out a CD4 count to check on her level of immunity and found that she had less than 10 cells – practically no immunity – and she was at risk of imminent death. It was surprising that she was still alive at all. By this time, due to manufacturers in India breaking patent and copying ante-retroviral drugs, the cost of the drugs had come down to around $2.0 per day. I looked at the girl sitting in front of me, and it occurred to me that I would spend that on a cup of coffee. The life of this human being was worth exactly the price of a cup of coffee a day. I paid for her treatment. I saw that girl irregularly over the next few years because she travelled to Yemen to work. She was doing well, but when she was in the Middle East it was more difficult to access her drugs, and I wondered about her long term future. I eventually lost touch with her and don't know her fate, but there were other patients whom I treated in those early days and then lost touch with, only to meet them again years later to find they were alive and well. No-one would have given much for their chances, and although some of my patients have since died, all of them had several more years added on to their lives through this hand to mouth existence.

The access to anti-retroviral treatment, which has now been made available to hundreds of thousands of Africans through American government funding and through foundations like the Global Fund and the Clinton Foundation, has resulted in restoring hope in this AIDS epidemic.

# The Role of Missionaries

We had been living in Luweero for several years and established a flourishing medical work, including a hospital and extensive community health programmes in the surrounding villages. Since we were being sponsored by Church Missionary Society Ireland, we were paid a courtesy visit by a representative of our sister organisation, Church Mission Society Britain. The visitor was the mission secretary for CMS Britain and had been involved in missionary and development work for many years. He looked around the project without much comment, but as he left, he was heard to remark, 'He is creating a dependency', meaning that we had started something which would need outside funds and personnel to continue and would never be self-sustaining.

Church Mission Society had an interesting history, regarded by some in Africa in a positive light and by others as a negative influence as it was considered to be the precursor of colonialism. There was no doubt that the various church missions, either Catholic or Protestant, were instrumental in proselytising for the Christian faith during the 19th century and, since the Arabs had introduced Islam at a much earlier stage, most African countries then had at least three competing religions. Perhaps it was because of this sensitivity to their own history that the modern day CMS no longer took the role as the 'big brother' or indeed any sort of paternalistic role in the church to which it had given birth. In Uganda, since the missions contributed much to the social fabric of society, particularly in the fields of education and health, they were generally regarded in a positive light, having left a legacy of hospitals and schools. CMS Britain no longer wished to build mission hospitals or extend their influence, and they certainly had no policy of sending missionaries to the bush to build new

49

institutions which could become a liability. But a renegade Irishman had done just that.

In church terms, there was a somewhat uneasy balance in the relationship between the parent and the child, with the child now having grown up. Phrases such as 'The African church has come of age' were politically correct, and anything with even a hint of paternalism was to be avoided like the plague. The African church was now master of its own affairs and indeed, in matters such as homosexuality, it took a completely different line from the mother-ship. However, it was evident that no matter whether the African church had come of age or not, it did not have the financial or professional means to support a network of hospitals, without support from abroad.

The Ugandan churches and religious communities – whether Protestant, Catholic or Muslim – were grassroots organisations, well placed to reach the common people, sometimes more so than the government institutions. But it seemed that in spite of this, donors and the aid world did not quite know where to place church based organisations in development terms –  that is, until they thought up the politically correct terminology. Then they were able to give churches a new legitimacy under the classification Civil Society Organisations, and under the Bush administration they even got their own recognised division within this classification as Faith Based Organisations. Church organisations could then be referred to as CSOs, FBOs, NGOs or PNFPs, like any other self respecting aid organisation which could not exist without an acronym (NGO was the ubiquitous Non-Government Organisation and PNFP meant private not for profit).

When the churches gained these various politically correct acronyms and titles, they were then seen to fit respectably into the aid world and could be accepted as players in the development system by the modern experts. Despite all this nonsense, the churches continued to reflect their own society in terms of the availability of finances or professional resources at grass roots, and many of the Protestant mission hospitals went into decline due to lack of resources. This was because the churches abroad had pulled out on the basis that it was time for these hospitals to be autonomous. Unfortunately, some of this 'Africanization' of the mission hospitals looked more like a rout than an ordered withdrawal, without much planning for the future or a well thought out strategy.

The Catholic Church planted many hospitals throughout Uganda with the support of religious orders from different parts of the world and, unlike the Protestant missionaries, who came for relatively short periods of time, many of the Catholic sisters and brothers stayed for thirty or forty years. The result was that the Catholic mission hospitals were generally better run than their Protestant counterparts since there was usually a Sister who provided continuity. The effect of this was not only to bring stability but to allow funds to be channelled from outside. But many of the Catholic orders were having difficulty recruiting new blood, and when the old timers died out their institutions were left in precarious financial and organisational straights.

One of the best hospitals in Uganda was Lacor Hospital in Gulu, Northern Uganda. Lacor was developed by a married couple, a French Canadian and an Italian, both of whom were doctors with close ties to the Catholic Church. The wife was a surgeon, and over the years she carried out vast amounts of trauma surgery during the numerous wars and rebellions which made up Uganda's history. They were often dealing with victims of gunshots and landmines, and she must have been repeatedly pricked by bone spikules in the course of her surgery. As a result of this, she contracted AIDS and died before treatment became available. Her husband carried on the work and then also died at the hospital for which they had given their lives. Today Lacor continues to be one of the leading hospitals in Uganda but struggles to get adequate staff coverage since there are so few Ugandan doctors available to work up-country, and a career for missionaries working in Africa is no longer fashionable. There were many stories of heroism by both Catholic and Protestant missionaries, and while there are those who feel that missionary activity was too closely associated with colonialism, I personally found that medical missionaries were not there to proselytize for their faith but were motivated by their faith to relieve suffering. There was something in them which drove them on, sometimes at great personal cost.

Although the old-fashioned Albert Schweitzer type of missionary is disappearing, there has recently been an influx of the American Pentecostal types who are there for purposes of spreading the gospel and church planting. Many of these missionaries do not feel their role is primarily humanitarian, but evangelical, and some missions have split between the evangelical camps and the humanitarian camps. Many developing countries deal with the spread of evangelical fervour by simply refusing visas to those who have no particular professional skills, but Uganda's visa policy is fairly open, with the result that there has been an influx of church based organisations. Although many are there for church building purposes, some have also carried out commendable work among orphans. The old fashioned humanitarian type missionaries seem to have been replaced today by consultants in development theory (McKinsey is a name that comes to mind) who travel round Africa, jetting into the country to advise the government and donors on how to tackle development problems, but such people no longer live at the grassroots among the people.

When we first came to Uganda, we met an Irish Protestant missionary known as Dr Donald Brownlee who had worked throughout the most difficult periods in Uganda's recent history. Donald was the sort of person who felt guilty if he was not pushing himself to the limit in order to help people. He would get up in the night and write letters appealing to supporters to send money for another borehole, or funds for a clinic in the bush. Donald and his wife, Una, were more at home serving in the heart of Africa than living a middleclass existence in Northern Ireland, which they could have chosen to do. He was an example of a person who literally drove himself to his death in his desire to serve others; he died of bowel cancer because he ignored his own symptoms while he looked after others.

Maura Lynch was a missionary sister who ran a Catholic hospital in western Uganda. She was a trained surgeon, one of the first who learned the technique of repairing vesico-vaginal fistulae (when the bladder develops a hole due to a prolonged obstructed labour, and as a result, the mother becomes completely incontinent). She ran regular courses to teach the technique to other doctors but lost an eye as a result of a serious infection, and since she was in her sixties, I thought she would retire at this point. But Sister Maura had no thought of retirement and continued to run the hospital and carry out surgery with one eye – you could say that she continued to keep an eye on things.

Recently there has also been a trend in 'Church tourism', where church groups visit developing countries for a couple of weeks and go into the villages to visit the local churches, build a school, or run a clinic. Some of these groups are on the American evangelical model, but many are made up of ordinary people who wish to see for themselves what Africa is about. I met one American group on their way to Uganda and asked what they would be doing during their visit.

'We are harvesting souls for the Lord,' was the unhesitating reply.

While this group may have been well meaning, they were certainly not worried about being politically correct. To say that you are coming to a country 'harvesting souls for the

Lord' has a certain ring to it, though it does conjure up images of the grim reaper.

Of course there are many Ugandan doctors and nurses, who work selflessly in up-country mission hospitals, but it is difficult to get a Ugandan doctor to serve in a rural area for a prolonged period, and the person who takes on the responsibility of running a mission hospital is also faced with the challenge of sustaining the funding. An expatriate might have built up a network of support during his term of service, but this funding often melts away if there is not a familiar face to continue to channel the flow of information. Whether it is a local person or an expatriate, they both face the challenge of sustainability. Perhaps the person who remarked that I was creating a dependency was right after all, but what was the answer? Was it to walk away from the glaring need and do nothing? And when one had become involved, what was the answer to sustaining the project? There was no simple answer, certainly not in terms of handing institutions over to local organisations which were themselves struggling with issues of financing and management.

# Payment by results

Finding the resources to run Kiwoko Hospital and all its programmes was always a challenge. The people of Luweero were not completely destitute; they had some cash since they grew coffee and other cash crops which were sold on the local market, but the little they had was not sufficient to cover all their medical costs. In theory, the government provided free treatment through the Ministry of Health, but in practice the delivery of this healthcare was patchy, to say the least, and there was always a cost attached.

Personally, I have always believed that it is right that patients should pay at least a small amount for medical services as this allows them to value the service. Otherwise the villagers had a tendency to blow all their cash on wine, women and song, (or the local brew). At Kiwoko Hospital we found that the proportion of the costs which people could reasonably be expected to meet was about 25% of the recurrent costs. Capital costs could usually be met through donors since it was not so difficult to get funding for capital projects, community projects, or preventive health programmes, but there were few mainstream donors who would meet the everyday running costs of a hospital. They referred to hospitals as black holes.

A few years after we had started the hospital, the government took a positive step by recognising that the work of the mission hospitals was meeting a substantial proportion of the healthcare needs of the community. They therefore began providing some financial assistance. Unfortunately, this assistance amounted to only 10% of any hospital's budget and was often late in coming, or even cut altogether if the government had a more pressing need. Taking into account the 25% from the patient and 10% from the government, the remaining 65%, therefore, had to be raised through voluntary donations. And while the government made a promising start, the public sector bureaucrats were not keen to part with this money, and the impression was that it was grudgingly given, and the mission hospitals should beg for it. The reality was that the mission hospitals were saving the government money, but despite this, the government subsidy shrank progressively over the years until in some cases it was as little as 3% of the hospital budget.

An important role which expatriates played was to keep the aid flowing since they had a much better network of friends and contacts than local people. In our case we had started a small support organisation for Kiwoko Hospital which evolved into a fully registered charitable foundation in the UK, known imaginatively as *Friends of Kiwoko Hospital*. This organisation continued to support the hospital for many years, and without this support it is difficult to see how Kiwoko could have continued to meet its running costs. But can a project be considered sustainable if it has to depend on funding from abroad, and what is the best way to reach sustainability? Can we ever hope for self-sufficiency when it comes to social infrastructure projects in developing countries, and what is our definition of self-sufficiency and sustainability?

In the UK it is the government which takes responsibility for the health and education of its citizens; could a country such as Uganda really be expected to meet such needs, especially when the population itself is growing at more than three percent per year? Various countries have differing models for the provision of health services, with some countries such as America and South Africa relying heavily on private medical insurance, mostly financed through the employers. Others like Britain have a nationalised health service, but is there any proven model for the delivery of health services for third world countries?

Accessibility to health services and reaching sustainability depends on which developing country one is looking at, since GDP varies greatly from country to country, and there is

56

probably no macroeconomic model to fit all. Even within one country, people's ability to pay varies greatly and hence a rigid model would not be appropriate for all levels of society, or even for different regions of the country. For example, Luweero was a post-war area, but by the time we arrived it was stable, which meant that programmes to install clean drinking water, rebuild schools or health-centres, or construct hospitals such as Kiwoko could get underway. The local population could also resume cultivation, and when cash crops were harvested, the money could be used for such things as school fees, medical bills, the purchase of a bicycle, iron sheets for roofing one's home, or it could be spent on frivolities. Income could be budgeted for necessities or spent on riotous living, and it was right to charge for, and give value to, healthcare at an appropriate level.

The government system in Uganda was supposed to be providing free healthcare, but comprehensive health services was a myth, and treatment was often delayed or not given, with the excuse of lack of resources. In government hospitals it was true that the bed which the patient occupied was free, but this was sometimes all they got, and if the medical personnel were not conscientious, they had a ready excuse for doing nothing by claiming lack of resources. The net result was long patient-stays, with no-one taking responsibility. The government hospital system resulted in the syndrome of 'hit or miss' medical services. If the patient was lucky, or had money, or encountered diligent medical staff, and there also happened to be drugs in the pharmacy, or oxygen in the theatre, things might go well, and he would score a 'hit', but these were many variables when no-one appeared to be in control. If the staff member had not reported for duty, or no one had replenished the drug supply, the patient scored a 'miss', and he would simply occupy the bed until the disease ran its natural course – he would get better without much medical intervention, or he would die.

In western countries we talked of the golden hour – that hour after an accident or an emergency when a timely intervention might save the patient's life. In most African countries there was no golden hour, indeed the patient would consider himself lucky if there was a golden day when he received treatment. Usually there was simply no time limit for medical intervention, and the patient was expected to feel grateful if he was treated at all.

A young clinical officer who worked for me died in the early hours of a Sunday morning, and if she had been in another place it might not have happened, but she was in the wrong place at the wrong time. Janet was attending a family function when she became dizzy and asked her friends to take her home, but her friends were worried and rightly took her to the clinic instead. At the clinic they carried out some tests, in the course of which they found that she was anaemic and had a low blood pressure. The staff started her on intravenous fluids, but she was going into shock, so they took her to the main government hospital. When they reached the hospital, they were told there was no blood. At this point her condition had become critical, but the hospital staff said they could not admit her and sent her away; she became unconscious and died as they tried to reach another small mission hospital.

The post-mortem showed that she had died from a ruptured ectopic pregnancy and had lost four litres of blood from her circulation into the abdomen. Ruptured tubal pregnancies are an emergency where the correct treatment is to carry out an exploratory operation and stop the bleeding. This is not a difficult procedure, and most Ugandan doctors can do it. It would have been reasonable to expect that when a patient was taken to a main regional referral hospital such an emergency could have been dealt with simply and efficiently. One would certainly not have expected the patient to be sent away on the basis that there was no blood, but in government hospitals there was often a shortage of something, or a reason why a procedure could not be carried out. Such shortages were real enough, but the system bred an attitude among public sector health-workers where there was always an excuse for postponement or procrastination, and everyone could blame someone else. It would have been fairer to advise patients that they would have to pay for part of their costs, but treatment would be guaranteed rather than to make promises and procrastinate. But as the government system stood, medical care was promised and not actually delivered, with the excuse of lack of resources.

At Kiwoko Hospital we carried out auto-transfusion in such cases, in which we saved the blood which had leaked out into the abdomen, put it into a bottle with some anticoagulants and transfused it back. This may sound a little unsophisticated, but we were not scooping the blood off the floor, we were simply taking it out of the abdomen and transfusing it back into the circulation. It was a sad reflection that in Janet's case a main government hospital seemed to be able to do less than a small rural mission hospital. Over the past twenty years the standard of medical care in some parts of Africa has actually fallen, and the gap in healthcare between many African countries and their western counterparts has widened. This is due to the fact that, while there have been significant advances in western medical practices, parts of Africa have been going backwards in real terms. Even if this was not the case and Africa was standing still, we would still have divergence, not convergence, in medical care between rich and poor countries.

If healthcare were delivered on the basis of paying for results, much of the procrastination, passing the buck, and the failure to deliver medical services would automatically change. But donors, in the form of western governments and multilateral agencies such as the World Bank, have been putting money in at the top of the system – the various Ministries of the recipient countries – with little being delivered at the grassroots. Yet the donors have signally failed to call recipient governments to account. These methods are the easy way to disburse aid since the donor government can simply write a cheque or transfer a few million dollars to a developing country. This does not require a large staff to supervise disbursement or reporting and, hey, we are in an age where paternalism or demanding accountability has colonial overtones, and governments do not have the responsibility to report on how they run their own affairs. Hence, assurances that the money has been ring-fenced for health, and not for the purchase of arms or the purchase of a new jet for the President, are taken to suffice.

This money, which is poured in to government ministries, is supposed to produce results measured in the Millennium Development Goals (the MDGs). Every few years, countries give an accountability of how they are faring in achieving these goals when indicators such as infant mortality, maternal mortality, and number of families in absolute poverty, are measured. Uganda and many African countries are way behind in achieving the MDGs related to health. Infant mortality has hardly improved, and maternal mortality is appalling, but despite these failures, donor governments just keep putting money in – usually because they apparently do not see an alternative method of financing. Or are they too lazy to look?

Would it be too much to ask that some of the many consultants would set attainable goals for the delivery of healthcare, and then donors could pay when measurable results are achieved? Many organisations at grass roots level could deliver such results. These might be private sector players, mission hospitals, or aid agencies, but they would all have to be willing to be held accountable. And if there is competition in the market place, even government departments and hospitals would then begin to deliver a credible service. As I travelled round Uganda, I noticed the remarkable difference between the industry of the artisans and tradesmen who had set up small scale businesses along the sides of the road and the attitude of public sector workers. Government workers themselves were often absent from their posts because they were running private businesses or consultancies on the side. It is a simple matter of capitalism; people in Uganda are not any different from anyone else in the world: they are motivated by reward and profit. I do not see why donors can not understand this simple characteristic of human nature and use this basic instinct to ensure that healthcare is delivered effectively.

# The Lord's Resistance Army

While we were working in Luweero, we heard many stories of atrocities that had been carried out under the previous Obote regime which had drawn support mainly from the northern tribes. When Museveni and the National Resistance Movement (NRM) took power in 1986, remnants of the previous army retreated to the north, and while the NRM dealt with most of these elements, a few diehards continued to foment trouble over the next twenty years. It was hard to see any clear agenda in their activities since most of the political activists had fled to Europe or America where they vociferously badmouthed the new government from afar, and the only people left fighting were those who had adopted bush war as a way of life. The worst of these groups had some sort of religious or superstitious bias which allowed myths to grow up around them, inflating their influence beyond their numbers.

During the eighties, a lady known as Alice Lakwena led *the Holy Spirit Movement*, based on an amalgam of extreme Pentecostal type religion and witchcraft. She anointed her followers with oil, or in this case ghee, a sort of fatty spread, and went into battle against the army in the belief that the bullets would bounce off. While it is true that Ghee is very slimy and slippery, the bullets were still not deflected, and that was basically the end of that rebellion. The Alice Lakwena rebellion thus fizzled out, and she spent the rest of her days in a refugee camp in Kenya – presumably improving her skills in the field of witchcraft; but amazingly, her cousin, Joseph Kony, took up her cause in Uganda. Kony came from an area in the North of Ugandan which had deep-rooted traditions in witchcraft, but he mixed this with religion, this time of the Anglican variety, since he had also been a lay-reader in the Church. He further developed Alice Lakwena's ideology into his own combined religious and political agenda, which he claimed was based on the Ten Commandments.

The movement was known as the Lord's Resistance Army, with the stated aim of overthrowing the government and the installation of rule by the Ten Commandments. Unfortunately, Kony's Ten Commandments were not quite the original biblical Commandments but were instead Joseph Kony's own perverted version. He was initially viewed as a crackpot and was not seen as a great threat by the government, which, unfortunately, gave the LRA the opportunity to gain support from the Sudanese government who saw this dirty little rebellion as a useful foil to counter Uganda's support for the Sudan People's Liberation Army. The SPLA, which was largely Christian, had been fighting the Muslim Khartoum government since 1983. They were routing supplies through Uganda, so the Sudanese government set out to undermine Uganda's support by destabilizing the North, using Kony as their tool. They provided him with arms and allowed him to set up training camps within the area of South Sudan which was still under their control so that he was able to consolidate his position.

Without Sudanese support, it is likely that the army would have contained the menace of Kony as there were few Ugandans who believed in his ideals, and he was brutal in his treatment of the local population. In his perverted logic he justified this brutality as punishment, in the same manner as there were certain punishments prescribed by Moses when the Jews broke the Old Testament laws. But Kony's punishments were draconian. He put forth an edict to the people of Acholi – his own home territory – that they should not work on Fridays, which he declared a religious holiday, and he also decreed that the villagers should not ride bicycles. The rationale behind this particular order was that bicycle riding villagers would be travelling faster than the rebels and could inform the army of their position. He was also irritated that the local population

63

did not appear to be listening closely enough to what he was saying, and some were even acting as informants to the army, so they deserved Old Testament style punishments for these transgressions as well. Thus, if a villager was found riding a bicycle, his legs were chopped off, or if the rebel group could not find an axe, they put the legs on a log and beat them so badly that they had to be amputated later. In the case of people who were not listening, their ears were cut off, and those who were talking had their lips cut off. Those who worked in the fields on a Friday had their hands cut off. The people who were mutilated or killed were the poorest and the most defenceless – often women or random villagers whom the rebels happened upon. I met and treated the victims of Kony's brutality: women without lips, amputees, and men without ears; they were ordinary villagers who could not run fast enough and had no means to defend themselves.

I travelled to Lira to see for myself what was happening, and the reality on the ground was so bad that there were hardly words to adequately describe it.

While I was there, I treated a fourteen year old girl who was horribly burned; when I dressed her wounds she winced with the pain, but she did not cry out. I suppose that her mind was numbed by what she had been through: the LRA punished children who cried by beating them to death. The rebels had attacked her village about 20 Kilometres outside the town, rounding up the people and tying their hands together, making them lie down and placing thatch on top of them. Then they took paraffin from the lamps, sprinkled it over the thatch, and set it alight, burning their victims alive in a funeral pyre. The girl had survived, but pretended to be dead, and for some reason one of the rebels came back and removed the burning thatch. Her mother, her two sisters and her brother were burned alive. Other villagers were taken to carry the loot, but most of them were beaten and hacked to death when their use was over. Her young brother was left for dead, but later rescued by the army; he had raw welts on his back where he had been beaten with a bicycle chain; his jaw was broken and his face bloated where he had been kicked. He was twelve years old.

I did not see any actual fighting since the town itself was under the protection of the army. But the problem for the army was that the LRA operated in small groups which picked on soft targets such as remote villages. It was for this reason that the government herded people into IDP (Internally Displaced Persons) camps to deny the rebels a source of food and to protect the local population, but these camps themselves became places of hopelessness and despair. People in the area surrounding the main towns of Gulu, Kitgum and Lira also abandoned their homes at nights and tracked into the towns because they were under military protection. The parents sent their children since they were the most likely to be abducted by the LRA. In the evenings great masses of children could be seen thronging the roads, hurrying to make it to the towns before nightfall, and in the early mornings there was another great exodus. They slept under the verandas, on the streets, or anywhere they could find a place to unroll their bedding. The movement of these children and the sheer pathos of the situation were captured by three young Californian film-makers in the movie 'The Invisible children.'

From a medical point of view, I diagnosed Kony from afar as a paranoid schizophrenic, suffering from delusions. He had all the signs of a type of schizophrenia in which certain trigger factors provoke an extreme paranoid reaction. In this state he then sought instruction as to what actions he should take from 'the Angel' or the spirits. Sometimes he was told that this was to be a day for death by burning. Another day could be a day of death by stabbing, or boiling, while at other times a village should be punished for not obeying him; an abductee could be killed because the angel had warned him that the person was planning to escape. So he would send out orders by mobile phone or satellite phone (which had been provided by his political supporters in London) that people were to die, according to the instructions he had received. Another mark of his mental illness was that Kony did not feel any guilt for his actions, nor empathy with his victims, since in his mind he was being instructed by a higher authority and dissociated himself from the suffering which he inflicted. He did not carry a gun personally, and the LRA did not usually use bullets to kill their victims; they were stabbed with a bayonet, hacked with *pangas* or beaten to death.

When word came into the main towns that another village had been attacked and more atrocities committed, such as a baby having been skewered through the stomach and thrown up into a tree, the news caused panic and mayhem among the local population, but the strange thing was that even while all this carnage was going on, those who lived in Kampala were detached from it and were poorly informed as to what was going on. I spoke to a few people in Kampala who had not been to the north for many years, and their perception of the war was: 'Those people are fighting among themselves.'

Nothing could have been further from the truth since the suffering of the people of the north was without their choosing. Lira hospital, with a capacity of two hundred and eighty beds, had five hundred patients and only five doctors, and the sight and the smell of the wards, packed with the victims of the LRA, resembled a scene from a First World War field hospital. Yet the people themselves were neither bitter nor full of recriminations; there was just an atmosphere of resigned despair. People would stand round the town in small groups and shake their heads.

'Pray for us,' they would say. They did not see an end to the war, they did not see what could stop Kony, but they were praying that God, the rest of Uganda and the world, would see their plight and come to their rescue.

Such a war, where a psychopath preyed on his own people, would probably have died out apart from the support of the

Sudanese, plus Kony's strategy of kidnapping children to replenish his recruits. He had refined this strategy over the years so that the children were indoctrinated into his cult through beatings, killings and fear, until they became hardened killers themselves. According to reports from formerly abducted children, Kony had a charismatic personality, to the point that one young abductee insisted that Kony was a kind man, and it was only the people under him who were cruel – this was despite the fact they knew the orders for the beatings and killings came from Kony.

From his base in Sudan, Kony would send bands of rebels into Uganda, composed mainly of abducted children, numbering anything from twenty to five hundred in size. A group would target a village or a school and abduct more children and students. They would then force them to carry the loads they had looted and set out for Sudan. These were arduous journeys in which the rebels could cover up to fifty kilometres a day in harsh terrain and extreme heat, and those children who did not keep up were simply killed. Kony justified such killings on the grounds that they could not allow anyone to remain behind as they would lead the army to them, but there was another more sinister reason for the killings. They were the first step on the way to the complete dehumanization and ownership of the captives. Some of the children were as young as nine when they were taken from their classrooms, roped together, and marched into the bush. Within hours many of them had swollen and blistered feet and cried out that they could go no further. Such children were first beaten by the rebels to encourage them to continue, but if they could not, they were told they could rest. This 'rest' had a particular meaning: the child could now rest permanently in death, but the death was not simply by a bullet – a group of friends would be made to beat the child. The children would be given sticks and instructed to hit their friend or family member. Of course they did not want to do this, but they themselves were beaten to force them, so they would tentatively beat the child around the legs.

'No, not like that,' the commander would instruct. 'Like this', and he would beat the child on the head. Then, crying and sobbing, the other children would beat their victim until his blood and brains leaked out over the ground.

By forcing children to kill in this manner within hours of their capture, they were made to share in the collective guilt. They had killed their own friends and family, and not only were they terrified that the same thing would happen to them, they were now killers and could not go back to a normal life. Once a child had been captured, there was an eleventh commandment which Kony strictly enforced: 'Thou shalt not try to escape', and the only punishment for breaking this commandment was death.

One group of children was abducted from a girl's boarding school in Lira, known as St Mary's College, Aboke. The rebels arrived late in the evening and broke into a dormitory, taking one hundred and thirty-nine girls hostage. They roped them together and herded them into the bush on their journey to Sudan, like the Arab slave traders of last century. Sister Rachelle, who was the headmistress, was unaware that the girls had been taken until the next morning, when she immediately followed their trail into the bush and caught up after several hours tracking. She pleaded with the rebel leaders to let her girls go, and eventually they decided to allow one hundred and nine of the pupils to return with her, but kept thirty, including the head-girl. Sister Rachelle and some of the parents of the abducted children spent the next eight years campaigning for the release of their daughters, forming themselves into an organisation, known as the Concerned Parents Association. Among the people whom they sought to bring influence on Kony were the Pope and Hilary Clinton, but Kony swore that he would never release any of the girls, and it was nine years before the last of them knew freedom. By that time several, including the head girl, had been killed and all of them had been abused physically and sexually, with many having borne children to rebel commanders. Kony himself had scores of children by various girls held hostage whom he euphemistically called his 'wives.'

The head-girl of the school never made it back alive because someone saw her talking to a local person while she was being held captive in South Sudan and informed Kony that she was planning to escape. Kony was then told by 'the Angel' to make an example of her, so she was beaten so badly that her teeth were knocked out, then tied up in the sun and left to die of thirst. The other girls passed her on their way to fetch water, but no one was allowed to touch her. She took several days to die, but neither Kony nor his senior commanders showed any remorse for the torture of this young girl.

One of the Aboke girls managed to escape from the LRA after four years in captivity. We came to know Alice after her escape since she became part of our extended family, and we sponsored her through the rest of her education. Slowly and painfully Alice's story unfolded, a tale of intense suffering and immense courage for a child.

After she was taken captive, all the children were force-marched towards the Sudan border, where Kony had his main camp close to Juba. The march took weeks, but finally they arrived at the camp where they were distributed among the rebels and used mainly in duties such as cooking and cultivating in the surrounding fields. She had been held for several years by the time she became sick and was taken to what was known as the sick-bay, located at another small camp some distance away. Here the sick and wounded were allowed to rest and given rudimentary treatment. The security at this camp was not so strict; she was left alone and was thus able to make her escape, but when she was hiding in a culvert beside the road, she realized that the choices now facing her were bleak. If she was recaptured, she would be beaten and killed, but she was also amidst a local population who were hostile to anyone identified as being part of the LRA since the rebels had stolen their food and slaughtered their cattle. The people in the town of Juba itself were not much better because they collaborated with the LRA and would return any abductee they found. Either way the choices were stark, but due to a complete lack of knowledge of the geography of the area or how to get back to Uganda, she decided to take her chances and head for Juba town.

As fate would have it, she was identified as an escapee by a local man who was a charcoal trader, but he decided not to hand her back to the rebels and instead took her into his own home as his 'wife' – she was fifteen years old. Coincidentally, another boy who had escaped was hiding in Juba when he realised that Alice was also there. He thus determined he would try to get back to Uganda and take her with him. He extracted her from the clutches of the charcoal seller, and they set out to walk back to Uganda. By this time Alice was pregnant, and the journey was arduous, the route taking them over harsh conditions through the Imatong Mountains. In the midst of this difficult terrain she miscarried, but somehow the boy managed to get her back to Uganda alive, though she was in critical condition. When she recovered, she came back to lira to be reunited with her mother, but shortly after returning, her mother died in an outbreak of cholera, leaving Alice's grandmother as her only surviving relative.

Alice went back to school – the same school from which she had been abducted, and the nuns looked after her tenderly, but she was so traumatized that she refused to speak. The sisters took her to Italy for a holiday to see if the change would help her to forget, but she was withdrawn and non-communicative. When she came back to Lira she had undergone some medical check-ups, including HIV testing, and was told the test was negative, but several months later a further HIV test was carried out, and this time she was informed that she was positive. This child was sixteen years of age, she had been abducted and held hostage for four years, she had been beaten and abused, had miscarried in the mountains of south Sudan without medical help, had come home to witness her mother die of cholera and finally been told she had AIDS. One wonders how much suffering a human being can endure. Prior to the night when the rebels attacked the school, she had been a normal high school student; the school was one of the best in northern Uganda, and the students were regarded as the cream. Years later, I met a Ugandan who was living in Manchester, married to an Irishman. She was a well educated young woman who was now a British citizen, and during the course of our conversation I found that she had also attended the same school and had been abducted with Alice on that fateful night, but she had been one of the 109 who were rescued. I was one of the few people to whom she talked of that night; she had put it all behind her and moved on.

When Alice had been diagnosed as HIV positive, the sisters from Lira called to ask if I could help, and I requested them to bring Alice to Kampala to see me. I met a small, withdrawn young girl, who would barely speak, but before I gave any medical advice, I decided to repeat the HIV test since I was puzzled as to why it had been negative and then apparently become positive. The test which I carried out was negative, and perhaps this was one of the few pieces of good news which Alice had received in her life to that point. When I told her, a silent tear trickled down her cheek. Alice said that she wished to study science for 'A' levels so that she could apply for medicine; her ambition after all that she had been through was to become a doctor. I was only too happy to facilitate her in her aspirations by sponsoring her through school.

Two years later, though she was still a quiet shy girl, she passed her 'A' levels and was given a place in medical school. Today she is a happy, smiling medical student and anyone who meets her would have no idea of what she has been through. They would simply see a beautiful young woman who speaks slowly and deliberately and has dimples when she smiles. When she started her clinical attachments I asked her if she needed anything, and she told me that she needed skirts and dresses to wear on the wards, as like most students she only possessed jeans. So I organized for her to go shopping, and the following day she came to show me her purchases. As she displayed her outfits, I felt privileged to be involved in her life; I could see that she was finally happy and surprisingly well adjusted. She had a new radiance about her; she was not only outwardly beautiful, but she had an inward glow. I thought about how much she had suffered, how much she had overcome, how much she had already achieved and would go on to achieve in her life.

Peace was fourteen years old and was studying with Alice at St Mary's College, Aboke, where she was doing well in class, but, unexpectedly, she asked to leave and go to another school. The Sisters did not understand this request and her older sister was particularly unsympathetic, accusing her of not wishing to apply herself to studying. But the reason for the strange request was that Peace had a strong premonition that she was going to be abducted. The fear was made all the more real by the fact that children were being abducted every day in northern Uganda, although St Mary's was thought to be secure. Within weeks, Peace's premonition became a reality, as she was one of the thirty abducted girls whom Sister Rachelle failed to bring back.

She walked for two months from Lira to the border and on into Sudan where Kony's camp was located. While they were in Uganda, they did not take a straight route but had to zigzag back and forth in order to avoid the Ugandan army. However, when they reached the border, they walked for two and a half weeks without stopping, usually starting at three in the morning. She had no shoes, and like the rest of the children, her feet were swollen, bruised and lacerated, but they had to keep moving, as the alternative was to be beaten or killed.

When they reached the camp, they were put to work in the surrounding fields to cultivate food, or were made to care for the scores of small children who had been born in the camp. The ground was rock hard and the work back-breaking, and since there was a general shortage of food, they were not even given the food they managed to cultivate. This was kept for the senior commanders and fighters, while they had to survive on boiled grass and wildflowers. For two years she went without tasting salt, so that when she tasted it again, she threw up violently for a whole day. Peace was slightly built, but was also emaciated and weak, so the commanders at first thought she was not going to survive, but when they realized that she refused to die, they gave her, along with another girl, to one of their rebel leaders who had twenty-one other women.

As I talked to Peace about these experiences, I realized that far from being weak, she was one of the toughest people I had ever met and that nothing she experienced had succeeded in breaking her spirit. I asked her about the man she had been given to, and she looked me in the eye and told me that she loathed and detested him.

'He was a ghost, he was the devil,' she said, and she added that she had never tired of telling him to his face that he was evil. The striking thing was that she could say how much she loathed him, yet she was not twisted or bitter in her own spirit and remained undamaged. It was as if she could correctly identify his evil and what he had caused her to suffer, without letting it affect her own purity. Death was an everyday experience in the camp, with children being killed because they tried to escape, but despite this, when Peace was questioned about whether she still had any notions of escaping, she told her captors that if she got the least opportunity she would take it. The Aboke girls were constantly guarded; they slept on the

73

bare ground, tied to a tree, or during rainy season in a mud hut, tied to the centre pole. Several years after she had been taken captive, Kony himself confronted her and told her that the Holy Spirit had told him she was planning her escape.

'I would escape at any opportunity,' she reiterated, 'but there is no organized plan, and if you are saying that the Holy Spirit was the one who told you, you are lying; that was not the Holy Spirit.'

No one confronted Kony like this, and within a few days she was awakened to be taken with two of her friends to be executed. This was to be carried out some distance away, in the area where Judith, the head girl, had been murdered the previous year. But before they could carry out the execution, the rebels received a radio call from Kony, telling them to bring the girls back. 'You are being given a second chance; admit that you are wrong and that Kony's revelation was true, and you will be spared,' she was told.

'You can kill me if you want, but I will not admit anything; there is no organized plan to escape.'

Peace had passed the fear of death and was prepared to defy Kony, even at the cost of her own life. The rebels then made her and two of her friends lie on the ground, brought a large bunch of sticks and ordered the junior ranks to beat them. She was given one hundred lashes on the buttocks, beaten with the flat of a *panga* on the back and kicked where she lay. After the first beating, she was hauled to her feet and given another chance to admit that Kony was right, but she still refused.

'Save your life,' they told her. 'You are going to be beaten to death.' But she still refused.

So she was beaten even more severely, but she was now numb and semi-conscious and could no longer feel the pain. The beatings had started in the morning, and she must have passed in and out of consciousness the whole day, but by the evening she awoke parched with thirst and screaming for water.

'We are not supposed to give you water,' was the response, but someone brought her small sips to moisten her lips. Over the next few weeks she was guarded in a hut and told that if she moved more than five meters outside, she would be shot immediately. It took months to recover.

The killings continued. At a meeting of the senior command, it was decided that the older people were no longer of any use and were eating food which was scarce, so the best policy was to get rid of them. This was not done by simply setting them free, or sending them to Juba, but by rounding them up and murdering them. More than fifty people were herded together and beaten to death or shot. Many of those who were slaughtered were not buried, but were carried some distance from the camp and their bodies flung on the ground to decompose. Others were buried in shallow graves, with the feet still protruding through the earth. It appeared that the leaders of the LRA had become so dehumanized that they considered death was normal, and much of their strategy involved punishment by death. They would never have controlled the camps otherwise since 90% of those in the LRA were abducted in the first place. They would not have obtained absolute obedience from their recruits through fear unless the consequence of questioning orders had been so draconian.

Infringements of other rules could also result in death. All the girls were brought together for questioning about an officer who was reported to have had sexual relations with an Aboke girl, without permission from the ruling command. No one was allowed to have a relationship without authorization, and it appeared that one of their senior officers had broken the rules. None of the girls appeared to know who this was, but the rebel commanders were becoming very upset and set up machine guns, threatening to shoot everyone if information was not forthcoming. One of the girls was a Karamajong and did not speak Acholi, the language which the rebels used, so Peace translated for her.

'It was me,' she said immediately. 'The guy took me, I had no choice.'

The officer was beaten on this occasion, but when it happened a second time, he was then executed.

Many children who tried to escape to Juba were brought back by the Arabs, and all of them were killed. Peace's mother, Angelina, Sister Rachelle and Ben Piri, the father of Joanne, travelled to Juba to meet Kony and plead for the release of their children, but the Aboke girls had been taken to another camp several kilometres away, and they were not allowed to see them. Kony declared on that occasion that he was inclined to let them go, but several of his other commanders saw it as a sign of weakness. One of Kony's senior commanders, known as Banya, had been part of the previous Ugandan army under Obote, another was known as Sam Kolo and both of these men appeared to enjoy the torture, killings, and gratuitous violence which they inflicted. Later Banya was cornered by the army and took advantage of an amnesty which the government had in place to encourage LRA defections. He was taken by the army but was later released and is still a free man, living the good life in Gulu, as is Sam Kolo, with neither of them having suffered any consequences for the killings and torture they inflicted on hundreds of children.

When Peace thought that things could not get any worse, they did. The Ugandan army launched a raid deep inside Sudan and struck Kony's camps, but the LRA were alerted and made their escape south towards the Ugandan border. They had to pass through the Imatong Mountains to get back to Uganda, but the army surrounded the foothills, trapping them in the higher reaches of the mountains. It was cold, food was scarce, and the local people, from whom they had stolen livestock and food, shot at them when they travelled through mountain passes. People around her would be shot randomly: the person behind her fell, and then the person two ahead; she did not know when it would be her turn; she just had to keep on moving.

The army's operation actually made things worse in the north of Uganda since Kony now had no safe base in Sudan and re-entered Uganda, where the LRA split into groups of various sizes, terrorizing the local population. The only advantage for Peace was that since she was now in her own country, it made the chances of successful escape higher. By this time she had been in captivity for eight years and was weak from constant beatings and starvation. They were in Pader District, in a group of about 120 LRA, and she determined that she would escape, come what may. She informed the boys who were guarding her that she was going to escape, and although they had the power to shoot her, she reminded them that they too had been abducted. Slowly she began to veer off the track and walk away from her guards while they looked on, but they did nothing, and gradually she was hidden from their view by the tall grass. She did not run because she had no strength, but she could hear that no one was coming after her and walked on and on. She was lost and didn't know where she was going until she finally heard the sound of a vehicle and headed in that direction, coming out in a clearing where a woman was hoeing.

The woman straightened up and looked at her intently.

'You are not from these parts, are you?' she remarked.

Peace felt very vulnerable because she did not know how the local people would react since they saw her as a rebel. There had been an incident where twins aged twelve had escaped, and an elderly lady found them and brought them back to the rebels, saying, 'Here are your children.'

The twins were beaten to death as a result. It was impossible to understand why this woman had acted in this way, but it demonstrated the alienation of the local population to anyone who was associated with the LRA.

As Peace stood trembling, other villagers came to see what was going on.

'You are not from here,' they asserted again. Then one of them lifted her long skirt and pointed out the lightening of her skin where she had worn rubber boots, which identified her as having been with the LRA.

'Yes, you are one of them,' they said. But they were not hostile, and before the day was over, one lady who knew her mother had identified who she was.

After eight years she was home.

The headline in the New Vision read '22 die in Teso Bus Ambush', and when I turned to the next page there was another small headline 'Rebels kill 23 in Lira.'

Forty-five innocent people had perished that day. These were not soldiers fighting against rebels; they were just Ugandans who happened to be in Lira or Teso. They were not caught in cross fire or even in friendly fire; they were just taken from a bus and shot through the eyes, or taken from their beds, made to kneel on the earth and hacked to death. Most of them were killed by children, not because those children bore them any personal animosity, but because they had been ordered to do so.

A boy came to see me, bringing with him a picture of his younger brother who had been abducted. I looked at the picture of a beautiful nine-year old boy whose eyes reflected innocence, fear and bewilderment. But he was one of the fortunate ones, having been rescued by the army within a week of being taken, unlike his friends who were beaten to death and never returned. In the picture, seated beside him was a twelve year old, who had been abducted more than a year previously and had been rescued. His expression was completely blank. This child was still only twelve years old, but he had already killed his fellow human beings. When I looked at the photo, I could not tell his age. He was not a child, he was not an adult;

he had become an automaton, a blank piece of paper on which anything could be written. This child had been told what to do by his rebel commanders, and he did it. If he was told to steal some food, he did it, if he was told to cut down a bunch of matoke, he did it, and if he was told to hack a person to death, he did it, in just the same way that he cut down the bunch of bananas. He was a slave sent out to kill other innocent, defenceless Ugandans.

Kony made a raid on Agora Market at the Sudanese border with Kitgum. At the time I happened to be in Kitgum to arrange orthopaedic surgery for some of the formerly abducted children who had gunshot and bomb injuries. I was travelling with Will Ross, the BBC correspondent, and in the course of ferreting out information, we met two children who had escaped during the raid. Because there had been a lull in the fighting before this time, many people had assumed that Kony was a spent force and that the Ugandan army, UPDF, were finally getting things under control, but according to the young people we spoke to, this was not the case. Kony had explained his lack of operations in Northern Uganda as an instruction from the angel, but, unfortunately, he was still very much alive and in good health.

According to the escapees, on this occasion five thousand LRA had been mobilized to march to the border to carry out the raid on Agora Market. They had marched for a week in organized columns, and when they reached the Agora hills they sent a few hundred rebels down to attack the market and the police barracks. Apparently they brought such a large number primarily to carry back the loot, as they expected rich pickings, but were also unsure of what resistance they would encounter along the way. The LRA were short of medicines and money, and it was well known that the Agora Market was a major trading centre where both would be available.

The other significant factor about this raid was that Kony himself travelled with them. This was unusual since he usually sent his minions to do his bidding. One of the children told us that she walked part of the way beside him and that he would make jokes, (though the jokes she told us did not seem very funny).

In the hierarchy of things, Kony was the absolute authority, known as 'the prophet', and under him were several chairmen, who would brutally see that his wishes were carried out to the letter. 90% of the 'rebels' were formerly abducted children who did not believe in Kony's cause but were kept under tight control, with radios being banned and little communication from the outside world. The children were brainwashed: they were told the UPDF would kill them if they escaped and, apart from that, the penalty for even thinking of escaping was death.

After years of war the senses of the whole of the population of Northern Uganda had become dulled because they could no longer afford the luxury of feelings. They did not have the basics of life, they had no homes, no plots to dig, they did not know when their children would be taken from them, and they did not know when those children might come back and kill them. All that was left was for them to creep through what remained of their lives in a state of half survival. Could they be blamed for living in this state of hopelessness, believing Kony when he said that he would come and kill them, but no longer believing the army when they said it would give them protection?

There were mixed feelings among the local population about the role of the government and the army. Many felt the government could have controlled the situation if it had the will, and that an army of over fifty thousand soldiers should have been able to deal with a rebel force which was tiny in comparison. There was immense suffering imposed through the dislocation and displacement of the population into the IDP camps, which nevertheless, continued to be targets of LRA attacks. Several years into the war there was an attempt at a peace settlement by a government Minister, Betty Bagombe, but the government appeared diffident, and the opportunity was lost.

Personally, I felt that it was not the case that the government wished to prolong the war, as was the theory put forward by some who said that the military were making money through the continuation of the war. The ineffectiveness of the army reflected its poor operational capability which was also seriously disrupted by a misguided foray into the Congo, and by the corruption and incompetence of generals and commanders. Inquiries into procurement and payroll revealed out-of-date rations, junk helicopters, and undersized uniforms. There were also ghost soldiers: whole battalions seemed to have disappeared, but were still on the army payroll. The various inquiries and resulting shake-up finally saw the replacement of the Army Commander by General Aronda Nyakairima, a man of integrity and competence. His appointment brought significantly improved operational ability, and the army began to gain the upper hand. However, this was not a conventional war, and the LRA had no agenda except to perpetuate its own existence, in which objective they had been very successful.

The Ugandan army was a conventional army, fighting a terrorist force which had broken into smaller and smaller groups, and even the British army, with all the resources and training available to it, were not able to break the IRA in Northern Ireland over a period of twenty-five years. The army was a moderately disciplined force, with a normal command structure, discipline, logistics and organization, but when they seemed to be getting the upper hand, Kony would retreat to Sudan and keep a low profile for some time. Then he would strike again, sending out bands of his followers to wreak havoc on the local population. In this way the war had lasted for twenty years.

Belatedly, the International Criminal Court issued arrest warrants for Kony and some of his top commanders. This action was a mixed blessing as, although it sent a message that the 'international community' would not stand idly by in the face of crimes against humanity, the court simply issued the warrants and did nothing to enforce them. This left the member states with the problem of actually arresting those who had been indicted. In the case of Kony, he was not about to give up voluntarily and place himself in the hands of the International Criminal Court. The warrant for his arrest simply fed his paranoia and became a stumbling block to any negotiated peace settlement. After all, it was this high level of paranoia which had kept him from capture for twenty years. Kony's mental processes did not function like those of any normal person; this was confusing for most people who actually met him or entered into negotiations with him. The paranoia was not always evident, so he could appear to be quite normal much of the time until the paranoia was triggered. Normal people relate to other human beings through shared emotional interchange: we pick up on the non-verbal signals and connect with them. Kony did not possess this ability to reciprocate emotions, and though he could appear to interact with people, he could then kill them without any emotional reaction. It was these characteristics which made him so dangerous and so effective.

By 2006 the Ugandan army had succeeded in pushing the LRA out of Uganda and South Sudan because Kony had largely lost the support of the Northern Sudanese government and been forced to take refuge in Garamba Forest in northeast Congo. Riek Machar, who was now the Deputy President of South Sudan, decided to initiate peace talks and made contact with the LRA. Kony was apparently amenable to negotiations and appointed a team, composed mainly of the Ugandans living in the Diaspora, to negotiate on his behalf. Such people had never accepted Museveni as a legitimate leader of Uganda and felt that they could use the LRA to gain some political leverage. Several had supported Kony from a distance through sending him money for airtime and satellite phones, but there were others whose reason for being part of the team was even simpler – money. The international community was paying a handsome allowance to the team carrying out the negotiations, so negotiating for the LRA was a lucrative business opportunity. Kony stayed hidden in Garamba though he made many false promises that he was coming to sign a peace agreement. In the end his paranoia got the better of him and, instead of signing a peace agreement, he murdered his own second-in-command, Vincent Otti, whom he believed was going to hand him over to the ICC. At least Kony's paranoia achieved something constructive in this case, since Otti was personally responsible for countless callous atrocities. The irony was that he was Kony's most loyal henchman and would have done anything which Kony asked of him. Finally, he paid the ultimate price for his loyalty, though he was one of the lucky ones who had a quick death by a bullet.

There was much talk about forgiveness of the LRA, in the light of the peace negotiations. I was somewhat confused by what people meant by forgiveness since my perception had been that forgiveness was a thing of the heart and not simply letting someone off the hook with no consequences. A murderer could be forgiven by the relatives of the person killed, but the murderer should still go to prison. I thought that the people in the north who had lost sons or daughters, or been disfigured by having their lips or ears cut off might choose to forgive, but the perpetrators should still be punished for their actions. But the great swell of opinion in the north of Uganda was to 'forgive' Kony, meaning to pardon him, in order that the war would end. Personally, I would have preferred a word like reprieve rather than forgive. How does one balance lawfulness and consequences, in such a case, against pardon and reprieve, given all the terrible things Kony had done? The people asked the government to forgive him for the sake of peace because they had suffered for two decades, and they desperately wanted the war to be over. The same situation had pertained in Northern Ireland where the government pardoned the members of the paramilitary organizations who had murdered civilians and policemen. It was hard for the families of the victims to see these men go free, but it was done for the sake of the greater good. Ultimately, both sides of the community had to enter into a process of dialogue and forgive each other.

In the end, all the efforts of the peace negotiators and the international community were for nothing, as Kony preferred to continue his cat and mouse game. But Northern Uganda was at peace for the first time in twenty years, and slowly the IDP camps emptied and people went back to their homes. Kony is still operating in the Congo and Central African Republic, looting villages, killing innocent people, and abducting children. He has merely moved the sphere of his operations. For those of us who have watched him wreak havoc among the poor and defenceless for more than two decades, we wonder why modern military technology has not been used to rid the world of this sick and dangerous man. A mobile phone and a drone are all that is required, but those who have the technology do not seem willing, or perhaps they have no strategic interest in the poor of Congo, Sudan or Northern Uganda.

# Are we really climbing this mountain?

Robbie and I had planned to work in Uganda for two years, though the period kept getting extended from two, to three, then four, to five years, but at this point we were overtaken by events. Over the years the work had evolved from the ad hoc clinics in the church vestibule to a health centre and then grown to a full hospital, Kiwoko. We had just gone through an arduous time in the work of the hospital – one of those periods when I had to grit my teeth and get on with it, because there seemed to be no end to all that needed to be done. Since we had recently received registration as a hospital, we organised an official opening by the Vice-President of Uganda, who was himself a medical doctor.

Unfortunately, we were also very busy with the medical side as the date of the official opening drew near – and very understaffed. I had been doing surgery during my time in Uganda and had become proficient at caesarean sections, exploratory abdominal surgery, and hernia repairs – which seemed to constitute the bulk of our work, but I was less experienced at hysterectomies and the removal of tumours. Just before the opening, we had a patient who had a large abdominal ovarian tumour, weighing several kilograms, which I removed (it was the weight of a small baby and the villagers thought she had been pregnant for two years). The patient appeared to be recovering well until my colleague, Dr Richard, told me on the very day of the opening that the patient did not seem to be passing urine. We went through the ceremony, but at the back of my mind I was worried about the patient, since failure to pass urine was an ominous sign.

On that day we also bade farewell to my friend, John Ando, who had been my right hand man in building the hospital. He had the opportunity to travel to Tanzania to train as a biomedical technician, which would ensure him a job in the future, but we were concerned about him because he was HIV positive and had begun having headaches.

Immediately after the opening, I rushed to Kampala to find a surgical colleague to review my patient. Dr Christina Dewind travelled around mission hospitals doing surgery on a voluntary basis. She was very experienced, and I was confident she would be the best person to sort out any complications of this case. Fortunately, I found she was still in Kampala and she came back to review the patient; a further operation was carried out and the patient, thereafter, recovered well – much to my relief. I was very stressed by the constant demands which were upon me from every aspect of running the hospital – I was the surgeon, the builder, the administrator and the general dog's body.

We were travelling every few weeks to visit our children at boarding school in Kenya. The long drive was arduous, but the trips were useful because we were able to buy supplies for the hospital which were not readily available in Uganda. During these visits we were able to spend quality time with our children and to escape for a few days and recharge our batteries. But the long journeys were becoming difficult because I had developed severe back-pain, which I attributed to hours of travelling on rough roads. At around the same time I noticed a breast lump – which was unusual for a man, but not unheard of – so to be on the safe side, I asked Christina to remove it and sent it for biopsy. At the end of a theatre list at which I had been assisting, I took off my surgeon's gown and hopped up on the table to become the patient. She excised the lump under local anaesthetic as I looked on, and after the surgery I did a ward-round before going home for supper.

When Christina finished in theatre she came back to our house, muttering to Robbie that she did not think I should be carrying on with work as normal since I had just had surgery.

'What surgery?' Robbie exclaimed.

She knew nothing about the operation since I had not told her. The tissue was sent for histology and showed simple breast hyperplasia, with no evidence of cancer, so I forgot about it.

Within a few weeks John Ando returned from his course since the headaches had become worse. It was evident that he had progressed to full blown meningitis, and there was little we could do to halt the progress of the disease. Over the next few days he went blind, then lost consciousness and died. My children kept vigil by his bedside and cried as they watched him sink; it was a tough experience for teenage kids – they were seeing life in the raw. Several years later, when Lauren was at school in the UK, a teacher found her crying alone in the corridor and could not understand what was going on. Lauren was crying for her friend, John Ando.

It was one of those periods when nothing appeared to be easy, and just getting through the day was a grind. To make matters more complicated, it transpired that Ando had another family in Arua, though he had never officially married. During his time in Luweero he had then married a young woman from the area and had a child. When the news of his death reached his other family, the relatives came down for his funeral but set about doing everything in their power to dispossess the new wife and child, including taking Ando's personal possessions and burying them in the coffin. This kind of confusion was not uncommon at funerals where another family might turn up to mourn the deceased husband and father. It was relatively common for children to discover that they had a number of half brothers and sisters at the funeral of their father, or for the wife to find that she had not been the only wife. In Ando's case, the dispute was so acrimonious that I had to intervene to ensure that his official wife was not beaten up and thrown out on the street.

Over the next few months the back pain persisted, and I started looking more haggard, until one evening the pain was so severe I needed an injection of pethidine. As I was now at the stage of requiring addictive drugs, Dr Richard suggested we should carry out more extensive investigations. So the next morning we held a case conference – with me as both the patient and the doctor – along with my two colleagues. I had already done an X-ray of the back which had not shown anything, so Dr Richard suggested that I do an ESR and a chest X-ray, though I had no chest symptoms. The ESR was abnormal, but this test is non-specific and can be raised in minor conditions such as a viral illness or more serious conditions like TB or cancer. However, the big surprise was that the chest X-ray showed I had extensive shadowing on the lung fields like bunches of grapes, occupying sixty percent of the lungs. When I looked at the chest X-ray, I knew this was not good. Of the diagnoses which could cause this kind of picture, there was a slight possibility that I had some exotic tropical disease, but the most likely diagnosis was cancer.

Robbie and I immediately packed our bags and went back to Ireland, so that I could have more definitive investigations. It was not a very happy homecoming since by this time it was obvious that I was very ill. I consulted with a chest physician who looked at the chest X-rays and organised a CT scan at the Belfast City Hospital. The scan was booked for one week ahead, and during that week I was left with my thoughts about life and my impending death. The cancer in my lungs was obviously secondary to another source, and it was important to identify that source in order to know the prognosis. The likely primary sources were either the kidney or the testis, but in the case of the testes one can normally feel a lump, and since I had checked myself several times and had no signs of lumps or bumps, I was sure it was not testicular in origin. This left a primary kidney cancer as the most likely diagnosis, and because of the advanced degree of the lung tumours, I reckoned that this cancer must be at a terminal stage. During the period when I was waiting for the CT scan, I had not the slightest doubt in my mind that I was going to die. I am not the sort of person who clutches at straws, and although I am generally an optimist, I am also a realist, so I did not give myself any hope, and the experience changed me; it put me in touch with my own mortality. Throughout that week I looked back over my life quite dispassionately to assess whether it had been worthwhile, and I reckoned that at least the previous five years of working in Uganda had been significant. Perhaps the rest of my life had been a preparation for those final few years before I died. I was forty years old, and although it had not been a long life, I believed that it had made a difference to others.

Facing one's own death can be an emotional experience. Of course the person facing death does not really know what he is going forward to, even though he may have faith. I had faith, but I was still facing the unknown. When I looked back over my life, it had not been perfect, and there were many things which I regretted, things which I could have done better, patients who had a bad outcome, and time that could have been used more productively. I had read the gospels often and identified with the faith of Jesus and the situations he found himself in everyday. They were very similar to what I experienced in Africa – the injustice, the poverty, the suffering and the unfairness of life. He viewed life through faith in the Heavenly Father who would one day right the wrongs of this earth and give people their true reward. There was a song by Chris Rea written about a child who had been abused, questioning the meaning of life and if the wrongs of this life would be righted in the afterlife. One line went 'Tell me there's a heaven, tell me that it's true.' I had a resonance with that line, as I had seen much injustice and suffering first hand and could not rationalise much of what I saw.

But the emotional part was not because I was facing my own death or what might lie beyond; it was leaving behind my family. Sean, my oldest boy, was sixteen, and as I looked at

Sean, I knew that I would never see him graduate, I would never see him marry, and I would never see my grandchildren. Death was the ultimate finality, and I would not bear witness to those parts of their lives; I would never see my children's children. Robbie had been strong, but as I withered away, she not only had her own sorrow and grief to deal with, she had her own fears: what was she going to do on her own with three young children, no assured income, and their lives strewn across Africa?

When I finally went for the CT scan, I lay in the tube and breathed in and out and held my breath as instructed. Then I was asked to wait while the doctor reported on the results. He came into the room within a few minutes to tell me that, as far as he could see from the pattern of the scan, the primary cancer must be in the testis, despite having no palpable lumps. He asked me to go to another department where they would carry out an ultrasound scan which would confirm the diagnosis. The next scan proved that my cancer had indeed originated in the right testis, with extensive secondary deposits in the lymph nodes along the spinal cord and throughout the lungs. The cancer had infiltrated throughout one testis in a uniform manner, such that there were no discrete lumps to be felt. Robbie and I sat in the corridor of the city hospital and laughed. No one would have understood why we were laughing since it had just been confirmed that I had advanced cancer, but we knew that at least there was now some hope.

The difference between a diagnosis of cancer of the testis or of the kidney at an advanced stage was simple: one was treatable while the other was not. Several years earlier a drug known as cysplatinum had been developed as part of a chemotherapy regime for cancer of the testis, and the results, even for an advanced stage, were good. Although my general condition looked so bad that those who met me were convinced I was going to die, I knew there was now hope.

The treatment itself was nauseating, prolonged, difficult and debilitating, consisting of cycles of chemotherapy lasting a week, followed by a few weeks of rest to enable the body to recover in order that it could be zapped again. However, the secondary deposits in my lungs and back melted away, and six months later they took another CT scan which showed that my lungs were completely clear of cancer deposits.

I was keen to get back to Uganda since I had left so precipitously, and although we felt that our time at Kiwoko Hospital was drawing to a natural end, we still needed to go back to tie up loose ends and hand the hospital on to the next person taking over. We would then return to the UK to provide for the educational needs of our children: Sean had gone as far as he could in terms of schooling in Kenya, and it seemed the right time to return home.

While we were preparing to go back to Uganda, I heard that some friends were planning to climb Mount Kenya and thought that climbing Mount Kenya would be a fitting celebration of being alive. Mount Kenya rises to 16,500 feet, and having previously climbed it with Sean, I knew that it was a majestic experience to stand on the top of one of the peaks. Robbie was not so sure that she wanted to go up this particular mountain and was secretly hoping that the whole trip would be cancelled. We flew into Kenya to meet Sean, who had returned to school ahead of us, and to hook up with the other climbers, but it had been raining heavily and the word was that the climb would be called off, much to Robbie's relief. We picked Sean up from school and rendezvoused with the other climbers, but the leader of the expedition told us that it was unlikely that we could climb because of the heavy rain. Instead, he proposed that we would stay at the base camp and do a hill walk if the climb was not possible. Robbie was OK with this since it was just a simple nature ramble. On the following morning we started walking, but we seemed to be climbing the mountain itself, so she asked me tentatively, 'We are not actually climbing this mountain are we?'

This question was a metaphor for Robbie's life because when she had psyched herself up for something which she thought was difficult, but attainable, like living in Africa for two years, she found that the goalposts got moved – she was still there after six years. When she thought her husband just had a bad back from driving over too many potholed roads, she discovered that he had advanced cancer, and now when she had been told that she was just going for a hill walk, she discovered that she was climbing another mountain – literally this time.

Somewhere along the line there were breakdowns in communication which never seemed to work in her favour.

'Ian, tell me that we are not climbing this mountain,' she said again.

'Sweetheart, I think that we are,' I had to reply, and so it was that we were on our way to the top. The vegetation on Mount Kenya was magnificent, and the mountain itself was vast, with many valleys running in different directions to the lower slopes. There was another camp at 14,000 feet where we stopped for the night, cooked and slept, before attempting the final ascent before dawn.

Sometime the next morning, in the biting cold and the dark, we set off again. This time I was shepherding Sean, Michael and Lauren. The boys were doing fine, but Lauren had mild altitude sickness and wanted to lie down on the glazier and have a sleep – not a good idea. I managed to keep her going, and we all reached Point Lenana safely. Being alive and standing at the peak that day was a memorable experience, and I savoured every moment of the life which I had been given back. My lungs, which had been totally infiltrated with cancer a few months ago, were now clear, and I was not having any difficulty breathing at this rarefied altitude. As it happened, my favourite surgeon, Christina Dewind, was one of the party, and she commented as she saw me reach the top, 'Not bad for someone who has just had a course of cysplatinum.'

On our way down we were asked to keep together since it was easy to miss the path, but a young doctor did not stick to this advice and took off at a fast pace, with Michael trying to keep up with him. Michael, who was fourteen, missed a vital turn and got lost on the mountain, a fact which we only discovered when the main group reached base camp. The guides turned on their heel and went back up to look for him, while someone went down to alert mountain rescue. Robbie was beside herself with anxiety; this trip had turned into a nightmare, but within two hours Michael had been found, unharmed. He had gone down a wrong valley but had soon realised his mistake, and although he was not able to retrace his steps, he could see the roofs of the base-camp in the distance and started making his way in the right direction. He told us of his experience on the mountain when he was thirsty and needed a drink; he discovered a stream, but within seconds realised that he was surrounded by rock hyraxes (the cousin of the elephant). These little creatures are very cheeky and can bite, so Michael got out his Swiss army knife and lunged at them. Apart from that, he had no other incidents with wild animals.

The next day we flew back to Uganda, but our plane was delayed and we were late arriving at Entebbe. Some staff from the hospital picked us up and drove us back to Luweero town, where we found men on bicycles waiting for us. Much to our amazement they rode along the dirt road, sprinkling rose petals before us. We realised that they must be part of a welcoming committee which had patiently waited all day for our arrival. We drove slowly towards Kiwoko, and all along the road little knots of people had gathered to wave and cheer. As we neared the Kiwoko Trading centre itself, the crowds thickened, completely blocking the way, so that we had to get out and walk with the crowd. People were waving, ululating, shaking hands, hugging. I had never experienced anything like it, and by the time we made it to the hospital, the crowd had grown to several thousand, all surrounding the Clarkes and giving us a hero's welcome, we were all rendered speechless – what were all these people doing? Surely they could not have come just to welcome us back? But they had; we were engulfed in a sea of people, all wanting a piece of us, to touch us and hug us and make sure that we were real. When we finally made it to the hospital, Rose, one of the nurses, came forward and placed garlands of flowers round our necks. Someone said a few words of welcome, and then they said simply, 'Ian and Robbie, we welcome you back, but you must be tired, you must go and rest.' Unusually for Uganda there were no long speeches, the people had just come to see us in the flesh and welcome us back.

I later learned that there was a special significance in this event: the people in the community had been shaken by the manner and the suddenness of my departure. One moment I was there and then I was gone, and the village people were told that I had gone back because I had cancer, so they had never expected to see me again. For them, the fact that I had survived and come back was a miracle – I might as well have risen from the dead because many of them were totally convinced that I had died. The rumour that I was dead was fuelled by the traditional belief that a sacrifice must be made when a person starts a new project, and I had started the biggest project in the whole district, yet I had not made the necessary sacrifice. Hence, the people said I had become my own sacrifice because I did not appease the spirits. When they were told I was coming back, many of them did not believe it, while for others it was a cause of celebration that the Christian belief had triumphed over the influence of the witchdoctors. Some came to celebrate the miracle of my recovery, while others came to verify that it was actually me, but as we were being mobbed by the crowd, I was wondering if it was all a dream.

# On not being a team player

After a further six months of living in Kiwoko, we said our good-byes once again, handed over the project to Dr Richard and moved back to the UK. We left Kiwoko Hospital in the hands of a British GP who had been working with us when I got cancer, and he fell into place as the next Medical Director. Over the next decade there were a number of excellent men and women – Irish, English and Ugandan – who offered their services to Kiwoko Hospital and kept things running smoothly. The hospital came under the oversight of the Luweero Diocese of the Church of Uganda which had a series of different bishops over the next twenty years, but far from wishing to sever the links with Church Mission Society Ireland, they appeared to feel more comfortable with a strong relationship.

I had applied to do a Master's degree in Public Health at the London School of Hygiene and Tropical Medicine, and there had been much debate between Robbie and me about whether we should live in Ireland or England, but eventually we decided to relocate to England, to a village in Buckinghamshire. Later we were having a discussion with our kids about the decision making process in the family and who had most say.

'Well,' they said. 'You divide the decisions. Mum makes the important decisions about the home, like what colour to paint the house. Dad makes the other decisions – like what country we will live in.' Personally, I would have been happy about this division of labour, but it was not really true, and such decisions were never one sided.

Several months earlier, during one of my free weeks from chemotherapy, we had made a quick trip to England to look for somewhere to live when we returned from Uganda. We had decided we would search within commuter distance of London and zeroed in on Buckinghamshire because we knew some people there, and the school system had a good reputation. I had only forty-five minutes before I had to leave for the airport – not much time to buy a house, but I asked our friends where I should look and was directed to a small development of only two houses being built in the next village, which also happened to be round the corner from some old friends, Kevin and Pamela Duffy, who were later to become significant as our work developed in Uganda.

I climbed inside the unfinished house where I found the builder himself.

'How is the property market these days?' I asked

'Bad,' he admitted. 'People have negative equity. The market is at a standstill'

He was obviously feeling the pain and was keen to make a sale.

'What would you take for this house?' I asked. He named a price which I felt was fair, and then I queried,

'How much would we get as discount if we bought the house without a kitchen and bathroom?'

This may have appeared to be a silly question, as although we might have managed in Luweero without either a built-in kitchen or a flush toilet, this was not how people lived in England, especially in a posh suburb of Buckinghamshire. He humoured me and named a price.

'OK,' I agreed and the deal was done.

The reason I bought a house without a kitchen or bathroom was that we could only raise a limited mortgage. Working in Uganda on a missionary salary for the previous six years did not qualify me for much of a mortgage. We represented those in the 'sub-prime' market since I could be classified as unemployed, a student, or a returning volunteer, none of which was a good credit risk. Being the eternal optimist, I thought that when we got back, we could scrape some more cash together, make a trip to the DIY store and buy a kitchen and bathroom for much less than it would have cost as part of the complete deal, and this is what we did. For several weeks we practically lived in the DIY stores, bringing home paint, toilets, shower, bath-tub and those ubiquitous flat pack kitchen units. I was a bit of a DIY man, but I wasn't a professional, so I made a call to the builder and asked him if he would come round and fit our kitchen and bathroom. And to demonstrate that there are still some understanding builders in the world, he came around and fitted everything!

Carrying out my Masters degree in Public Health was like a half way house in terms of transition back into western society since on that particular course the school accepted only students who had worked in, or originated from, developing countries. Thus, everyone brought their unique experience from various countries, and there was a certain sense of camaraderie and shared experience. Having finished the Masters, it would have been relatively easy for me to get a job again in General Practice, but I could not face the thought of going back to a job where the experience which I had built up over the previous six years would be largely irrelevant, so I did not make the sensible financial choice and opt to become a well paid G.P.

Settling back in the UK was not easy for any of the family. Over the past six years the children had moved from schools in Ireland to home-schooling in Uganda, to boarding school in Kenya, back to Ireland, then to Kenya, then back to England. Sean was first year 'A' levels, while Michael was doing 'O' levels, and Lauren was a year behind. The boys were taken into a large single-sex grammar school with over one thousand students, and the transition was a culture shock for them all. Despite the fact that they were getting an education in a relatively affluent area of England, they were also exposed to the problems of peer pressure and adolescence which we had previously only read about in newspapers. Lauren lost a friend to an overdose of 'E', while another developed anorexia; soft drugs were readily available in the schools, and smoking was regarded as cool.

The kids were at that stage in life when children become somewhat embarrassed by their parents. Lauren brought home one of her friends who was Eurasian in appearance. I was interested in where the young lady came from and asked innocently, 'And what is your ethnic origin?'

If looks could have killed I would have been dead on the spot.

'Dad,' they all chorused 'You don't ask such questions.'

Lauren was never good in the mornings, and we were supposed to tip-toe around and not disturb her. One morning I broke the golden rule by saying cheerfully, 'Good morning Lauren.'

She just gave me a look and answered, 'Don't be so silly.'

Perhaps this was a reasonable response from someone who did not find anything good about mornings.

After the completion of the Master's degree I didn't know what I would do next. Most of the options which I tried did not work out, and I felt like a complete failure; this was compounded by failing a public health examination which I had expected to pass. This feeling of anti-climax and failure was not an unusual scenario for people coming back after working in a developing country. When I was working in Africa, I felt I was doing something useful, my skills were needed, there was a buzz about life and I was not only getting satisfaction from what I was doing, I was receiving a certain amount of approbation. Then I came back and people didn't even register that I had been away.

'Did you have a nice holiday?' someone asked.

'But I have been away saving the world,' I inwardly fumed.

I had witnessed life in the raw, been involved in life and death situations, engaged in a foreign culture and even saved lives. But when I returned to the mother-ship for some mundane reason like getting my children educated, no-one

99

even noticed. On one occasion I did forget that the sphere of interest of the normal neighbour was bound by the *Mail on Sunday* and inadvertently engaged in a conversation about our experiences in Africa. Gratifyingly, the lady immediately appeared to identify with me.

'Oh, I was once in Africa,' she told me.

Finally I had found someone I could talk to.

'In Morocco on holiday, it was ever so nice.'

I applied for jobs with aid agencies, with the rationale that, even if I had to be based in the UK for a couple of years while we took care of our children's education, I would be able to focus on matters concerning development, but I was singularly unsuccessful.

One well known aid agency were interviewing for a medical advisor, so I thought I was in with a chance. The interview appeared to go well, and I explained all that we had done in Luweero in going to the bush, starting a clinic under a tree, and developing it into a hospital. I probably failed to register the growing look of apprehension in the eyes of the members of the interview panel as the story unfolded.

'We will call you,' they reassured me, as I left with the feeling that it had not gone all that badly and that they must have at least been impressed with my experience. True to their word, they did call.

'We are going to re-advertise the job,' they said. Then they came straight to the point. 'We think you are not a team player.'

I thought I was a great team player – as long as I was leading the team. They had actually been appalled by my story since it did not fit in with any good theory of development, and what would they do with a person who had just gone out to Uganda and founded a hospital? It would set a bad precedent – other people might launch themselves into helping people and what would that do to professional development agencies? I was getting the impression that some aid organisations were pretty comfortable in what they were doing, and the last thing they needed was someone to rock their boat.

While we had been working at Kiwoko, we lost so many friends and colleagues due to AIDS and other diseases that it seemed that almost everyone we loved was bound to die. Someone with whom we had built up a close relationship was Janet Kalungi, the World Vision project worker. Janet's sister, Sarah, was eighteen years old and had worked for us at the hospital as an auxiliary nurse, but she was found to be HIV positive, and was dead within a year of diagnosis. It was as if the first wave of HIV hit Uganda with such extraordinary force and virulence that it carried off its victims rapidly and without mercy.

As part of my Master's thesis I had done some research into the community's response to HIV to design an appropriate community-based and community driven intervention. For this I had been awarded a small grant and made forays back and forth to Uganda for focus group discussions, documenting case histories and distributing questionnaires in the community. After I had completed the Master's, I went back to Kiwoko several times to continue more research in the community and looked up Janet who agreed to come back to facilitate a community workshop. We both travelled to Kiwoko by bus and on the journey from Kampala, she told me her own story as it had unfolded since I left.

She had planned to get married the previous year and, as was routine, the couple were asked to go for an HIV test by the church pastor. Neither of them felt they were at risk nor were worried about the result, and they had the test carried out at the blood transfusion service because a friend worked there. But the results showed that Janet was positive while her boyfriend was negative. The friend found it difficult to give Janet the result and procrastinated, then decided to repeat the test. During this time the preparations for the wedding were going forward, and the date was drawing near. The repeat test was also positive, and it was now within a week of the wedding date. The couple were finally informed, but a further confirmatory test had still to be carried out, the result of which did not come back until the very eve of the wedding. All the results showed that Janet was positive, and they decided to call off the wedding – difficult to explain at the eleventh hour. So not being able to face people, Janet simply left Kampala. No one knew where she had gone or why the wedding had been called off, though there was a large amount of speculation.

Although a rumour went round that Janet had gone to Nairobi, she had actually travelled up-country to a remote village, so Christmas day found her desperate and alone – a girl who had found she was HIV positive on the eve of her wedding day. When she should have been enjoying her honeymoon, she was standing alone in a village church, staring out over the hills. Then her fiancé appeared in her field of vision; he was the last person she expected to see, but he had come to be with her. But despite their love, they were still unable to marry because his parents objected srongly.

All these events had taken place during the previous year, and as Janet talked to me, she shared that she was now having some symptoms of AIDS: she had lost weight and was having diarrhoea. We travelled on to Kiwoko together where we held the community workshop in which we discussed how the community could deal with the scourge of AIDS. Janet was leading the discussions while all the time knowing that she herself was infected and probably did not have long to live.

In the evenings we would sit and talk late into the night; she was an educated and informed young woman of exceptionally high calibre who had already risen quickly within the ranks of her organisation. Later we parted in Kampala, and I went back to England while she continued with her project outside Kampala. I was not in Uganda during the next six months, and then I heard that Janet had died. She developed the classic 'slim', due to one of the many opportunistic infections common in those with low immunity. She was admitted to a mission hospital, but the progress of the diarrhoea and wasting could not be halted, and she became dehydrated and emaciated. She died a slow and undignified death. Janet had seen it all before and was well aware what was happening to her.

When Janet died I was traumatised and her death brought back all the ghosts of others who died of AIDS or other diseases which I had not been able to halt during my time in Luweero. I saw Sekatebi, our carpenter, Edward the lay-reader, Sarah, John Ando. I saw the girl in a yellow dress who called me *Daktari* and who died of post-partum haemorrhage. I saw the woman who was bright yellow herself, with jaundice, and died of rampant hepatitis. I saw Ruth, the nursing auxiliary, who refused to believe she had AIDS, but still died. I saw Rachel, the nurse, and Darlington, the medical assistant, all of whom died of AIDS. I saw all the friends and colleagues I had lost, and there was something in me that desperately needed to hang on to those who were left – one of whom was Rose.

Rose had worked at Kiwoko as an auxiliary nurse, and Robbie and I then sponsored her to study at Kuluva Hospital in the north of Uganda to do a nurse training course. So while I was travelling back and forth to Uganda to carry out the community research, I took the opportunity to visit Rose. We also made arrangements for her to travel to the UK to visit us, but the evening before she was due to arrive, she called to say that had missed the flight. We were so disappointed – it was the classic Ugandan story of a driver who turned up late, and then his car broke down on the way to the airport. But she was able to travel later and this time she made sure that she was camped at the airport several hours before the flight.

Rose had become the embodiment of our time in Kiwoko and epitomised the hope that we sought to bring to that place. We wanted her to continue to be a part of our family and our lives, and so she became our daughter, Rose Nanyonga Clarke.

Of all the young people whom we met and worked with in Luweero, Rose's start in life made her the least likely to succeed because of the training which her family had forced upon her as a child. Her father was a medical assistant who worked in the Luweero Triangle during the war; he was polygamous with five wives and over thirty children. Rose's mother bore him nine children, but then died in childbirth, so Rose was brought up by aunties and step-mothers. The family identified Rose as a 'special child' from an early age because she appeared to exhibit certain unusual powers, so she was selected to undergo intensive training as a witchdoctor. She did not have a mother who could object to this course of action, and the clan needed a person to bring them good fortune and act as a medium for the spirits. As a young child she was subjected to many kinds of rituals, being taken to the witchdoctor and left there for days at a time. Most of her training would rank as child abuse and not the kind of thing that any of us would subject our children to. She was also made to tie many fetishes onto her body which were not to be removed for any reason. This made activities such as PE at school very embarrassing since, when she undressed, the other children would laugh at her.

Part of her training was to listen to the spirits, and she was taught to sit still for long periods of time and hear the spirits. She was also the keeper of the family shrine which needed to be attended on a regular basis with small offerings and the performance of certain rituals. Rose would go into trancelike states, and the family treated her with respect because of her perceived powers. However, her art of listening to the spirits appeared to backfire because she felt that she was being told by the spirits to go to church. She knew this was odd, but nevertheless she started attending church. She was now a young teenager, and the family did not really object to her going to church as long as she also tended the shrine and did her duties in witchcraft. This state of balance continued for two years, but gradually Rose began to realise that Christianity and witchcraft were incompatible and stopped tending the shrine. Co-incidentally a number of family members died, and the family deduced that the spirits must be displeased and narrowed down the blame to Rose, due to her failure to tend the shrine. They then tried to persuade her that she could still attend church as long as she continued with the witchcraft, but she was not prepared to compromise, so a family meeting was called, with her father leading the meeting as head of the clan.

Her father put it to her that she must continue with her duties in the traditional religion, or she would be excommunicated from the family. They gave her one day to think about it, but when they reconvened, she told the clan she was still not prepared to continue. Her father began to speak in the vernacular, and she at first did not understand what he was saying, then she realised that she was being officially thrown out of the family with the words: 'I divorce you, I divorce you, I divorce you, as a Muslim man divorces his wife.'

She was seventeen years old.

That night she slept at the school because she had nowhere to go. But soon, thereafter, a school friend sent word that a missionary couple had arrived in Kiwoko, (about forty-two kilometres from where she was living) and had started a hospital, for which they needed nursing assistants. The candidates would be trained, and free board and accommodation provided. For a girl who had just been thrown out of her family, this must have sounded like an offer she could not refuse. She decided she must come to see us but had no money for transport, and she asked a friend, who was a veterinary officer, to give her a ride on his motorcycle. But the evening before she was due to travel, he came with the news that he had to visit a sick cow, which obviously took priority over her. The following morning she set off to walk the forty-two kilometres and made it to the hospital by nightfall.

When I met Rose for the first time, I thought there was something about her which was special: she was more thoughtful and articulate than any other village girl whom I had met. We gave her a place on the course for nursing assistants, and then I suggested that we would take her back home since we were travelling to Kampala that day. Not wishing to tell us her history, she accepted, and we drove her back to Wobulenzi, about ten kilometres from her own village. When the car was out of sight, she turned and walked back to Kiwoko – she had nowhere else to go.

The next few years were difficult for Rose. Although she was a very talented individual, her past caught up with her in the form of bizarre behaviour, and since we did not know the underlying reason, we didn't know how to deal with it. She would develop headaches, leading to a complete change in personality, when she would become sullen and non-communicative or disappear into the bush. The next day she would reappear again, having no recollection of what had happened. The situation came to a head when she lapsed into a state of unconsciousness, from which she could not be aroused. She was admitted to the ward, and later that evening some nurses came running to my home with the news that Rose was dying – her blood pressure had fallen, and her level of consciousness had deteriorated. We did all the investigations we could think of, but none were positive, and we could not establish a diagnosis. Gradually she regained consciousness and over the next few days she told Robbie her story of deep involvement with witchcraft. But the episodes continued, and her behaviour became disruptive to the whole hospital. One of the senior nurses took me aside and said that I should send Rose away for the sake of the other staff.

'This girl will run mad,' she said, using the local term for those with psychiatric or behavioural problems. 'Running mad' was not uncommon in the village and from a medical point of view could be due to many conditions, ranging from hysteria to schizophrenia. All such conditions were, of course, put down to witchcraft, and the suggestibility of Ugandans to the powers of witchcraft certainly made things worse. During these episodes Rose was an entirely different person from the Rose we knew.

Over a number of months Rose slowly began to change; the episodes became less frequent and then ceased altogether. She later shared with me that it had only been by a supreme effort of will she was able to stop the pattern of behaviour and had to consciously fight every day to maintain a normal life. It took a year for Rose to overcome the witchcraft influences completely and become a normal balanced human being – with no tendency to 'run mad.' I think that some of the determination to overcome all obstacles, which we witnessed in Rose in later years, was honed and strengthened by the experiences she had as a teenager. Perhaps one has to live in Africa to understand how many people succumb to the powers of superstition and how hard it must be to pull out of it and take another road. Rose was not only successful in overcoming these influences, she went on to accomplishments way beyond our expectations.

During the period while we were living in the UK, I was keeping body and soul together by working for one of the agencies which covered out of hours work for family doctors. I would report for work at ten in the evening and then work through the night, travelling round London doing GP house calls. I was paid ten pounds for each call and had a small car and a driver, who was usually of Indian or Pakistani origin. I got used to the smell of the tobacco which the drivers chewed, and I even got used to them opening the door and spitting. But I was a bit surprised when one of my drivers launched into a diatribe about how the 'bloody Pakis' were ruining everything in Britain.

'But where are you from?' I asked, somewhat bemused. 'Are you not from Pakistan yourself?'

'No,' he barked at me, 'I am from Sri-Lanka.'

I was now being exposed to life in inner London and learned that the poverty and dirt of the city was sometimes worse than the poverty I had known in Africa. Some of it was avoidable and some self inflicted, but those who lived in the tower blocks of London were trapped in a vicious cycle. I would stand in the lift of a tower-block (if it was working), watching where I put my feet since there was usually a puddle of urine in the middle. When I visited my patient, I was careful not to sit down since I did not know what I would catch from the settee which usually had years of ground-in filth. Sometimes there was nothing to sit down on anyway because all the stuffing had been pulled out from the settee, leaving only the webbing. During one house-call a very obese lady had a heart attack while I was standing beside her. She was in bed and weighed at least two hundred kilos. I had to get her onto the floor to carry out resuscitation and somehow managed to drag her off the bed and do mouth to mouth and cardiac massage, but despite my best efforts, I was unable to revive her.

I was also called to visit some the more prestigious areas of London, one of which was Golders Green. The reasons for the calls were variable, and few of the calls were true emergencies. Some were because people were lonely or insomniacs and a visit from the doctor brightened up their long night. I met two old Jewish gentlemen who were sitting in the kitchen reading the newspapers about two in the morning.

'What seems to be the problem?' I asked, since they both appeared to be in good health.

'I was just wondering,' asked the younger man, 'What age gap would you think is reasonable if one is going to marry?' So we had a discussion about marriage; it appeared he had a girlfriend who was fifteen years his junior, and he needed some reassurance.

While the job allowed me to pay the bills, it was one of the most soul destroying I had ever done, mainly because I had no patient continuity. I would fill out a small pink form with the history and findings of the patient, and the regular GP was supposed to follow up. Most of the GPs were simply annoyed that their patients had called me out at all since it was costing them money, and I rarely had any meaningful contact with the regular doctors.

During this time, while I was on one of my regular visits to Uganda on the community research, I met a British GP who had been working in Kampala for over thirty years treating the expatriate community. He was one of the few expatriates who stayed throughout Uganda's turbulent years, often risking his life to see his patients. Dr Gibbons made me an offer of a job in Kampala through which I could meet my financial commitments, stay involved in tropical medicine and infectious diseases, and continue to work in a developing country.

'What do you think?' I asked Robbie when I was back home.

'Just go,' was her immediate response, because she saw that I was a fish out of water in the U.K. This may not have been the noblest reason for moving countries yet again, but she had a valid point, and the job would allow me to practise tropical medicine, continue the research on AIDS in the community, and be involved in sub-Saharan Africa.

I arrived back in Uganda with two suitcases and a bunch of questionnaires on the community's response to AIDS and settled into life as a GP in Kampala. But within a few months I began to have doubts about the job I had accepted, since the practice was primarily serving the expatriate community, and I no longer felt engaged in Ugandan society itself. The upside was that living in Kampala allowed me to understand the healthcare system in the city. I observed that, although there were a number of clinics, plus the large government hospital, there were few clinics and no hospitals catering for the emerging Ugandan middle class, which had been growing since political stability returned. The mission hospitals had rendered heroic service during the years of civil war, but now that peace had returned, there was the opportunity to improve the standards of medical care. After I had been working in the practice for three months, I had to make a decision about whether to stay permanently or leave, and I decided that it would be best to move on. I wished to be more engaged in the Ugandan community and the idea of building another hospital in Kampala was growing. I was grateful that Dr Gibbons had given me this opportunity to return to Uganda, but realised I did not fit into a medical practice.

It was all very well to dream of starting a hospital, but I was now in a position where I was unemployed and had no fixed income. I decided that if I started a clinic which targeted middle income Ugandans, I would earn a salary, and I could use any surplus to improve the medical facilities. I had a dream of building a hospital, but the dream had to start somewhere. I had to raise money, find suitable premises for a clinic, hire staff, buy equipment and then hope that patients would come. The practice in which I had been working was financially secure, but I was leaving for an uncertain future. I was setting up a private clinic in a developing country, aimed at paying patients, yet this was a country where only a few years previously people did not know where their next meal was coming from. And I expected to earn a living in such a place.

# Private sector led development

It was a sad fact that the gap in medicine and healthcare between rich and poor countries was growing. Medical technological advances were moving so fast that even if developing countries managed to stand still, the gap in knowledge and practice was getting wider, and countries such as Uganda had fallen further and further behind in the delivery of healthcare. Uganda did not see healthcare as a priority so the medical sector was starved of cash. In the provision of healthcare the government rightly focused on the essentials for the masses such as immunisations, the prevention of HIV, and treatment of malaria, but there was little development of sophisticated facilities such as intensive care, cardiac surgery or high level diagnostic services. Those who needed such facilities either flew out of the country or died because the service was not available within Uganda.

When I decided to start my own clinic, I was making the conscious decision to switch from the aid/mission sector to the private sector, which was generally not perceived as driving development in third world countries, and certainly not seen as helping the poor. I could easily have gone back to work in the mission sector or for an aid organization, but I was also beginning to question accepted perceptions as to how sub-Saharan Africa would develop. There was a stereotypical image of 'poor Africans' reinforced by regular television pictures of emaciated children and harassed aid workers, bringing relief to the suffering. Indeed, the aid agencies depended on such images in order to keep funds flowing. But was aid the only model for sustainable development?

Ireland was a good case study of a country which had shown significant development in the recent past by effectively using a combination of aid (or grant funding) and private sector development, although one could say that Ireland developed to the point where the economy overheated and imploded in the global financial meltdown. The Irish, being Irish, found ways to laugh at their own predicament:

'What is the difference between Ireland and Iceland? One letter of the alphabet.

What is the sound of the Celtic Tiger? Meow.

The Irish did get carried away with their own success, particularly in the construction and housing market which were stoked by cheap loans from the banking sector. A certain amount of correction was inevitable, and perhaps it has served to bring the Irish back to their essential core values again, like having time for people, rather than being preoccupied with making huge amounts of money. But having recognized the mistakes of recent years, one should also accept that not so long ago the Republic of Ireland was a rural peasant economy in which most of the population lived off the land, and it was generally regarded as lagging far behind England, or even Northern Ireland. Ireland has made remarkable progress in development over a relatively short period of time.

In my childhood I witnessed the farmers making haystacks with pitch-forks, and a common mode of transport was the donkey and cart. While this was very picturesque for American tourists, it did not add much to the growth of the economy. But thirty years ago the economy began to take off, particularly when Ireland became a member of the European Union. Since I lived in Northern Ireland, which was traditionally more prosperous than the Republic, I heard much muttering by the farmers in the north that those farmers in the Republic were eating up all the subsidies from the EU. These were special grants for member states which were regarded as being on the fringes – which Ireland was, both geographically and economically. Such member states could benefit from large agricultural subsidies for hill farming, beautification of the countryside, and construction of infrastructure. It was in effect, EU aid, and Ireland grabbed all that it could. The richer countries were supposed to be shouldering the burden for the development of the poorer states, such that large economies like Britain and Germany were net contributors and smaller states like Ireland were net beneficiaries.

So like Uganda and most third world countries, Ireland benefited from aid. At that time Ireland also had a serious problem in collecting sufficient taxes to balance the budget as it had a narrow tax base, with certain sectors of the economy such as construction, not contributing much. This was because there was a parallel black economy, where many of the construction workers were paid cash. They also claimed unemployment benefit, so the government suffered double jeopardy, and some of these workers who lived near the border, claimed unemployment benefit from Northern Ireland as well!

With all these sources of untaxed income and benefits, construction workers were the richest people in Ireland at the time. The government grew the tax base by aggressively going after foreign investment and bringing those outside the system into the tax net. They did this by a carrot and stick approach: allowing tax avoiders a grace period, during which they could put their house in order, but after which they would be liable for stiff penalties. They marketed Ireland as a destination for investment by offering generous incentives and tax breaks to foreign investors to set up businesses and factories. This may seem counterintuitive, since the point of bringing investors was precisely so that they could collect more revenues. But the real goal was to create employment and then tax those who were employed, which they did – heavily.

In order to provide suitably trained candidates for employment by these new industries, the government expanded their higher education programme enormously. Ireland had a young population, but the classic problem had been limited employment opportunities, so young people tended to emigrate to all parts of the world. If Ireland was going to market itself as a destination for investment, it needed a skilled and educated workforce, which it set out to provide through increasing the number of secondary and tertiary educational institutions, but also ensuring that standards remained high. Of course, the plan had many other elements, not least among them the gift of the Irish blarney, but it was essentially a combination of the wily and productive use of aid to build the infrastructure; the production of a well educated young workforce; giving incentives for foreign direct investment; and widening the tax base. All of these initiatives contributed to the development of the Irish economy.

There are those who espouse the slogan 'Trade not Aid', and while this is part of the answer for development, in that it emphasizes the importance of trade, if one examines Ireland's rise from poverty, Ireland used aid as a means of development. Of course when developed countries gave aid to their neighbours, they did not actually call it aid, they referred to it as subsidies, incentives, agricultural ceilings and any other term which appeared to legitimize the aid. On the other hand, when it comes to Africa, developed countries trumpet how much aid they are handing out. The judicious use of aid is an essential element in the development of any country, but such aid must be targeted, and the country which receives the aid needs to be called to account for how it has been spent. Generally speaking, aid should be used in infrastructure projects – improving the roads, bringing electrification, delivery of health services to the grass roots community, and improving the education system.

Like Ireland, raising the level of education, and making an educated young population available for employment in cutting edge fields of technology were also key elements in the development of India. Uganda also has a significant programme of Universal Primary Education and a programme of Universal Secondary Education, but while making education available to all has been a noble vision, the standards must be sufficiently high to meet global demands. Uganda made a large budget available for education, but despite this, the standards have remained relatively low by international standards. The teaching methods have often been old fashioned, and the quality of students produced after tertiary education is poor in terms of problem solving skills. Such graduates are often trained in subjects that are irrelevant to the job market. This is not the fault of the students themselves, and indeed, many of those who have continued their education abroad have done well. The difference is in the detail: all the elements of the educational system must be just right if we are to provide an appropriately educated workforce which will stimulate development.

The new factories and IT companies in Ireland provided job creation and offered employment to the young people who were gaining employment due to their higher education. Had there been a mismatch, where students were not trained in the right skills mix, the result would have been thousands of graduates on the streets for whom there were no jobs, while at the same time the new companies would not have been able to find suitably qualified candidates to meet their requirements.

Unfortunately, this has been the state of affairs which has prevailed in Uganda, where thousands of graduates are spewed out every year, but with qualifications irrelevant to such sectors as finance, engineering, or telecoms; hence, there are not enough appropriately trained graduates to fill such positions, and companies end up poaching staff from each other, paying over the odds and getting poor value for money.

Ireland is not the only destination which has brought dividends for investors, and some of the large multinational companies such as Unilever have done well in sub-Saharan Africa in terms of profitability, while also succeeding in bringing jobs and development to the country. Unilever not only procures raw materials in Africa but manufactures household products for the local market, such as Blueband margarine, at a price point which is affordable to peasants in the rural areas. They are thus making their products available at the base of the pyramid and doing profitable business at the same time, which means paying more tax to the government.

The development of the mobile phone industry in Africa is another example of a sector which has been profitable and made communication in Africa move forwards by a quantum leap. Prior to mobile phones, developed countries had extensive fixed line networks to all parts of their countries, but it was almost impossible to communicate with the more remote areas of Africa. Today one can talk on mobile phones right across Africa for a price that ordinary Africans can still afford – just.

The private sector not only provides employment and pays tax, but in certain sectors it relieves the government of the burden for provision of essential services. The number of people who access private medical care outside the government sector in sub-Saharan countries is estimated to be between 40 – 60%. Governments are therefore being relieved of up to 60% of healthcare needs by the non government sector. This is very significant and something to be encouraged, particularly when the government budget for health is only a few dollars per head, and most of that money does not appear to produce results

Unfortunately, it is not all good news regarding private sector development in Africa, and there are some interesting perceptions and attitudes which need to be addressed. I found that many Ugandans regarded business as some sort of war where anything goes as long as profit was achieved. I have heard statements such as 'One has to be ruthless to be a successful businessman.'

Such a perception allowed some local businessmen to justify crooked practices and certainly did not foster the growth of ethical principles, or good business practices. I also witnessed sharp practices in the private medical sector, where certain clinics perceived the most important driving force, not as scientific and ethical practice, but making a quick buck. This was seen in over-diagnosis and unnecessary treatment with a spurious medical justification, while the underlying incentive was actually financial gain. Of course, such financially driven practice can also be seen in western countries, but there is normally a stricter regulatory environment, and the abuses are less flagrant. A common practice was that of private clinics inflating their medical insurance claims, sometimes with the collusion of the patient who shared the profit or by the clinic claiming for treatment which was not actually given.

Many people in western developed countries have difficulty seeing private business as driving development or being in the best interests of the poor. Hence, if someone defines himself as an aid worker, people know how to classify him, but if he uses that word 'profit' this brings confusion. I sometimes had discussions with well meaning people who asked me how I was funded, and when I mentioned that the organization was private, they were taken aback since they assumed that it must be charitable, or at least a 'private, not for profit' company. I could see that their first thought was that I was a capitalist let loose in Uganda, fleecing the poor and making a fortune for myself. Sadly, I was not making the fortune, but neither was I fleecing the poor, and far from being a rampant capitalist, I simply believed that private sector development was the key to sustainable development and to leading the poor out of poverty.

Some years later I was in a meeting with the Minister of Health and the Director General of Medical Services, along with some other high powered officials from CDC and WHO, and introductions were being made. When they reached me, they did not quite know how to classify me, and the Director General finally stepped in and said, 'Dr Clarke is an investor in this country.'

By that time I had made a significant investment in the medical sector in Uganda, and I thought that was as good an introduction as I would have wished for.

# The disbursement of Aid

Although the private sector is critical in the development of any country, one cannot write off the role of aid, but the manner in which aid is applied can be a problem. Much aid is given to the government with little or no accountability, thus supporting a system which is mismanaged and sometimes corrupt. In the eighties, Uganda was an economic basket case similar to Zimbabwe under Mugabe. There were currency controls, hyperinflation, and scarcity of goods in the shops. When Museveni came to power, the IMF and World Bank advised the abolition of currency controls and the liberalization of the economy, which was their standard recipe. The government accepted this advice and inflation died overnight, with the Ugandan economy then growing at a rate of 5 – 8 % per year for a sustained period. This was an impressive achievement, and Uganda, for a time, was the favoured child of the IMF and the donor countries.

However, everything was not as rosy as it seemed since the government budget was being heavily subsidized by the international donors. Five to seven percent growth in any economy seemed to be impressive, but there had been stagnation for so long that it would have been hard for the economy not to grow through rebuilding of the infrastructure. Also, since Uganda was seen to be an example of good macroeconomic policy, and the President had been very open about the AIDS epidemic, Uganda became a favourite destination for donor funding for AIDS projects.

Many donor countries channelled their aid through budget support. What this meant was that the Ministry of Finance worked out the budget for public sector programmes and how much they were short, and the donors met the shortfall. Certain countries did not take part in this process, the most notable being America, which was not so trusting as to simply hand money over to a foreign government. But governments such as Britain, Ireland and Italy bought into the concept and contributed generously – the budget of the government of Uganda was subsidized by foreign governments. Donor governments favoured this process because they had the perception that it gave them leverage in prioritizing the recipient government's budget and of course, developing country governments were in favour since it was a grant.

Ideally the budget of any country should be balanced by the collection of taxes from its own citizens. But what happens if there is not enough economic activity and the government cannot therefore collect enough taxes for its essential programmes of health, education, and the development of infrastructure? Normally it either does not carry out the programmes, or it borrows the money, or in the case of developing countries, aid agencies fill the gaps. In Uganda's case, at one point donors were putting more money into the Ugandan government's own budget than the government itself, and up to 60% of the budget was paid for by foreign governments. This was not sustainable for various reasons, the first being that, although the budget was balanced, there was always an imbalance of foreign currency flowing into the country. This had the effect of keeping the local currency strong, not because there is an export surplus or a healthy balance of payments, but because aid dollars were continually being mopped up in the local economy which in turn was bad for the promotion of exports.

The other negative effect of budget support has been less obvious in pure economic terms but more insidious and destructive in the long run. Free money handed to the government strengthened the public sector and weakened the private sector. The bulk of the money in the economy was coming into government coffers; hence, civil servants and politicians knew that this was the gravy train to ride on – their income was assured. Those working in the public sector, instead of having an attitude of facilitation towards the private sector, knew that the private sector were not their paymasters. Of course, politicians paid lip-service to the private sector as being their constituency and those who were paying taxes etc, but in reality, the whole tone of the public service, in the creation of bureaucratic obstacles and lack of accountability, told another story, and this picture has been repeated all across Africa.

Politicians and public servants have debated this with me and disputed this assertion vigorously, but the public sector well know that it is the government who are their paymasters and that their pay is assured because of the role played by the donors in budget support, grants and cheap loans. If this free money were not there, many of the programmes would still have taken place through the voluntary sector or through donor support of independent programmes, such as those supported by USAID. But there would have been less arrogance and more accountability. The real answer was to extend the country's tax base, but this could only come about by developing sufficient private sector investment, creating jobs, and then collecting more taxes. There is a balance between trade and aid, and while it is right to avail aid to developing countries for infrastructure, it must be done in a way which promotes accountability, value for money, and the growth of the private sector.

One person who was instrumental in campaigning for debt relief for developing countries was the rock star, Bono, from the group U2. The large loans given by the World Bank and its partner organizations to poor countries over the past fifty years means that current governments are saddled with the sins of their fathers. Hence, a significant proportion of their income goes into servicing debt. Bono campaigned to wipe the slate clean, with a large degree of success. If this had the effect of allowing countries to reprioritize their finances and address important infrastructure needs, it was a positive step forwards, but all too often countries just used debt relief as a means to redirect their finances into non productive areas such as public service expenditure, including purchasing new vehicles, giving parliamentary allowances, and adding more jobs for the boys.

I had never met a real live Megastar and, being the groupie that I am, when I heard that Bono was in town, I was anxious to meet him. He was my fellow countryman; U2 was launched in the mid seventies, which was my vintage, and the fact that my children were also fans demonstrated the longevity of this particular rock group. But even though U2 was popular in the west, it seemed that hardly anyone in Uganda listened to rock music, and when I told people excitedly, 'Did you hear that Bono is in town?' the usual response was 'Bono who?'

The programme manager of the popular Capital Radio station had arrived from Australia with his western ideas about music tastes, but his choices were met with a big yawn and decreased rating, so he had to make adjustments to local tastes. Sometimes I attended the jam session at the National Theatre which was a fair barometer of what local musicians liked, though if I heard another rendering of 'No woman, no cry', I was about to burst into tears myself. Taste in music ran more to reggae, lingala, raga, rap, pop and hip hop, but there were few people who liked rock music. Africans liked music that had rhythm, while whites liked beat. So though Bono may have been a Rock Star legend, he did not excite much attention in Uganda. I inquired where one might get to meet the great man and was told that there was a reception at the American Ambassador's house, but I didn't appear to have an invitation, and there was no way I would get past security. An insider suggested that I look for him at the Rhino Bar of the Sheraton later that evening. So around 10.00pm I wandered in there and inquired if anyone had seen an aging rock star.

'He's over there,' said one guy, jerking his thumb at the corner of the bar with little interest.

'But Chris Tucker is here,' he added excitedly.

'Chris who?' I said, and went off to find Bono.

'I'm one of your fellow countrymen,' I introduced myself.

He was surprisingly easy to talk to and at one point I commented, 'Why have you not become seriously weird like some of your fellow megastars?'

'I can get weird sometimes,' he replied.

I asked why he was campaigning for debt relief and for more help for AIDS in Africa and why he was spending so much of his time on such causes, and he replied that Bob Geldof had been an inspiration when he raised money for the famine in Ethiopia in the eighties because he used his position to focus people's attention on what was going on in the world.

Bono impressed me because he had made it by any standard – even if no one in Africa listened to rock music. He could have developed such a big ego that he was only concerned with himself, but he was using his position to make a difference. It could not have been all that much fun to trail around Africa campaigning for debt relief – he missed his youngest child's first birthday because of the trip – but he used his influence to do good for others. He may go down in the history books for having been at the top of the rock music industry for a quarter of a century, but what made him a great man for me was simply that he still cared about people.

# Starting Over

I was now on my own in Kampala; I had no job and no assured income. I had a dream of starting a hospital, but I had no money. I needed to earn an income, and the first step in fulfilling my vision was to set up my own clinic, for which I had to locate suitable premises. I had seen a vacant space off the foyer of an old cinema complex which was now being used by a large Pentecostal Church. The area had been an ice-cream parlour in a bygone age, but the whole complex had fallen into disrepair, and although the cinema itself had been repaired, this portion was still derelict. When I had first come to Uganda in 1987, I attended a conference in the same cinema building.

'Put up your umbrella,' I was told.

This was a strange instruction since I was inside the auditorium, not outside, but I could see that everyone around me had come equipped with their umbrellas, and they were sprouting all over the stadium. It looked funny to see everyone sitting inside with their umbrellas up, but there was a reason – it was raining and the roof leaked badly. The church later repaired the main auditorium, but the room where I wished to set up the clinic was still in its original condition. The church agreed to rent me the space, and I set about making it suitable for a small clinic. This was the first time that I became involved in building work in Kampala itself, though I had supervised much of the building work at Kiwoko. However, I reckoned that if I could organise the renovations myself they would be much cheaper, so I used my pick-up to fetch sand, cement, tiles and paint; I hired some tradesmen, and within a few weeks we had transformed the dank space into a modern clinic.

The first day I sat in the clinic I had one patient – who wandered in accidentally – and for the first few weeks it was a nail-biting experience to see if anyone would actually turn up.

Of course, if I had been working in the slums, giving free treatment, I would have had no shortage of patients, but now I was charging for my services, so would anyone feel that they were worth paying for? I would come home in the evenings and count the number of patients I had seen that day – two, three, five, seven. Under the laws of Uganda I could not advertise medical services, so it was a question of word of mouth. Fortunately, the numbers built up quickly, and I soon had as many patients as I could handle.

One difference between practising medicine in Kampala and Ireland, or even Kiwoko, was that I had to carry out my own laboratory investigations, many of which involved looking down a microscope at a blood slide for malaria parasites, or looking for organisms in a stool or urine sample. At the time the professional sample bottles were not readily available, so I would hand patients an empty film canister and an orange stick and ask them to bring me a small sample of their stool. This worked reasonably well as the canister was well sealed, but there were some patients who found other innovative ways of supplying their bodily samples. One guy brought his stool sample in a matchbox, which was leaking by the time he handed it to me, while another patient thought I wanted the whole delivery and arrived with a full jam pot. I did have to make some rapid disposals of samples at arm's length.

I had financed the renovations of the clinic with money I raised through increasing the mortgage on our house in the UK. Now that it had a kitchen and bathroom, the house was worth more than when I bought it, and since I was working in the private medical sector (even if it was in Uganda), I appeared to qualify as a better credit risk. But I had been so thrifty in doing my own renovations for the clinic that I had some money left over, so once the clinic was operating successfully, I began to look around to see if I could buy somewhere to live. I was renting a house at the time but wished to put down roots in Kampala since this season of my life was

125

beginning to look like a long term project. I did not have enough money to buy a complete house, which seemed to be a habit, but on this occasion I didn't even have enough to buy any of the house. I could only afford the site, with the hope that I would earn enough money later to build the house on it. So I put the word out that I was looking for land in Kampala.

There were no official Estate Agents, as we know them, with pictures of houses in the window, but there was an informal network of land agents who shared information among themselves and who seemed to know which properties were on the market. When the word went out that I was interested in buying land, random people kept turning up at my clinic, offering to sell land or act as brokers, which they pronounced *bloakas*. One of these agents, known as Ben, took me to the area of Kampala called 'Tank Hill', aptly named because the tanks supplying water for the city were situated at the top.

'There is a site somewhere there,' he said, pointing rather vaguely at a bushy part of a hill. Despite the fact that we were not far from the city centre, there were still large areas which were undeveloped.

This particular site was very steep, located on the side of the hill overlooking Lake Victoria. No-one appeared to wish to buy it because construction was more expensive on a steep site than at the bottom of a hill. I brought along an engineer to give me an opinion as to how I would gain access, and I then understood another reason why it had not been sold.

'It would be impossible to make a road from below, it is too steep,' he said. 'And neither can you gain access from the top because that incline is also too steep.'

However, since the land was cheap, and I was not able to resist a bargain, I thought there must be some solution and bought it anyway. I then discovered yet another reason why the site was not selling. Since it was on one of Kampala's hills, which were revered as being the homes of the spirits, many of the Baganda tribe believed that one would suffer ill fortune if these sites were disturbed. This was the reason that sacrifices were made at the beginning of such construction projects: at the very least a goat would be sacrificed, and in many cases the sacrifices were much more sinister, some involving body parts and even child sacrifice.

After I bought the site, our belongings from the UK arrived in a twenty foot container, and when the contents had been unloaded, the shipping company asked where to leave the container.

'Take it to the top of the hill, tie it to a tree and pull it off the truck,' I instructed them – as one does when one has an empty container to unload. My calculation was that it would be easier to push the container down the hill to the site once I had begun construction than to drag it up from the bottom. The container was left lying near the top of the hill, and I forgot about it until one day I had a visit from the police. Apparently, I had left the container on someone else's land, and not only that, it was blocking his access. The owner was understandably unhappy that there was a random container blocking his entrance and had gone to the police to complain. Fortunately, the container had some identification on the side and they had been able to trace it back to me. I apologised for the inconvenience which my container had caused, but since he was the owner of the adjacent site, I took the opportunity to offer to make him access into his site if I, in turn, could use the road to get to my own land. He was agreeable and all that remained was for me to hire a bulldozer and begin.

Sinani, who was my main man at that time, located a small bulldozer which appeared cheap to hire (we later found out the reason). It was transported to the top of the hill with the instruction that he excavate a road down to the neighbour's site and thence on to mine. This could only be achieved through considerable excavation in order to attain a slope of not more, nor less, than one in five – which is the steepest angle that a vehicle can climb for a short distance – and would allow us to have a driveway to the site.

The young man who owned the bulldozer was from the Baganda Tribe and was also a devout Catholic, and it was evident that he was having some conflict between his Catholic faith and his belief in the traditional Kiganda witchcraft. On the one hand, he felt that appropriate rituals were not being performed to appease the spirits who inhabited the hill, while on the other hand he felt that we should pray to God to keep him safe. I was never quite sure if he had more faith in the traditional beliefs or in his Catholic religion. Either way, he greeted me every morning with the words, 'Pray for me doctor.'

And it seemed that the things that he feared befell him because his old bulldozer broke down on a regular basis, almost every day. He believed that this was because he had disturbed the spirits who were therefore resisting this work, while I believed that his bulldozer was old and in poor mechanical condition. Sinani had the job of ferrying diesel to the bulldozer and reporting to me how the work was going, and a job which should have taken a few days was taking a month. We reached a critical point where we had to construct the part of the road which was exactly a one in five gradient in order to allow a vehicle to turn on to the site where the house would stand. I left the instructions in the morning and returned in the afternoon to find that the bulldozer operator had become somewhat over-enthusiastic and had gouged out a one in three gradient – which would have been good for abseiling, but not for vehicle access. The problem was serious and could only be rectified by a week's work of back-filling, but eventually we had a driveway which we could use.

Events took an interesting turn when a solicitor's letter arrived from my neighbour, claiming damages in the region of $60,000. It appeared that the old gentleman had a lawyer in the family who felt that he could extract some money from the *mzungu*. Fortunately, I also had a good lawyer who had been involved in the initial negotiations and took it personally that someone was trying to go back on his word. This kind of behaviour was not uncommon in Uganda, or any sub-Saharan African country where, unless one knew one's way around legal matters and had friends on the inside, one could become prey to unscrupulous practices. My lawyer stood his ground, and the other party dropped his case.

It was an exciting day when I was able to drive my car down onto my own site – I finally had access to the land which I had bought, and I didn't need a helicopter! Now I had a site on which I could build my home and, having already built a hospital in Luweero, I didn't think that building a house in Kampala could be all that difficult, though another expatriate warned me not even to try as I would get into all sorts of problems.

I was inclined to take his warning as a challenge and, as it turned out, it proved to be easier to get things done in Kampala than in Luweero since there was a greater pool of skilled labourers and cheaper access to materials. The kind of building work which I had carried out in Luweero was fairly basic, involving only single storied buildings, but I was planning to put up a two-storied house on a very steep site, and I did not want to see any cracks developing after a few years, nor see my home sliding down the hill, so I went to a friend who had worked in the building trade for many years. Terry was now retired, living in the boathouse of what had been his former home in the Amin regime. One of Amin's colonels had taken a fancy to his house and simply moved in. Terry considered himself lucky to have escaped with his life since someone had warned him that he was about to be picked up, giving him time to flee the country. When he came back to Uganda after Amin had been ousted, he found it very difficult to get his home back. The house had been sold through several different owners; papers and titles had been changed, and it was virtually impossible to prove who had the authentic deed. So he just moved into the former boathouse and renovated it as his home.

I enrolled Terry to act as my site manager, but the problem was that Terry smoked like a chimney, and although he was built like an ox, the smoking had destroyed his lungs, so despite his strength, he did not have breath to walk up a flight of stairs, much less around my site. Despite his short stay, Terry taught me a few things about building and gave me the courage to tackle this new project, even without ongoing professional help. My home, therefore, turned out to be a self-build, where I supervised the construction, hired the masons, the carpenters, the tilers, the plumbers, the steel fabrication squad, or any other craftsmen who were needed.

It was more common in Uganda for people to launch into building projects themselves than to engage a contractor. There were several reasons for this, one being that there was no shortage of bricklayers, or *fundis*, as they were called, and unlike developed countries, labour was cheap. The other reason was that many people acquired their piece of land and then started to put up a house as and when they had the cash. Hence, when they had some spare cash, they dug the foundations, then the work might stall for a year until they got some more money when they would put up the walls and so on. In the past, many Ugandans did not trust banks and did not keep their money in a bank since those who did lost it due to hyper-inflation. Thus it was more sensible to put money into bricks and mortar, and when they had some more cash they bought a few more bags of cement. Of course, the time frame could be very variable, and if unforeseen events intervened, the house might not get finished in the person's lifetime. I saw many unfinished houses as I drove around Kampala, the reason often being that the person had died before he could complete the project, and if there were disputes over the will or the ownership, as was often the case, the house was neither sold, nor finished.

Another outcome of all this self building was that standards of building were rather low, with poor finishes and dangerous structural engineering, which meant that it was not uncommon for buildings to fall down. Of course, some of these structural problems could have been remedied if the cement had not been stolen while the building was going on, the result being that there were some very weak mixtures of concrete. Putting sufficient cement in the mix was a novel idea to some masons who preferred to pilfer the cement and use it to build their own houses. There were many projects where the budget resulted in the building of two houses – one for the owner and one for the masons.

I was now acting like many other Ugandans and had started to build my house with no clear budget and no timeframe since I was also doing it when I had some surplus cash. If I did not supply money, the work came to a halt. Fortunately, the clinic began to attract more patients, and I found myself earning enough to buy the requisite amount of cement, although it was preferable if I supervised the actual mixing myself. Running the clinic and constructing the house at the same time was hard work; I may not have known where my next bag of cement was coming from, but it was exciting to establish a business and to build my own home. Robbie, who had now joined me from the UK, was a little more sceptical about this whole project, but as the house began to take shape, even she could not contain her excitement.

I have always believed that we are capable of more at the workplace if we have our own home to which we can retreat for solace. When we were in Luweero and had begun the development of Kiwoko Hospital, Robbie was happy to see all that was happening, but we were still living in part of a Ugandan farmhouse. We were supposed to go back to Ireland after two years, but it was obvious that we were on the brink of developing a significant project, and I wanted us to stay.

'OK' she told me, 'I will stay, but only on condition that you build me a house which I can call home.'

'Deal,' I said, and the first house which we built at Kiwoko Hospital was our own home. Building our home in Kampala was a statement that we were putting down roots and were there to stay. We were investing our own money, and we did not see ourselves running back to Ireland at the first sign of trouble.

# Third world, third rate?

Cement was expensive, with the cost in Uganda being relatively more than in western countries, partly due to lack of manufacturing capacity and partly to the fact that the huge international construction company, Lafarge, controlled large sections of the business in East Africa. Lafarge bought up the largest cement producers in both Uganda and Kenya, and since there was also an overall shortage of cement in the region, the prices were high. There were certain business sectors in Africa where multinational companies could make much higher margins than in a developed market, including banking and cement production. The justification given for these high margins was usually related to increased risk or cost of operations, but while such arguments may have been true when Uganda was unstable, they were beginning to sound hollow.

Fortunately, when I was building my house, I did not need to borrow money from the banks, but I did need cement. Two storey houses in the UK or the USA are usually built using a wooden floor for the upstairs floors. In Uganda, houses were built with cement, including the first-floor slab. During construction, the floor is held in place by a complex system of scaffolding, which is not actually scaffolding as most people know it, but a web of eucalyptus poles. While I was in the process of building, I had to watch the sand/cement mix since the workers had the tendency to hide a few bags of cement outside the wall and then come back to retrieve them after nightfall. Therefore, I had to devise elaborate systems of counting empty bags and employing watchmen to lie in wait at night, though the safest way was to be there while the cement was actually being mixed.

On one occasion, I was building a wall at the bottom of the garden and was obviously too trusting because I woke up one morning to find that the wall was a pile of rubble. It had rained during the night, and the strength of the wall was obviously not sufficient to hold back the mudslide. Whether this was due to bad design or to lack of cement, I will never know, but other Ugandans were in no doubt about the cause, and they did not think it was a design fault. They also had to chuckle at my predicament since most of them had had similar experiences.

The serious side was that it was all too common to read about the collapse of buildings which reflected poor building controls, poor design and poor structural reinforcement in the building. A school collapsed while being built, burying scores of workers, and for two days relatives scrambled through the wreckage, trying to unearth bodies. One of the relatives tried calling the mobile phone of his brother who was buried, but there was no answer, then he had the bright idea to buy airtime and send it to his brother's number and try again. The next time they heard the phone ringing under the rubble, they continued digging and found the brother alive – after three days.

Although I was an Irish doctor, not an Irish builder, I liked building and was closely involved in the details of building our own house, becoming familiar with the ways of tradesmen and craftsmen in the process. Perhaps I enjoyed building because of the sheer visibility of seeing what I had achieved, whereas as a doctor, I did not always get the satisfaction of seeing such measurable results. Tradesmen in Uganda were capable of producing world class workmanship, but they could also produce substandard work, and if high standards were not set, they were never reached. I met an Irish property developer who was building houses in Kenya and felt that the skills of the local builders were so deplorable that he needed to import skilled workers from Ireland to do the job, but this approach did not do much to build capacity in the local industry. I was more of a hands-on, or perhaps a mouth-on person, who believed that if I shouted loud enough and made enough fuss, the local builders were quite capable of achieving the necessary standards.

The world economy no longer accepts excuses for sub-standard workmanship, even though there may have been a time when Africa, Asia and China were looked upon as poor countries for which allowances could be made. China has produced more than its fair share of sub-standard goods, but as it has emerged from the debilitating control of the Maoist era and strict communist control, the label 'made in China' is no longer synonymous with poor quality, and the Chinese can compete at global standards, while in the world of IT the Indian tech companies have learned to compete at an international level. But what about Africa? When will it catch up with the rest of the world in terms of attaining the necessary international standards in areas such as education, service delivery and product provision?

Standards in Africa are not homogenous, and there have always been large differences between regions and even neighbouring countries. For example, the work ethic in Kenya is different from Uganda. As a generalization, Kenyans tend to work harder while Ugandans are more laid back, possibly because Kenya is a more unforgiving country, with large stretches of barren land and lower soil fertility than Uganda. If a person does not work, he will not eat. Uganda's terrain and climate are fertile, and there is generally something to eat – even if it is only cassava roots from the garden. This appears to have bred an air of contentment among many Ugandans who are satisfied with life as long as they have something to eat and drink. It could be said that as one moves from Kenya to Uganda and on to Rwanda and Congo, the further one gets inland, the more laid back are the people. But like all generalizations, there are many exceptions.

Despite these stereotypes, Ugandans are industrious. One only has to drive along the highways to observe the artisan's workshops at the sides of the road which are a hive of activity.

Ugandans are very good craftsmen in steel fabrication, woodwork and crafts. They are also innovative in car mechanics, though this was not necessarily to the advantage of every customer. One friendly mechanic explained that if I needed a new (or at least a different) starter motor at a good price, he could simply swap my faulty one for one from another vehicle which had come in for another repair. While I appreciated his concern and acknowledged that this might indeed save me money, my conscience would not allow. For the mechanic, it was an entirely logical solution since he would be solving my problem and creating some more work for himself at the same time. If the other vehicle was a government vehicle, or belonged to a UN agency, then he believed that no one was really getting hurt since it was all off a broad back. It was for this reason that I sent my own man to stay with my car when it went in for any repairs – just to ensure that my vehicle was not donating parts for another worthy mechanical cause.

Craftsmen were skilled, but also liked to cut corners, and since there was no benchmarking, the finished product could be lacking. The finishing of items such as window frames, doors, or the paint job on a vehicle, was usually below international standards, but acceptable by local standards. Hence, local people bought the service or merchandise, but little of it would have been fit for export. Although there are few manufactured products which are exported from sub-Saharan Africa, there is much natural produce which is successfully exported. Flowers from Kenya and Uganda are significant in the international markets, as is coffee and tea. But even in these products more value could be added if more care was taken in their preparation. For example, if coffee beans were cleaned and sorted properly, the coffee would be of higher value.

Tradesmen were not used to producing to standard dimensions. When I was building the house, one sub-contractor had the job of making burglar proofing for the windows, since we did not find that glass by itself was much of a preventative in stopping thieves. I wished the burglar proofing to be made in a diamond shaped design, which gave the impression of leaded glass and did not make the rooms feel like prison cells with bars. However, in order to achieve the diamond effect there had to be very precise measurements to preserve the diagonal lines. We were behind schedule in finishing the house, and I decided that if I did not set a date to move, it would never happen, but the burglar bars for our bedroom window were still not ready. Since the guy doing the job had made many unfulfilled promises, I went and camped at his workshop until the job was finished, and in the process I discovered the problem was that my work required precise measurements. Michael was not used to this degree of precision, so he couldn't be bothered, until he had to do the work in order to get rid of me. None of the other windows which he made had any precise measurements, with the result that they all had small variations. Although I put pressure on Michael, it must not have been such a bad experience because he later came to work for me.

Standards of workmanship were seen in simple things such as ensuring that a plug or a light switch is level. It appeared that many tradesmen could not appreciate levels, and if things were crooked, no one was particularly bothered. I could not get used to walking into people's homes where the pictures were crooked, yet it seemed very odd if I went round straightening the pictures – there was definitely something obsessive compulsive about such behaviour. The other problem was that they were often hung so high I couldn't reach them, and it was very annoying to be seated under a lopsided picture of the President staring down at me. This made me wonder if the ability to see levels was a learned behaviour which people acquired through being brought up in houses which had straight lines, whereas inability to distinguish levels might be related to being brought up in a traditional house. I did ask myself from time to time what was wrong with a picture being crooked anyway because one could still see it, but I could not help myself – crooked pictures bothered me.

I found that if attention was paid to detail, tradesmen were very good at their jobs, but there could also be other factors which were responsible for poor quality. Wood which was not properly dried made it difficult for anyone to produce a good piece of carpentry. Uganda was heading for a severe shortage of wood because there was inadequate conservation or reforestation, so natural forests were dwindling. It was not uncommon to see hardwood trees being felled and the wood used for low level types of carpentry. Also the manner in which such trees were logged caused maximum wastage so that only a relatively small percentage of the tree was productively used. Since timber was rarely adequately dried, it continued to twist after it had been made into a door, door frame, table or cabinet; thus a dining table would open up a crack several months after the customer had bought it, or the door would not close properly. One could overcome such problems by stacking and drying the timber for several months, but this required forward planning which was not a business skill much in evidence among the small scale carpenters.

The world today is 'flat', so it is no longer possible for poor countries to hide behind practices which are sub-standard. International markets demand international standards, and inferior workmanship, the practice of cutting corners, or producing low quality products, is no longer acceptable. But Uganda and most of sub-Saharan Africa still have a long way to go, though things are changing slowly. I do not know where the term 'Third World' came from; there are countries which are labelled 'first world', those that are 'second world', and the rest are 'third world'. Some of the previous third world countries have now been reclassified as 'Least Developed Countries' or LDCs, most of which happen to be on the African continent. Others, which were previously third world, have rapidly developing economies, and some countries which used to be in the third world category now have first world GDPs. In the minds of many people the term 'Third World' is automatically associated with third rate. But I have never believed it follows that just because a developing country is classified as Third World, third rate is then automatic, and I found that if I insisted on high standards, they were usually forthcoming.

Over the years I applied this principle, not only to building and craftsmanship, but also to standards in the provision of medical care. The sad thing was that many people, both Ugandans and non-Ugandans, made excuses for poor standards by saying they were due to lack of resources. While one has to take the available resources into account, the two are not the same thing, and lack of resources should not be used as an excuse for poor performance.

# International Medical Centre

It may seem that I spent most of my time building, but building was a hobby, and my day job was still as a family doctor. I spent the vast majority of my time seeing patients, fitting the other activities into early mornings, lunch-breaks and evenings. I enjoyed the work since I was treating much in the way of infectious diseases and was able to apply the experience I had gained in Luweero. Also the patient base was young, so instead of patients with arthritis, gout, and high blood pressure, I was seeing patients with malaria, bilharzia, dysentery, tick fever, pneumonia, TB, and of course AIDS. I was also doing antenatal check-ups, but since I was working in a clinic with no inpatient beds, I did not do deliveries – except in special circumstances such as when an American couple, John and Margaret, asked me to carry out the delivery of their second child. Fortunately, it was the evening when Margaret went into labour, and we were able to use the whole clinic without disturbing other patients. Margaret was a perfect patient and delivered a healthy baby without complications. After the delivery had been completed, her husband was fussing around and brought some orange juice – I think as a kind of celebratory drink. He had found some plastic cups and had served everyone else by the time I asked, 'Where did you find those plastic cups?'

'They were in the lab.'

'Those are the ones I use to collect the urine samples,' I told him. I passed on the drink.

I had only two rooms at the clinic, one which acted as the reception and waiting area, with a small laboratory tucked in the corner; the other was my consultation room from which I also dispensed drugs from a cupboard behind my desk. Despite our cramped conditions, with the patients often having to sit in the corridor outside, the clinic rapidly became busy. One problem was that Ugandans patients were generally not accustomed to making appointments although this was perceived as normal for expatriates. Therefore, when someone had not made an appointment and a foreigner was seen first, the patient got very annoyed and complained.

'I was waiting and then you took him first,'

'Yes, but he had made an appointment,'

But patients did not accept this as a good enough explanation and interpreted it as racist since I was seeing the white patient first. We got so much 'stick' about this that we had to abandon the appointment system and accept patients on a first come, first served basis, but then they complained about long waiting times.

As with any family doctor, I got to know my patients well, and there were times when I got so engrossed in conversation with one patient that the nurse would knock on the door and remind me politely, but firmly, that the waiting room was full of increasingly irate patients. The funny thing was that when I would eventually see them and apologise for the delay, they would wave it off. 'Not at all doctor, we can see you are busy.' But outside they had been giving the receptionist hell.

Many of the patients who needed the greatest support were those with AIDS. At this time there was very little in the way of sustainable treatment for HIV, though dual therapy with two anti-viral drugs had just become available. This combination slowed up the progress of the disease but did not halt it because the virus mutated and became resistant – usually within six months – although I found clinically that dual therapy gave the patients a boost for up to one year.

I had one patient who had practically no immunity, but she continued to fight on. Her husband worked on engineering projects and was often away, so she would call me to visit her at home or else come and see me on a regular basis. She had developed a neuropathy of one leg and had difficulty walking. I saw her over a period of several years with many different illnesses, and at times I was sure that she would not make it, but she always pulled through. On one occasion when she was extremely ill, I admitted her to a small hospital in Kampala and the staff acted like they had seen a ghost. They could not believe that she was still alive, since when they had last seen her several years previously, she had been at death's door. Her CD4 count dropped to 2 cells (It should be 1000 in a normal person), with the result that she had no resistance at all. I put her on the combination of the two drugs which were available at that time, and she rallied, but her CD4 count did not even make it into double figures. Finally, it seemed that we had run out of options. Her husband sat in my office and cried because there was no more hope

'Why Rachel?' he said through the tears. 'She has never done anyone any harm; she is just a sweet kind person.'

I did not have the answers and could only tell him that I had done all that I could in Uganda, but perhaps if he could get her to the UK (he was British, she was Ugandan), other combinations of drugs might be available. This was at the time when triple therapy was just emerging but was scarcely accessible in Uganda. Somehow her husband managed to get a visa and to get her onto a flight, even though she was very sick at the time. In Manchester she was given a combination of several antiretroviral drugs and again defied the odds. She was able to move around with the aid of a stick and used to call me every year to let me know how she was doing, but one day it was her husband who called to say that Rachel had finally succumbed. He was sobbing over the phone as he told me that his beloved Rachel has passed away. She had died of lymphoma, a form of cancer closely associated with HIV.

One of the common conditions which I treated was malaria, and I found that there was an interesting cultural dimension to the treatment of this disease. The Luganda word for fever was the same word as malaria – *musuja* – so every time a Ugandan said they had *musuja*, they were giving me the diagnosis and expecting to be given anti-malarial treatment. On the other hand, if a non-Ugandan had a fever, they just wanted a test to find out if the fever was due to malaria or something else. If the test was negative, they were relieved, but many Ugandans would doubt a negative result since they felt their symptoms were proof enough that they had the disease. There was an added complication in that the malaria parasite could be incubating, and although one might not see parasites that day, they could appear on the blood slide the following day. Therefore, it became common practice for doctors to treat malaria on the basis of clinical symptoms, even without finding parasites in the blood.

Some clinics had such poor laboratories where the microscope was not clean and the stain so poorly filtered that it was hard to tell what one was looking at. Malaria parasites show up as small rings, but if they have not absorbed the stain properly, they can be seen as incomplete rings or even dots. If the stain was not filtered, a dust particle could be mistaken for a malaria parasite, and many lab technicians had a habit of reporting 'scanty' parasites if they were not sure what they were seeing. My colleague, Dr Paula, was asked to consult on a patient who was not responding to anti-malarials. The doctor pointed out a parasite on the slide.

'Yes, I see it,' Paula responded. 'But that is odd, it stays in the same place if I move the slide.'

The parasite was an artefact on the lens, so every slide seen under that particular microscope was diagnosed as malaria. I only treated patients if they were parasite positive, and if the slide was negative, I advised the patient that he should return the following day for another test if he still had symptoms. Although this was the correct procedure, many Ugandan patients left the clinic, muttering that our machines did not work.

Since this was a recurrent problem, I thought I would pro-actively visit some of the companies where our patients worked and carry out health education on the subject. Hence, I was seated in the boardroom of the National Environmental Management Authority discussing malaria with some of their top management and explaining that *musuja* was not always due to malaria. I went on to say that I had been trained at the London School of Hygiene and Tropical Medicine, so I was treating malaria correctly according to international standards and the scientific evidence.

'Dr Clarke,' one of the senior managers interrupted, 'we know that you have international training, but this is Ugandan malaria, so we suggest that you treat our Ugandan malaria the Ugandan way' – which was to give anti-malarial drugs to everyone who complained of 'fever' or *musuja*. I thought that if a senior manager could not accept the scientific basis for treating malaria there was not much hope for the man in the street.

The net effect of all the over-treatment was that the malaria parasite itself became resistant to the cheapest drug available at the time: chloroquine. When I came to Uganda in the late eighties, there was very little resistance to chloroquine, but within a decade there was widespread resistance, necessitating the introduction of a range of drugs which were at least ten times the price.

One morning a member of a group of street children who hung around outside came into the clinic, holding a tiny baby wrapped in newspapers, claiming that she had found the baby in a dustbin. The baby weighed less than two kilos and was already cold, but we rushed the baby to hospital and put her in an incubator. The street children hung around the traffic island near the clinic and spent the day sniffing glue, aviation fuel, or petrol fumes and were usually 'high'. They slept in the shade of a tree or begged from passing motorists. It was likely that one of these young people had given birth and dumped the child, though we never identified the mother. The baby only survived for a few days; it was too tiny and premature, so the lungs were not properly developed. It appeared that the existence of this child was doomed before she was born.

Another newborn baby had a traumatic entry into this world but survived because of the kindness of a neighbour. This little mite had been born to a house girl who did not want the child, and after giving birth, she dropped the baby down a pit-latrine. Fortunately, the gentleman who brought me to see the baby found out what had happened and called the fire brigade, who dug down beside the latrine and then broke through to pull the child free. This unfortunate infant had spent the first eight hours of her life lying in human excrement. When I saw her she was ill but, miraculously, looked like she would pull through. Her rescuer decided to adopt her and touchingly named her 'Blessed'. She began her life in shit, and if it had not been for someone who took swift action, she would have ended her life there.

Such situations made me ponder the ability of ordinary people to do evil. We feel we can distance ourselves as ordinary people when we can attribute evil to a monster such as Amin or Hitler, but when a house-girl puts her baby down a pit latrine, what does that say about ordinary people? Was such behaviour simply a reflection of the harshness of life in Uganda? Was this girl evil? Because it appeared that she was callous enough to murder her own child. But was this due to ignorance or desperation, or did she just want to be rid of the thing that had grown inside her? Reports of murder were all too common in the Ugandan press, and it seemed that the perpetrators could easily dissociate their actions from the consequences and move on. Stories of atrocities were common: a woman waited for another woman and then hacked off her head; a man chopped his wife into pieces. When I read such things I wondered what kind of people could perpetrate these acts, but they were just people; some were ignorant, some were superstitious, some were callous and others were desperate. Life in Uganda was hard and people did terrible things

My office was right above the street. One morning I was disturbed by the sound of a loud crash just outside my window. I ran downstairs to find a woman lying under the very wheels of a *matatu* while the passengers were still seated inside. The driver had already jumped out – not to give help, but to flee – and he was nowhere to be seen. We pushed the taxi off the lady and gave first aid, but she was badly injured and died within minutes. The taxis were in such a hurry to get to their destination and then get their next batch of fare-paying passengers that they flouted every basic law of the road. Thus, when this particular driver had seen a way to pass the stationary traffic by mounting the pavement, he hurriedly drove right up on the curb; but he was going so fast the pedestrians did not have time to scatter, and he hit the lady. It was likely that since he escaped into the crowd, there were no consequences for him personally – apart from having someone's death on his conscience, but he would probably find a way to deny that it ever happened. Later the church put bollards on the pavement to prevent the same thing happening again.

Some time afterwards a young woman came to see me, telling me that it was her mother who had died, and she wanted to thank me for what I had done. I had been able to do little, but she appreciated that we had tried to give her mother some dignity in her death. Her mother was dead through rashness and stupidity, but unfortunately, this was not the first and would not be the last time that such an incident took place.

When I started International Medical Centre, Rose was one of the key staff, as the nurse, receptionist and administrator all rolled into one. But she was getting itchy feet and wanted to do a higher qualification in nursing. We discussed the possibility of her doing registered nursing in the UK, but she was not drawn to this idea and wished to explore the options in the USA. Coincidentally she had been asked to travel in the States

146

to supervise a Ugandan children's choir which was raising money for orphans, so she had the opportunity to sample life in the USA. When she returned, she told us that an African American couple wished to sponsor her to do nursing in Texas, and she would like to take up this opportunity. As it turned out, the couple did not have any connections in nursing and simply wanted to tout Rose in front of black empowerment meetings as a poor African whom they had rescued. Since Rose had white Irish parents and did not identify closely with the issues of the Deep South, she was not all that comfortable in this role. So she made her escape and went to stay at a youth centre with friends, from where she made over fifty applications to various nursing schools. But she was singularly unsuccessful, mainly because she could not get the necessary evidence of her education from Uganda.

Finally, she was about to return when she was asked to speak at a church group and tell her story. One of those present was a doctor working in Russellville, Arkansas, Dr Mike Hendron. He told Rose about a university in his home town and the Hendrons made the extremely generous offer that if she was accepted into their school of nursing, she could live with them. She travelled for the interview and met the dean who happened to be doing her last interviews for admission to the school before retirement. This lady wanted to assist Rose as one of the final good deeds she would be able to do before leaving the job, and she made the offer of a place, on condition that Rose achieved good grades during her first semester. Rose did not need a second chance.

Rose went on to win numerous awards from the nursing school and graduated at the top of her class. From there she moved to Dallas, where she joined Baylor University to do her Master's degree. She once again won awards and was the valedictorian speaker at the graduation. After graduating with her Master's, she came back to Uganda and worked with me again, then earned a full scholarship to Yale University to do a PHD.

This was the girl from the village who had struggled against witchcraft.

# Starting a hospital

While I was running International Medical Centre I had not given up the dream of building a modern hospital, and after a few false starts, I was able to secure a long lease on a building in Kampala, which I felt could be renovated into a small thirty-bed hospital. In the distant past, the building had been used by an Indian association as their community centre, and when the Indians were expelled, it had become a school, but had fallen into a sad state of disrepair. I met with a group of elderly Indian men who constituted the association's committee and listened as they argued among themselves (I had once heard it said that if there were two Israelis, there were three opinions, and roughly the same principle seemed to apply to these old Indian gentlemen). Eventually, we were able to agree a long-term lease, and I was free to start renovations in order to convert the building into a hospital. It seemed that in every phase of my work I was building, and when I finished one project, there was always another on the horizon. Maybe there had been a dodgy Irish builder somewhere among my ancestors and building was in my genes.

By this time I had also secured another room to expand International Medical Centre and employed a very capable Ugandan doctor, David, to work with me. This eased the burden somewhat, but I still spent most of the day seeing patients, and visited the site at lunchtimes and in the evenings to supervise the work, which was progressing slowly. Since Kampala is a city set on hills, this building was also built into the side of a hill, so the ground floor was considerably smaller than the first floor. Therefore we planned the layout with the ground floor serving for consulting rooms, while the first floor was allocated as the wards. The first floor was just one big empty space and we planned the wards by laying bricks along the lines for the proposed internal walls and corridors to measure if we could wheel a trolley through the doors. Everything about the building was a compromise since it was not purpose-built and was far from ideal. After we had planned the wards, there remained the question of providing for an operating theatre suite, a mortuary, staff canteen, kitchen and laundry, and there did not appear to be enough space on the site to fit them all in. The only way in which we could create more space was by digging away part of the hill at the back and putting up another small building to act as the theatre suite – which we did. This new building had to fit the available space, so when the theatre was designed around the dimensions available, it turned out to be pentagonal. During this whole process we were not overburdened by city planners or hospital planners because the project was not classified as a new building and did not need much in the way of planning permission. But I had just got into the flow of the renovation work when everything ground to a complete halt due to a more serious problem.

One morning I was talking to my colleague, Dr Paula, in the car-park outside the clinic, when she reached out and touched my neck

'What is that?' she asked.

'What is what?' I replied, since I had not been aware of anything. I quickly retreated to find a mirror to take a look at myself, and there I saw a large egg shaped swelling on the left side of my neck, rising up from under my collar bone. I knew what this signified – the cancer had returned.

My immediate feelings were not so much concern for my own health, but that the timing of this recurrence sucked, since I was in the midst of building a hospital. Also from a financial point of view, getting cancer now was actually worse than the first time because if I was not working I had no income and no fallback position. Fortunately, I now had Dr David so the clinic could continue, but there was nothing worse for the interruption of the continuity of patient care than for the doctor himself to get sick – unless of course he died! Patients are loyal, to a point, but if they realise that the doctor might not be coming back, they make other arrangements. The fact that I had been there for my patients day in and day out meant that much of my impact depended on that one on one relationship. If I died, everything died with me, and I determined that if I survived this recurrence of cancer, I would learn how to replicate myself. If I wished to create a legacy, I would have to bring about institutional development.

This was not a happy time for me, as I was the one who had pushed out the boat, and it seemed it was about to sink. That evening, when I told Robbie that I had a recurrence of the cancer, she was extremely distressed. She was not only upset that her husband had a life threatening illness, but did not know how she would cope if I died and left all of these unfinished projects in her hands. I was annoyed that the cancer had returned when I had so much to do, and we were both worried about how we would survive financially. Throughout all of this, the thought was also in the back of my mind that it was an extremely serious turn of events that the cancer had recurred at all, and there was a real possibility that I would not survive. I was also worried about facing chemotherapy again, because, unfortunately, I knew exactly what lay in store for me.

The day before I left for treatment, I met with Tim Lwanga, who was a Member of Parliament. We had known Tim and his family for many years; his children had gone to school with ours, and he was one of the founder board members for the hospital project. We walked round the building works and then I said to him, 'Tim, you know the board is legally responsible if I am not here; look after all this and look after Robbie.'

The truth suddenly dawned on Tim that I might not return and that he would be responsible for what I had started in Kampala. The seriousness of my statement struck him like a thunderbolt. Tim never forgot that moment.

# Cousins.

According to the text books I had been cured, having survived five years, but despite this, a dormant line of cancer cells had reawakened and was growing vigorously in my lymph nodes. One interesting medical aspect to this cancer was that it was a different cell line from the first time round. On the first occasion I had what was known as teratoma, while this time it was diagnosed as seminoma; they were cousins, but they were different. When the cancer occurred the first time the diagnosis was so sudden and unexpected that I barely had time to take stock of my life. And when there was hope for recovery, I was too sick to think about anything outside of the bucket I was puking into – my world having narrowed to my immediate pain and discomfort. But all that was supposed to be in the past and the cancer should not have recurred again – theoretically.

I travelled back to Belfast, nursing my lump, which appeared to be growing by the minute, got off the plane and went straight to see my friend, Jim McGuigan, a thoracic surgeon. Jim had no idea I was coming, and as far as he was concerned, I was working on the far side of the world; but he found me standing on his doorstep about seven o'clock in the evening.

'Do you think you could do anything about this lump on my neck?' I asked, without preliminaries, not being in the mood for small talk. I don't know if I expected him to take me to theatre then and there, but I was desperate for something to happen. Despite my abrupt appearance, Jim was sympathetic and was able to arrange for a fine needle aspiration to be carried out by a colleague the next day.

In this procedure some fluid is sucked from the lump through a needle, spread on a slide, stained and examined through a microscope. In my case I became a walking sample and went to the laboratory myself, where the doctor stuck a needle in my neck and aspirated a little tissue fluid from the lump. Since it was a teaching laboratory, the microscope had an extra lens where the student could also view the sample and I was able to view my own cancer cells, as the pathologist explained what I was looking at. It was a surreal experience. I could see sheets of normal cells just like I had seen in histology textbooks, but the cancer cells had lost the inhibitory factor which ensured that they grew in an orderly fashion and instead were heaped up haphazardly. As I looked at the slide, I was looking at the enemy – the very cells which would kill me, if given the chance.

Subsequently, I met the consultant oncologist who had treated me the first time. I don't think he was delighted to see me again! Obviously doctors do not like to see their failures – they take it personally – but besides this, I had not been an easy patient. Doctors never make good patients, and I'm sure he did not relish the thought of having me under his care again, especially since this time I was already militating to get the treatment started.

'Let us just get one thing settled at the outset,' he said. 'Am I treating you, or are you treating yourself? Because we can only have one doctor in charge of this case.'

That was putting it rather bluntly, but he was right. I had to stop being a doctor and resign myself to being a patient – even if I did know what was going to happen and how the treatment would progress from first-hand experience. He was also right to have addressed the issue at the beginning since it allowed me to be the patient and let him get on with managing my case.

He decided he would start the treatment the following week as the drugs had to be sequenced with the pharmacy over the period of the working week from Monday to Saturday; this left me with time on my hands, while I awaited my fate. Lauren was now a student at Edinburgh University and had flown over to be with me. Since there was nothing more that I could do in the way of getting treatment, we hired a car and travelled to

153

Dublin where we stayed in a small hotel in the centre. In the morning we lay on top of my bed, watching cartoons, until we almost missed the full Irish breakfast, then we drove out to the Vale of Glendalough, had lunch in a pub and walked by the waterfall at Powerscourt. It was bright cold sunshine and the beauty of Ireland impacted me strongly again. I did not want to live permanently in Ireland, but I loved to visit and drink in its beauty. It was the intensity of my life which allowed me to appreciate the light and the colours, and that weekend I was seeing in glorious Technicolor because I knew that when I came within site of the tower block of the Belfast City Hospital the feelings of nausea would return. And by the time the automated voice in the lift said, 'Going up, third floor, Oncology', I would already feel like throwing up.

Rather than wait for my hair to fall out, I went to the barber and had my head shaved – preferable to waking up to find your hair beside you on the pillow. At least taking that decision gave me a sense of empowerment. I had a bad moment when I was waiting to start the treatment. We had some good friends, Heather and Andrew, who lived a stone's throw from the hospital. He was the vicar in charge of the Anglican Church at the university, and they invited me out for a meal just before I was to commence the treatment. While we were walking back, I decided to stop off at a large pub we happened to be passing. I was depressed, being very aware of the lump on my neck and afraid of what I was about to go through.

I also felt like a stranger in my own land since I had now lived in Uganda for thirteen years, but in Belfast I had lost touch with people, and on that night in that pub I felt alone. I tried to strike up a conversation with some people seated nearby, but they just looked at me suspiciously, because unlike Uganda, one could not just engage in conversation with random people. Subsequently, since I was alone, I must have dozed in my chair, because I woke up to find that I was in a head lock, being propelled out the door by the bouncer. I was in shock and wondered why the gentleman had not tapped my on the shoulder and told me that I was dozing and should go home. This experience came at a low point; the gesture summed up how I felt at that moment: I was no longer part of normal society and was being thrown out.

Perhaps all cancer victims find it hard to sum up their feelings because we are divided into those who survive and those who do not. I have always felt somewhat guilty when I meet others whom I know will not make it. Those who survive have a sense of good fortune that they are alive, while at the back of their minds they wonder when it will be their turn again. Most have a strong grasp on life, and, on the basis that another day of survival is still life, cancer patients allow themselves to be subjected to all sorts of horrendous medical treatments in the hope of gaining another few months of life. They develop a grim determination to hold on and go through the next thing that science has to throw at them – for they know that therein lies the possibility of a future. The first time I had cancer I went from having no hope to gaining hope, to being past caring because I was so sick. The second time I never lost hope, but the thought of going through it all again left me terrified.

My treatment involved going into hospital for a week at a time, during which I was filled up with intravenous fluids and chemotherapy drugs. Then the following week I was allowed to go home to lick my wounds, and by the third week I was on the road to recovery. If my blood had held up or recovered by the fourth week, then I could go back to the hospital to repeat the cycle. While I was in hospital I was on a drip, continuously receiving fluids, chemotherapy and steroids. The chemo made me so nauseous that the only thing I looked forward to was sleep and, though I was given anti-nausea drugs, nothing could take it away entirely. Before such drugs were available, they used to give the patients strong sedatives, and each time the patient woke up and started vomiting, they just knocked him out again. I would happily have been put to sleep for the entire course of my treatment. Not surprisingly, I lost my sense of humour and did not crack any jokes or even smile for several months. Then one day I made a lame joke, and Lauren knew that I was getting better.

After I had received treatment on the first round of chemotherapy, I insisted on going back to Uganda during the break in treatment. I so longed to be back in my home because, even if I was in bed, I could look out over Lake Victoria. There were also many pressing issues to which I had to attend because I had left so precipitously. One of the side effects of chemotherapy was that it also killed the blood cells, so it was important to have regular blood tests to keep track of the state of the blood. My tests showed that the platelets were falling; a level of less than 10,000 was considered dangerously low, and mine were falling towards that number. So an appeal for blood was made to the Irish community at the St Patrick's Day ball, which happened to be taking place that week-end. Quite a number of people volunteered to give blood, but fortunately, the blood count began to rise and a transfusion was not necessary. When I returned to Ireland for the second round of treatment, the Professor in charge of the unit came to see me personally and sternly warned that there would be no more trips to Uganda until the chemo was entirely finished.

Since there was a danger of wiping out my ability to make blood altogether through the chemotherapy, it was decided to take off some stem cells and put them in the deep freeze. Hence, I was sent to the haematology department between the bouts of chemotherapy, where I sat in a big chair and was attached to a machine which apparently filtered out the stem cells. They called it harvesting and, after each session, the nurses looked pleased and told me that they had harvested another good yield. I had grown up on a farm and associated harvesting with crops like wheat and barley. I now have stem cells stored in liquid nitrogen in Belfast – should they ever need them to clone me.

During all this time Robbie still had to hold down a teaching job in Uganda since that was our only regular income, but she would make trips to Belfast to hold my hand during chemotherapy sessions. On some occasions this was just about all she could do since I would not talk. People would drift in and out to visit me, but I was not very good company. Those with whom I had most contact were the nurses, some of whom had just the right touch to help me through the chemo, but there was one nurse who got it wrong. She would come into the ward in the mornings, pull back the screens and announce to all and sundry, 'OK happy campers, let us have you all up!'

For a start there was no one on the cancer ward who was happily 'camped' there, and secondly, to make matters worse for this inordinately cheerful nurse, all of us had lost any semblance of a sense of humour.

When I had received the final round of chemo, I had to wait in Belfast to ensure that my blood count was recovering before flying back to Uganda. After a couple of weeks I checked my blood in the local health-centre and noted that the count was rising, so I boarded a flight for London. Unfortunately, the hospital had not been kept up to date with the results and thought I was not ready to return. Hence, when I arrived in London, there was a stewardess waiting for me as I disembarked, with the instructions that I should return to Ireland immediately. You can run, but you can't hide, I thought. But on this occasion, since I knew that my blood was returning to normal, I carried on home.

Since I still had no hair and the treatment had made my face bloated, no-one recognised me when I got back. I sat in the office of a friend as he walked in and out past me, looking at this bald man and wondering who he was. I was a regular columnist in the Uganda national newspaper, the *Sunday Vision,* and it was their practice to publish a picture of the

157

columnist alongside the copy. They had been publishing an old picture, but when one of their photojournalists bumped into me at a cocktail and realised that I was bald, the newspaper then insisted that they publish the up-to-date picture, which was very confusing to most Ugandans. But regardless of how I looked, I was so glad to be home.

When I went back to work, I found that the clinic was still running and still solvent, but that the flow of income was greatly reduced. I had called the renovation works to a halt while I was away since I had no money, and now it was a question of whether I could crank things up to get going again. I had been knocked down, but I was not about to give up. However, it was not a pleasant return: I had some low level bureaucrats from the Uganda Revenue Authority who immediately descended on me as a sort of welcome back; many of my patients had gone to other doctors, and I had a half renovated building for which I was paying rent, but receiving no income.

The Uganda Revenue Authority officials had a rather unsophisticated strategy for getting people to pay tax. Their philosophy was that if they shook the tree hard enough, some apples were bound to fall out. So I was given an assessment which bore no relationship to reality, and it was my job to prove that the figures were wrong. Alternatively, one could negotiate, and in the negotiations there were two choices: one could pay the tax authority itself, or one could pay the tax official, the latter amount being considerably less than the first, but contributing to the official's personal welfare fund. I was able to show what was due, and they finally accepted my figures, but it was all added stress. I was trying to renovate a building which would improve the level of medical facilities, I was motivated to make a difference to the standards of healthcare, but in the process I had to deal with petty officials who saw me as a legitimate target to be shaken down. I could have set out to build the hospital through the aid sector, and then I would not have had any personal liability, but I was an entrepreneur, or perhaps a social entrepreneur, and risk taking was part of my nature, so even if I felt sorry for myself, it was all self-inflicted

I got back to work and continued the renovations. Since the building was built into the side of the hill, we were able to make access to the first floor by landscaping a road round the side of the building. This solved our problem of getting patients to the first floor without a lift. The building also had a flat roof to which we could add another floor if we were to expand in the future, but to do this we needed to make provision for a lift. Hence, we gouged out a hole in the side of the hill and built a concrete structure for a lift shaft, but as we were not going to install this lift immediately, we put wooden floors in the shaft and made two offices and a store. I shared one office with two other people, while the other became our finance and billing office. We never did expand beyond the first floor and never installed the lift, and from experience I can verify that a lift shaft does not make an ideal office.

Gradually we completed the building: first the ground floor, then some of the wards on the first floor, then the operating theatre suite, offices and staff canteen, kitchen and laundry, generator house, mortuary, small workshop, hospital incinerator and fire-safety system. Every square inch of space was used, and everything fitted in snugly; we were even able to make a small garden, and by the time we were finished we had created a credible thirty-bed hospital with single, double and four-bed rooms, each with en-suite facilities and a nursing station at the centre of the complex.

Though we did not face onerous regulations in renovating this building into a hospital, there were regulations with which we had to comply in order to obtain the license to run a hospital. This involved an inspection from a Ministry of Health official who came armed with a form and a list of boxes to tick.

'Do you have a mortuary?' We had now solved that problem and the mortuary was beside the generator house. Tick.

'Do you have an operating theatre?' Tick.

'Do you have a laundry?' Tick. And after all the boxes were ticked, and payment of the appropriate fee had been made, we were officially listed as 'International Hospital Kampala.'

# The patients are shagging in the beds

I employed many young people at the clinic and the hospital, on the basis that they were bright, they were keen, and they were fast learners. They were also usually unemployed and needed someone to believe in them to give them a start in their careers – and they were affordable. I discovered that the job title for the position was important to these young graduates and learned to my cost that the title of receptionist was unacceptable, as this had connotations of a low level person, sleeping over an empty desk, or lethargically answering the telephone. After one young lady had been employed as a receptionist at the clinic, she jumped ship to take a job which was similar in pay and responsibilities to the one I had given her.

'Why did you leave?' I asked, peeved, when I met her again

'Because the other company gave me a job as an administrative assistant.'

'But you are doing the very same job you were doing for me, and the prospects are better in my organisation,' I said.

'Yes, but I was a receptionist for you, now I am an administrative assistant,' she answered.

I couldn't argue with that – she now felt she had a better title. This young woman kept in touch with me over the years and later told me that the job to which she moved was inferior to the one she left, but that she had been under pressure from her family who felt the position was more prestigious because of the title.

Despite having keen young people to work for me, I did not have many systems in place; I was just a doctor after all, and doctors are not generally renowned for their proficiency in management skills. And to make matters worse, I was a doctor who liked building and had a strong entrepreneurial streak. My management style was to find a person who I felt had the

161

potential to do a certain job and then let them get on with it. This strategy worked most of the time in that people rose to the challenge because I believed in them, and they did not want to let me down. Belief in people was not common in Uganda, where it was more usual for the boss to sit behind a big desk and bark orders at his staff. Of course, I have been let down on numerous occasions, but despite this, I still believe in people, and many young Ugandans have rewarded me by fulfilling their potential and going on to great things.

I had employed Pendo and Hannah, two university graduates, in administrative positions at the clinic, and as the new hospital got to the stage where the ground floor was nearing completion, I asked Pendo if she would move with Dr David to that location in order to get a clinic going, as the first step towards operating a hospital. This would establish the location as a medical centre and would also free up David's room at the clinic so that I could employ a third doctor. Dr David and Pendo had never had such a challenge in their lives; they had no previous experience in starting a clinic and there were no systems in place, but they did their best and got things going.

It was also my style to grow the business organically by taking one step at a time and seeing how that worked. Then lessons could be learned, and one could go on to the next step. Dr David and Pendo were the guinea-pigs in starting the hospital and I did feel sorry for them, but they performed valiantly. Years later Pendo wrote to me to say that she had been looking back over her life and wanted to thank me for believing in her and allowing her to develop as a person. At the time, she just thought that I had thrown her in at the deep end.

After completion of the first ward, we were able to admit patients for non-surgical conditions, and co-incidentally, an Australian nurse, who had married a Ugandan lawyer and come to settle back in Uganda, was looking for a job. She was very well qualified and I was happy to hire her because I needed a nursing officer to take charge of the nursing side of the hospital. We discussed terms and conditions at my office at the clinic, and then she agreed a date when she would start, but on the day she commenced I was not able to spend time with her because I was busy seeing patients, so Julie was left to get on with things as best she could. She started the new job without an office, a desk, or a computer and with workmen banging and hammering overhead; she was supposed to be in charge, and the man who had given her the job was too busy to see her. Julie gradually settled in, but she was not impressed with her induction.

The first baby to be born at International Hospital was a boy, and the parents named him Ian Clarke, since I was the one who delivered him. So somewhere in Uganda there is another Ian Clarke, as there are a number of Bill Clintons, subsequent to his visit. I should clarify that such names do not signify any biological link! We installed an X-ray department, consisting of a second hand Ultrasound scan and X-ray machine (it cost more to bring a technician from South Africa to calibrate the X-ray machine than the cost of the machine itself). The operating suite was equipped and made fully functional, and offices were equipped. We even had a computer network, and Julie eventually had her very own desk and computer, though she had to share an office. We purchased new laboratory equipment and hired staff; we were on a steep learning curve.

As we became functional as a hospital and admitted surgical patients, we also needed blood. Here we met some challenges, particularly if we ran out of blood during the night. Normally we would send the ambulance to the National Blood Bank when blood was needed, but the night staff were not used to being disturbed, and the watchmen were particularly difficult. The first hurdle was actually getting through the gate, the second getting someone to open the door, and the third hurdle was getting the right blood group from the fridges. The blood bank itself did the best they could, but there was a shortage of blood, and there were obviously some people who did not appreciate what an emergency was and who felt they should hold onto the blood they had in stock.

On one occasion, knowing that the ambulance driver would encounter such difficulties, I went with him in order to give added weight to our mission. Predictably, the response of the watchman was, 'We are closed, why don't you come back in the morning?'

'Because it is an emergency,' I shot back. 'Now open up and give us some blood.'

Reluctantly, he opened the door, and eventually we were able to get some blood, but not before there were many abusive exchanges. The watchman really did feel there was no reason why we should not wait until the morning like everyone else. I had heard so often that a procedure could not be carried out, or that someone had died because there was no blood, and it seemed that medical staff were prepared to accept the shortage of blood as a legitimate reason for someone's death. But I sometimes felt that people did not push hard enough to get the blood at the time it was needed, or perhaps make themselves obnoxious, like me, when a patient's life was in danger.

I had arrived in Uganda after the horrors of the previous regime in the eighties, during which it was an everyday event for people to be kidnapped or killed in order that ransoms could be extorted from their relatives. I even met some of the people who were responsible for atrocities during these regimes, though when I met them, they were genial and friendly, and it was hard to believe that these same people had committed crimes against humanity. During this period, ordinary people lived from day to day and survived as best they could. There was no such entity as a middle-class in Uganda; there were only survivors who made it through that day. That was also the time when AIDS took hold and why worry about AIDS, which might kill you in five years, when you could be dead tomorrow?

Terrible things happened then, but survivors had no time to shed tears; it was only those who were insulated from the harsher realities of life who could afford the luxury of emotion. At that time Ugandans accepted that one could go to a hospital and die because of the lack of blood, the lack of drugs, or even the lack of a doctor. It was not anyone's fault because that was just how it was, and people accepted it because there was no alternative.

When Museveni marched into Kampala with his boy soldiers, he brought hope, but not much else, and though Ugandans were grateful for the peace, most people still had nothing. They knew that when they went to hospital, the pharmacies would still have no drugs, so they still expected people to die unless they could afford to go to the private pharmacies. Doctors wrote prescriptions but felt their responsibility ended there, and instead of being more in touch with their patients, they became less so because they prescribed in a vacuum and gave them pieces of paper to heal them. They prescribed without relation to cost or availability; they prescribed the latest and most expensive drugs because these were the ideal, and the fact that they were not there was not their responsibility.

Even when there had been peace in Uganda for many years, health still did not seem to be a priority, and the drugs and treatment were still unavailable so that while other facilities and services improved, medical care remained underdeveloped. The general public, particularly those who could not afford to purchase treatment, became so inured to this state of affairs that they did not expect anything better. So when there was something which could be done, like fighting for blood to save the patient, people did not appreciate the issues, and when a doctor came pleading for blood at midnight, the watchmen saw it as unreasonable since normally no-one bothered them at this time.

'Go away, why can't you use the proper system and come back in the morning?' I had been told. By that time the problem would indeed have resolved itself, and the blood would not be needed because the patient would be dead.

Susan was someone whom I had known for several years; she had a loud infectious laugh and was usually the centre of attention, but she kept getting sick and turned to me for help. The first time was quite straight forward: she developed abdominal pain which I diagnosed as appendicitis, but she was frightened to undergo the operation and asked if I would go into theatre with her, so I assisted the surgeon in the appendicectomy. She made a good recovery, but she was in and out of my clinic so often with other diverse complaints that I named her Sick Susan. There was no underlying relationship between the various illnesses, such as severe migraines or recurrent sore throats, but she was at the clinic on a regular basis and developed a thick file. Later she was admitted to International Hospital with severe measles, which was unusual in an adult; she also developed acute pain in the abdomen, with signs of obstruction of the intestine. Since she had a previous operation, Dr Moses the surgeon, thought that she might have developed adhesions which were causing obstruction. However, when he operated he did not find any evidence of this, but discovered that she had a generalised inflammation of the organs and oozing of blood. The measles had caused the platelets in her blood to drop to the point where she was not clotting properly and was bleeding into the abdomen, into the joints and the skin. She needed fresh blood and platelets urgently. I was group '0 negative' and my blood could therefore be donated to anyone, so I was able to supply a pint of fresh blood which replenished her platelets sufficiently and gave her some clotting factors, preventing her condition from deteriorating until we were able to obtain more platelets. The

166

blood which I donated was instrumental in saving her life, and she went on to make a complete recovery.

Over the years, since my blood group made me a universal blood donor, I was called on to give blood on numerous occasions. I think that the lab treated me as a sort of walking reserve blood bank, so today in Uganda there are a good number of units of Irish blood mixed with Ugandan blood.

As the years went on, the Ugandan Blood Transfusion Service became better organised, and they were able to obtain, and screen, a large amount of blood so that there was often sufficient amounts of blood to supply all the hospitals. But one still found the excuse of 'no blood' being used, and one felt that the problem lay, not with the blood bank itself, but with the lack of organisation of some medical staff and hospital administrators in making arrangements to ensure they had sufficient blood supplies for their patients.

During our staff recruitment for the hospital, we appointed a nurse to be in charge of the wards, whom I found to be a very serious minded person and who did not appear to have any sense of humour. But she was good at her job and had the best interests of the patients at heart. One morning she came to me about a problem with the beds in the hospital. Some of the beds were from an American field hospital and had wire springs supporting the mattresses, so if they were not tightened properly, the beds squeaked and sagged in the middle. Ugandans from different parts of the country have different pronunciations, with some getting Ls and Rs mixed up and some substituting Sh for S. The priest at Kiwoko always prefaced the communion by saying, 'Let us play for the blade and the wine', but we knew what he meant. When elections were held there were usually some light moments when someone contested that the erection was very rigid (the election was very rigged). The Mayor of Kampala had his own interesting grammar and vocabulary and when he was

167

challenged about 'bird flu' during the time of this pandemic, he responded, 'Bad flu, good flu, we will handle it.'

My nurse was concerned about the bed springs sagging, so she approached me and said, Doctor, you must do something about it, the patients are shagging in the beds.'

They must be recovering, I thought.

# The Man with the Key has gone

Life was not all work, and we were often invited to cocktails and receptions to celebrate various international days. These events were held at the different Embassies and were an excuse for free drinks and the opportunity to socialize with a wide variety of people from different walks of life. But sometimes while we were socializing inside, thieves were having a field day outside, stealing parts from our vehicles. On one occasion, after celebrating Bastille Day at the French Embassy, I came back to find that my car had been broken into yet again and the electric window switches stolen. This was the third time this had happened in a few weeks (the electric window switches were a preferred item, along with the wing mirrors and side lights). After the last episode, I had bought new electric switches and fitted an alarm, which had obviously made no difference at all. That was the problem with car alarms; they were set off by the slightest disturbance, so everyone ignored them; they were set off when a breeze blew or by a passing pedestrian breaking wind. So even though the car alarm might have been ringing merrily, thieves could strip the vehicle, and no one paid the least bit of attention.

On the previous occasion when the car was broken into, we had gone to see a movie and were comfortably ensconced in the theatre, secure in the knowledge that the cinema had guards watching over our car. But, apparently, we had parked two spaces away from the guard's line of sight, so no one saw or heard anything. Of course I was apoplectic when I realized that my switches had been stolen, and shouted at anyone who cared to listen, which included the guards, the police and any random passers by. I could see people shaking their heads and staring at me pityingly, not because of the theft, but because they thought, 'The Doctor has finally lost it.' After the theft at the embassy, the French Ambassador himself must have heard because he sent me a bottle of good French cognac, presumably to drown my sorrows, or perhaps this was the civilised French way of dealing with such problems.

By the following morning I had calmed down, but determined that I was not prepared to accept this recurrent theft, so I went right to the top and phoned the IGP – the Inspector General of Police.

'How are you Dr Ian?' he inquired politely

'I am not a happy man,' I told him, coming right to the point. 'My electric switches have been stolen again while the police are still investigating the theft of the last ones. What are the police doing about all this rampant theft of car parts? It is now not safe to leave one's car on the streets of Kampala.'

The IGP is a very nice man – he must have been to put up with calls from me. So he sympathized and assured me that the police had already taken action and had raided one of the local markets where second-hand, or should we say, recycled car parts were sold and they now had a whole stash of stolen parts at the CID offices, including switches. He suggested I should go along to the CID and identify my stolen parts, and then we could apprehend the criminals.

This seemed like a good plan, so I got in touch with the head of the CID who brought me into his office and assured me that there was, indeed, a room full of car spares, right next door, but there was one small problem. There had been a death and a funeral to attend, and the representative from the police was also the man who had the key. Unfortunately, the man with the key had gone.

'Would the police happen to have another key?' I inquired half heartedly, knowing the answer already.

'No, for reasons of security there is only one key and only one man who stays with it.'

So this went to prove the general principle that in any organization, it was not the man at the top who was important;

the man who really mattered was the man with the key. He was the one you wanted to cultivate the relationship with.

So I drove around in my car for a few days, with windows that would not open and air conditioning that did not work and became very hot and sweaty, until the man with the key returned. He opened the room to reveal that, indeed, the police did have sacks full of stolen car-parts, including electric window switches. I rummaged through the sacks until I found mine, or at least one that looked like mine and emerged triumphantly clutching the electric switches.

'I am taking these ones,' I announced

'But you can't do that,' said the officer. 'They are evidence.'

'You have a whole room full of evidence,' I insisted, 'but I don't have any switches, and I am dying in the heat, so I am taking these ones.'

And I did.

### The cow is stiff

Rose's brother was getting married, and she had to travel with the prospective bridegroom's party for the *Kwanjala* – the traditional wedding where haggling over the bride-price was carried out, and the deal was struck. The bride-to-be was from the west of the country, and the groom was from Luweero in the central region, so the party set out from their village to travel the long distance, complete with all the presents and goods necessary for the function. On this occasion they had been instructed to bring some goats and a cow as part of the price demanded for the bride. I had been to *Kwanjalas* where goats were transported physically, but cows being larger were usually left at home and just pledged as virtual cows. On this occasion the groom's party had been instructed to bring an actual cow.

The cow was duly loaded on to the back of a pick-up truck in Luweero and tied securely – perhaps a little too securely. On

171

reaching the bride's home, the groom's delegation were disembarking and getting organised, when the driver of the pick-up approached Rose and whispered to her that the cow was stiff.

'Well, we are all stiff after that long journey,' Rose replied. 'Give it some water.'

'But the eyes are protruding,' added the driver.

Rose, being a nurse, felt this was probably not a good sign and went to investigate, only to find that the cow was indeed stiff – rigor mortis had set in. The eyes were also bulging because someone had tied the cow so tightly that the poor creature had been asphyxiated on the way. As the groom's party now gathered to gaze at the dead cow they had inadvertently brought along as part of the bride-price, information leaked out to the family of the bride, and the news was not well received. So the delegation was instructed to remove the creature from the property forthwith before coming near the home. When they then presented themselves at the gate, minus the dead cow, they were severely reprimanded, since the death of the cow was regarded as a poor omen for the marriage. However, after the payment of a heavy fine, the function went ahead and negotiations were successfully concluded, but they were told to take their cow back with them. As they travelled back they looked in vain for anyone in all of Masaka District who would like a recently deceased cow, but no-one was interested, and the party travelled back to Luweero, carrying their dead cow.

There were numerous times at Kiwoko Hospital when I was called with the information that the patient's condition had changed, only to find that the patient was not only dead, but the body was cold. I understood that sometimes the terminology used in Uganda to describe basic bodily functions, or events such as death, could result in misunderstandings, and I needed to understand the nuances (perhaps some of it was lost in translation).

An English nurse was volunteering in our clinic, and while she was administering IV fluids to a patient, the patient became agitated and expressed in broken English that she wished to go for a 'long call'. The nurse, not understanding the request, reassured the lady and kept on administering the IV fluids, but the lady became more agitated and repeated the request. The nurse was baffled as to why her patient needed to use the telephone, but helpfully offered her own mobile phone. At this the patient became even more agitated, and the situation was obviously deteriorating sharply, until a local nurse, understanding the problem, escorted the patient to the bathroom. The English nurse then understood that the term 'long call' had nothing to do with making transatlantic telephone calls and neither was a 'short call' related to the length of time spent on the telephone. I learned over time that if I was informed that the patient's condition had changed, it probably meant the condition had changed from one of being alive to being dead.

On the other hand, if you were informed that your cow was stiff after a long journey, you could be forgiven for not twigging that this was due to rigor mortis.

# Building a team

Several months after I had started International Medical Centre, the HR manager of the American Embassy walked into my office and told me that the Embassy was looking for a clinic to take care of the medical needs of their local staff, but that they could not find any takers. He definitely had my attention. He wanted a doctor who would take care of the staff on a capitation basis for a fixed fee per person per year. Being from Northern Ireland, I was familiar with this method of payment for medical services since I had been paid on a capitation basis when I worked as a GP – the bigger the practice the more the GP earned.

Hence, within a short time I had my first medical scheme, in which I had the care of several hundred Ugandan American Embassy staff and their families. Such schemes are excellent from a cash-flow point of view, as they give an assured predictable income, allowing one to budget for expenses. It also meant that I was treating families across the social spectrum as the scheme covered all levels of staff, from guards to managers. Having the experience of such a medical scheme made me realise that I could replicate this for other organisations, and I simply needed a sales and marketing team to design and sell the schemes.

It was not rocket science, but a matter of working out my costs and then agreeing with the company what they would pay on a per person, per year basis. Since I employed more staff at the hospital than the clinic, I had relatively higher fixed costs at the hospital, so the more patients I brought into the system the better, and once I had met my fixed costs, I was then only meeting the marginal extra costs, such as medications, investigations or procedures. Like the principle of car production, if I did not have enough patients, I lost money, but if I crossed the threshold, I broke even and then only had to meet the marginal costs of the extra materials I used. Better still, if I had already reached this threshold through my cash paying patients, I could offer the medical schemes at very good value for money indeed.

The only problem was that I was not a salesman and had neither the time, nor the inclination, to sell medical schemes, and moreover, the regulations of the Ugandan Medical and Dental Practitioners Council did not allow me to advertise as a doctor in any way. This meant that I had to set up another company to market the medical schemes and find some sales people to sell them. Someone recommended that I meet a lady, called Donna, who had lived in South Africa for some time with her husband, who was working in the Ugandan diplomatic service. She had just returned to Uganda and wanted to get to know the situation before she established herself in business; hence, she wanted a job which would help her to understand the local market conditions. Donna proved to be one of the most astute business-women I have ever met, and hiring her was one of my better business decisions as she would not let a sale go past her. We then set up a Health Maintenance Organisation (HMO), but called it International Air Ambulance (IAA), because the company also ran an ambulance service and organised air evacuation when necessary. However, its main business was to market medical schemes, based on yearly capitation fees. Now there were three parts to the organisation: International Medical Centre (IMC), International Hospital Kampala (IHK), and International Air Ambulance (IAA), and I felt that we were finally beginning to get the right business model and establish traction.

The greatest demand from the patients on the medical schemes was for GP services, and the space at International Medical Centre and at the hospital was still limited, so we set out to look for other premises for another clinic to meet the needs of our growing number of patients. The demand was mostly in Kampala, but it was preferable to have the second

175

clinic located at a different end of the town from the existing clinic and the hospital. One of the well known local banks had just gone bust, leaving a number of former banking premises empty, and there was one property which was ideal for our purposes. It still contained the counters from the banking hall and the safe, but the counters were modular and could be rearranged and put to good use. The landlord was agreeable to us leasing the building, and we set about transforming the former bank into a clinic. The cashiers' counters became part of the pharmacy and the reception area, but one would never have guessed their previous function. The clinic served mainly the corporate clients from the IAA medical schemes, so it was named IAA Clinic, which also gave us a High Street presence in a prominent position.

There were many lessons to be learned as the organisation developed from a single-handed practice to two busy clinics, a small hospital, and an HMO, one of them being that I needed to put in systems and have good management in order to run the business efficiently. Some of the young people, such as Hannah, whom I hired as a fresh university graduate, had now spent several years working for me and were good at their jobs. But Hannah felt that she lacked exposure and wanted to pursue a Master's degree in the UK in organisational psychology. She had obtained a partial sponsorship, and I decided that it was a good investment to sponsor the rest, so she went to the UK for a year, and when she returned, she took up the position as HR manager for the group. We now employed around one hundred and fifty people and were getting too big to do HR management in an ad hoc manner. She immediately started putting in appropriate HR systems and procedures.

We were joined by another manager, Judy, who first worked as the hospital administrator, but I saw that she had exceptional talents as a trainer, and we needed her skills in that area even more than in administration. At first she was reluctant to move into training, thinking that she might be sidelined within the organisation, but as she got into it, she realised how vital it was for the development of our young people in a fledging organisation. There were areas, such as communication and customer care, which many of our staff had never even thought about and which certainly were not part of the curriculum for nursing or medical graduates. Judy found that, far from being sidelined, training became a central part of the organisation.

While a hospital needed buildings and equipment, the most important part of the service was the people. We knew we needed to develop three things within the organisation: the facility, the equipment and the expertise, in order to attain the standards we desired. In terms of facilities we had taken the first step by setting up a credible hospital. We also needed modern and appropriate medical equipment and, although we had some adequate equipment, there were still many gaps in that field. Lastly, we needed expertise; if we had good staff in terms of nurses, doctors, managers and administrators, this would really make the difference. There had been no private hospital in Uganda for many years, with the result that we all had to learn from scratch; there were no professional Ugandan hospital managers; there were no hospital systems in place; there were no manuals; there was no-one who had experience of setting up, or running, a private hospital in Uganda. We were the pioneers, and we were learning as we went along; we had to train our own people and gain the expertise as we grew organically.

While there were many who appreciated the services which we were rendering, there were also those who wanted a private hospital equivalent to a smart South African private hospital. I explained that this was not something that one could transplant to Uganda since the prices would be well beyond what ordinary people could afford. We could not just hire South African personnel and transport them to Uganda; we had to train our own people and bring them up to the appropriate standard. Uganda had to develop its own expertise, though along the way we could fill the gaps with foreigners, especially when they were able to train and pass on their skills.

One day the hospital had a visit from the President who came to visit his elderly mother, who was our patient. When he had seen his mother, he came down the stairs very informally, and as he reached the bottom, he was mobbed by our staff who wanted to meet him and shake his hand.

'You have a lot of nice young people to help you run your hospital,' he remarked as he left, and his observation was correct. But the challenge was to make these nice young people into world class professionals.

I had the tendency to think of a new idea, digest it and act on it simultaneously. Most people separate these processes into three different and distinct phases, but for me it all flowed together and this tended to give those who worked with me difficulties in keeping up. When I shared a new idea, people would naturally think that I was in the first phase and was still ruminating, but they did not realise that I could move on to the next step almost immediately, and they were likely to be confronted with the implementation of the idea within days, or even hours. Even my wife had difficulty in getting used to the speed at which I moved from idea to reality.

'I didn't know you were going to do that,' she would tell me.

'But I told you about it.'

'Yes, but I thought that you were only thinking about it, mulling it over.'

'Yes I was, and I have, and now I've done it.'

But I was in danger of getting so far ahead of my team that they would not even see where I was going, and we would lose the connection. I needed to slow down and take people with me. Thus we began to have weekly management meetings, at which all decisions were discussed and agreed before they were implemented. I looked to the other managers, both for input and implementation. I found it rewarding working with these young managers who were, incidentally, mainly women. The reason for the gender imbalance may have been the way in which we hired staff for entry level positions, who were then promoted within the organisation as it grew. Girls were more likely to apply for such jobs in reception or administration, and if the guys did apply, they tended to be impatient in their rush to make money and left prematurely to do their own thing. In Africa there were many people who hustled for a living, making small deals and looking for the next opportunity; some did well at times, but their income fluctuated widely.

We were developing systems and putting them in place. Hannah was an excellent communicator, Judy was a great trainer, Anita was an astute finance manager, and Dr Moses was our medical director – though we had to change that title since he was a surgeon. Dr Moses had worked with me in Kiwoko and had since moved to Kampala and trained as a surgeon. He was very committed to the vision and interested not only in surgery, but in the complete development of the hospital and in medical education, and his input was always insightful.

We were joined for several years by a British nurse, Rona, who was completely committed to our vision of developing a professional Ugandan workforce. Her role was to implement protocols and key performance indicators for the nursing team. But one of the nurses was entrenched in her ways and took offence at being called to account by Rona. She therefore resorted to witchcraft and sent a letter with chicken feathers, blood and fetishes, warning of dire consequences for Rona and her family. Although Rona was somewhat shaken by the incident, she was not intimidated and continued to press for high professional standards. Rona's other main contribution was to slag me off mercilessly to keep me from getting too far ahead of myself and everyone else.

There were also many desirable objectives which could not be achieved because of lack of resources, or the fact that we were not big enough to support certain specialties, or simply that the expertise did not exist in Uganda. Since I had now lived in Uganda for many years, I understood the gaps and limitations, so if someone appeared in my office who could fill such a gap, I tended to hire him on the spot. Rona wanted a more strategic and systematic approach, but the practicalities often dictated the pragmatic method.

'So what random blow-in have you hired today?' she would banter.

Dr Zina was a Russian cardiologist who had worked in Uganda for many years and carried out cardiology clinics at International Hospital. She asked if I would be interested in hiring a Russian obstetrician who had recently come to Uganda.

'Sure,' I said, 'Let me have a look at him.'

But looking at him was all that I could do because he did not speak English, and we could not communicate. He claimed that he understood English, but as far as I could tell the only word which he used was 'Humph', which he pronounced at intervals throughout the course of the conversation – really a one sided monologue. I think that 'Humph' is some sort of a Russian expression which means – well I've still not figured out what it means, but he uses it throughout conversations, especially where there is an element of confrontation involved. Dr Alex did try to work at the hospital, but he found that it was difficult to build up an obstetric history or communicate with the patient through a series of short grunts, so I explained to Zina, (because I couldn't communicate with Alex) that he would have to learn English to a higher standard before I could employ him. Six months later he was back, with passable English which became fluent over time, and we employed him. He proved to be a very experienced and capable obstetrician.

My daughter, Lauren, had graduated from Edinburgh University with a degree in Social History, and asked if she could come to Uganda to work for me as an intern for a period of one year. Lauren was a people person and usually travelled in a pack, and so two of her friends also asked if they could come and, of course, I said, 'Why not? I'm sure we will find something for them to do.'

So we also got Cara and Michelle, both of whom helped in administrative functions. Michelle had that Northern Irish no-nonsense approach to life, where she expected people to just get on with the job, and she could never understand the 'faffing' about that went on – though those of us who had lived in Uganda for some time accepted it as normal. Cara had red hair, curves, and pale skin, and was like a honey pot for bees as far as Ugandan men were concerned. They would stop her in the street or buy her drinks in bars; random men would buy her presents and make her proposals of marriage – she was fighting them off. I had never witnessed such a phenomenon; I think it was something to do with her unusual hair colouring and pale skin, or else she had very strong pheromones for African men.

So Lauren became my PA and started coming to the weekly management meetings, where her main contribution was to bully me into stopping at Nando's Restaurant to buy donuts for the meetings – a practice that I soon put a stop to when she left. The meetings were lively and enjoyable, and we all had a sense of satisfaction in a shared vision and in building an organisation together. Building a team may have slowed me down a bit, but I enjoyed the interchange thoroughly, and the fact that it was young Ugandans who had bought into the vision and were making it happen. One unexpected side-effect of Lauren's time in Uganda was that she began to consider doing nursing as a career, and by the end of the year she had enrolled in a graduate nursing course in London and was on her way to becoming a registered nurse. I was very happy about this decision – I now had two daughters who were nurses, both of whom had many other options, but had chosen nursing as a career above any other profession.

The problem with nursing in Uganda was that many of the nurses were there by default, not out of a sense of vocation – they had not been able to get into the university course they wanted, so they did nursing. As such, they did not see it as their chosen career and did not take pride in nursing as a profession. This was not helped by patients who didn't show respect for nurses, so a vicious cycle was established in which the nurses did not have self respect, they did not take pride in their jobs and, as a result, were poor professionals whom the patients did not respect.

At International Hospital we were striving to give all our young staff a sense of worth and value, but we determined at a relatively early stage that, when we had the means, we would set up a nursing school and train our own nurses so that we could inculcate in them a sense of pride, vocation and professionalism.

# Guaranteed maize prices

Uganda's social scene was fairly vibrant, and apart from the night life and the usual round of Embassy receptions, there were many corporate functions, one of which took place annually on board a ship in Lake Victoria (this was before someone managed to sink it). As the ship sailed into the sunset, I felt it was one of those magical moments: there was a slight breeze, the islands slipped past, and the sky was imbued with the colours of the sunset. It could even have been a romantic moment, except for the fact that I was surrounded by bankers, accountants, and economists, and I was deep in conversation about grain prices! This was the 'booze cruise' – I mean the *Bell Sunset Cruise,* sponsored by one of the Breweries in Uganda, which made a lager by the name of Bell, and it was supposed to be a relaxing social event, but I was getting my ears burned with an economic overview of Uganda's agricultural policy. My informant was John Magnay whose family had lived in Uganda for many years and knew the agriculture sector better than most.

'Do you know how many millions of dollars of food support Africa imports every year, and yet 80% of Africans work in agriculture?' he asked me.

There was something not quite right with this balance – if Africa had so many people who worked in the agricultural sector, how come it had to import so much food?

'Part of the problem,' he went on, 'is that those countries, such as Uganda, which produce a surplus, sell it only on the local markets, and that is not where it is needed. Every harvest time in Uganda there is a glut of maize, and the price plummets, so the farmer gets precious little for his produce. Consequently, he feels it is not worthwhile growing any for sale the next season, so he grows only enough for his own consumption. Of course the following season everyone has

183

done the same thing, so there is not enough maize, and the price rises, but the local farmer does not benefit as he hasn't produced anything for sale. It is these huge fluctuations in price that discourage farmers from growing,' he said, pausing for breath.

'Why should they, if they are going to have to sell their maize for thirty shillings a kilo? As a result, there is not enough food overall in the whole continent, and billions of dollars are spent on importing food to one of the richest agricultural continents in the world. Doesn't make any sense, does it?'

'The same thing used to happen in Europe,' he went on, 'so they formed the Common Market, which later became the EU, and introduced price support for farmers. This means there is a minimum price for agricultural products, and the EU will buy up any surplus the farmers produce, which is great for the farmers but costs the EU vast amounts in subsidies and has distorted world markets.'

I was getting this lecture in agriculture free of charge, but there was no stopping John as he was passionate about the topic

'Now if Africa, and Uganda in particular, could solve the problem of price fluctuations, and therefore under-production, without recourse to subsidies like the EU, we would take a leap forward in ensuring constant production to meet the food production needs of the region.

'Uganda has taken the first steps in doing this,' he went on. 'A handful of commodity traders – the merchants who buy the crops produced – got together and built a huge warehouse. They then persuaded the banks to lend them money to buy up grain for export. The banks agreed, partly because they can get 50% of the risk guaranteed under an aid agreement. The merchants then went out and bought up maize from all the little farmers all over the country – a bag here, half a bag there. The merchants then stored the maize in their warehouse under the proper conditions so that it did not get fungi, and all the stuff that happens when it is stored in poor conditions in the village. They sent thirty-five boat loads of the stuff to Zambia, they got paid, repaid their loans and were ready to start again for the next harvest.'

This time he took a swig of his drink.

'This scheme is effectively acting as a price support system for the farmers; these merchants can guarantee a minimum price for the farmers and wipe out the huge price swings that destroy the market. Instead of the farmer getting thirty shillings, as they did last year, they are guaranteed at least two hundred shillings and more, depending on the competition'.

'What about cheap imported maize?' I asked, knowing that maize was sent from as far as the United States for food support.

'Although it is cheap at the port, it still has to be transported inland to where it is needed, and this adds greatly to the cost,' he replied. 'And this is where the local farmers have the advantage. For once our land-locked status is working for us and not against us. Now 80% of Uganda's population are subsistence farmers and at present they grow enough to live on, and not much else, as there is little incentive; they basically live off the land without cash. With a guaranteed price, they can grow more for sale and have a disposable cash income, with which they can pay medical bills, school fees, buy airtime, iron sheets or whatever. As the spending power of the rural population increases, the country develops from the grass roots up; this is real self-generated development, not handouts,' he finished.

So as we sailed on into the sunset and the band played, I missed my romantic moment, but I understood how building grain silos, storing grain, and giving village farmers a guaranteed price could make a big contribution to the development of the economy. Unfortunately, despite John's enthusiasm, I later learned that the scheme imploded within a

185

few years, and the market for maize is still plagued by price fluctuations with oversupply and undersupply, while Africa has continued to import subsidized American grain. The theory seemed sound, but it collapsed because there was little political support, and some of the merchants decided to by-pass the scheme and make their own arrangements. It seemed that such a scheme needed government support to see it through the lean years and, as with so much in Uganda, the theory was good, but the implementation was lacking.

However, several years later the government did invest in setting up grain silos for storage and provided a scheme where farmers could borrow against receipts of grain stored. This was a definite step forwards.

# It takes a village

I was now dividing my time between clinical and management duties. My role was to give leadership and motivation, but I had also learned that in Africa it was not possible to take a completely hands-off approach, and I needed to pay attention to the details and the implementation of our plans and strategies myself. It was not uncommon for the President, or the government, to articulate their willingness to deal with Uganda's needs, but even if the political will existed at the top, there appeared to be limited ability to ensure implementation of these good intentions, perhaps because there were too many Chiefs and not enough Indians. It was this signal failure of implementation, more than anything else, which made the delivery of healthcare in the government sector so poor.

One morning I was checking the wards at the hospital when I saw a child in the children's ward with a tiny body and a big head. He had been brought to the hospital by a local aid agency which specialised in child rights. A member of the community had reported that a child had been abandoned, and they found Joel in a neglected condition, so they brought him to the hospital for treatment. He was not difficult to treat since all he needed was food, and he ate everything we gave him, but Joel was emotionally starved and wanted to be with people, so he cried when he was left alone. That morning I took him in my arms, and he stopped crying, but when I tried to put him back in the cot, he started sobbing again, so I took him with me and held him on my knee when I attended the management meeting. He snuggled in my arms, and perhaps that was when a bond was formed between us. He stayed at the hospital for months and was no longer a patient, but had become every-one's child, and therein lay the problem: he was claimed by everyone but no-one was taking ownership. Joel was still tiny, but he now had a big head and a big stomach and could be found walking around the hospital by himself, usually carrying a piece of bread in each hand. One night I was called to see a patient after midnight, and as I drove through the hospital gate, there was Joel standing in the middle of the car park. It had been the habit of the night nurses to allow him to stay with them, but on this occasion he had escaped and gone outside. I decided that there was obviously no-one taking personal responsibility and something had to be done, so I asked Robbie if we could bring Joel home.

Up to this point we had sponsored children for school fees, but apart from Rose, we had not fostered or adopted any children. Taking on Joel would be a big commitment, but neither of us had the time to do all that was required in bringing up a small child. Fortunately, with the set-up of our household, it was still possible for Joel to be with us if Reste, our long term housekeeper, was also agreeable. Then we could share the responsibility of seeing that this little boy got a fair chance in life. I told her Joel's story and my proposal to bring him home.

'This is a good thing, let us do it,' she said immediately

So Joel became the child of the Clarke household, which also included Reste and her own son, Stephen. Although we did not take in any more small children, Alice, Peace and Joanne also became part of the extended family. We had enough rooms in the house, such that some of the young people could stay with us during school holidays or at week-ends. The older kids looked after Joel – taking him swimming or to get his hair cut, while Reste cooked and cared for us all. My job was just to provide financially, oversee how the kids were doing, read their school reports, and try to get them into appropriate schools or universities. Robbie, being an excellent teacher, got involved in Joel's education and ensured that he learned to read and developed a love for books. Indeed it was funny to see this little boy (because he was always small for his age), sit down and read the newspaper fluently. As the saying goes, 'It takes a village to raise a child.' Everyone had a hand in raising Joel.

Our extended African family was possible because we had made Uganda our home; we were not there for a limited period, so when we took children in we knew that we would be there for them indefinitely. Thus we were able to become meaningfully involved in the lives of Alice, Peace, Joanne, Asaph, Moses, Lawrence, and a number of others who had remarkable, and sometimes painful, stories to tell. It was great to be part of their lives and facilitate them on their journey, through ensuring that they had education, financial support and advice. We also provided something which was more important, but less tangible – we gave them stability and an identity. I was their Dad: that person who gave them roots and a reference point in their lives.

The extended family has largely died out in modern western societies where the nuclear family has taken over. The household has also died out because there are so many labour-saving appliances and gadgets; labour is expensive and there is no longer a role for household help. In Uganda few people have such labour saving devices, but 90% of the population has some sort of live-in home help. Even those who cook or keep the house as an occupation often have another person who does the same for them – the house-girls have house-girls. Developing countries have a big pool of cheap labour, and there are so many people unemployed that paying a person to do a task is a much better solution than buying a machine. So in many households there is someone to look after the garden and someone else to cook and clean the house. Having house staff is not colonial, it is just commonsense and good for employment.

One of my duties was to read the end of term reports for our other African children, so Joanne had brought home her school report and fee account. She was attending a secondary school

189

just outside Kampala which had a good Catholic name, Our Lady of Good Counsel. It was similar to many other such schools scattered across Uganda which were started by the Catholic sisters in colonial times and had subsequently become part of the government system. The fees were a bit cheaper than the purely private schools, and they were recognized as being 'good schools'. The fees came to around three hundred and fifty thousand shillings, about $200 per term, which wasn't that much, considering it included board and lodging, although boarding schools in Uganda were not known for their culinary variety, and the meals tended to be a rotation of *pocho* (maize porridge) and beans or beans and *pocho*.

On one occasion, when we attended for a visiting day, the guard searched the car as we entered. I thought it was very strict security and that perhaps he was checking for arms, and then discovered that he was looking for cooked food which was strictly forbidden. Maybe the school could not allow any pupil to taste home cooked food as they might not be able to stomach *pocho* and beans again.

Joanne was doing well academically and coming near the top of her class – this time she came eleventh in a class of eighty-seven students (the upper limit of class size was how many could fit in the classroom). During my own education I had a clever strategy to stay in the anonymous middle, since I believed that if you were at the top, you would get in trouble with your fellow classmates because you were teacher's pet, and if you were at the bottom, you got in trouble with the teachers. In truth, I never had to consciously strive to avoid being at the top. But apparently this habit of constantly grading students according to their place in the class does not accord with modern educational philosophy, and they should be graded according to other criteria which give the student insight into their strengths or weaknesses. But this modern way of education had not yet percolated through to the schools. Joanne's report consisted of terse comments such as:

190

'Try to improve.'

'More effort required.'

'Pull up.'

'Try harder.'

'Good effort' – thrown in when she had got 89% in that subject.

The teachers had several phrases which they used in rotation in the reports. Personally I favoured 'pull up', since it had that terse, matter of fact tone that really gave the student the right mentoring and direction. As a generalization, Ugandan students were bright, and given the opportunity, they excelled in academic learning. One only had to look at the number of Ugandans who fled the country during former regimes and attained eminent positions abroad. Uganda had a tremendous human resource at its disposal, but in many schools the teaching methods were so antiquated and the format of reports so old fashioned, they only succeeded in putting down the students, squeezing out their self-esteem, and then making them cram until they hated the pursuit of knowledge. All too often initiative was stifled, and the ability to think for themselves and be problem-solvers was lost, which made them ill equipped for the real world.

One weekend, when Joel was old enough to attend boarding school, I called into school to visit him and was just sitting there on a wall with him, watching other kids play. Have you ever noticed that kids are never in a rush and that the world slows down when you are with them? His school had children from various African countries, one group from South Sudan was playing with another group from Uganda. Some other children were lolling on the swings, and some were swimming in a small pool nearby. It struck me how normal it all was, and how good it was that we should have such normality in Uganda since this, by no means, had always been the case. A couple of decades earlier, such kids could not have gone to school without fear and been able to play with children from other

191

parts of Africa. In fact, the children from South Sudan still did not have such a school in their own country. There were few enough occasions when one had time to sit with a child and watch the cumulus clouds scudding across the blue sky. It was at those moments that I enjoyed Africa most, perhaps because I had lived in Uganda long enough to appreciate how it had changed. Sometimes when I was walking in the downtown shopping mall, I was struck by the nature of the multicultural crowds of people, doing their shopping, eating ice-cream, or just hanging around. When I did stop rushing and took the time, it was the ordinary things which gave me most pleasure: striking up a conversation in a pub, having a game of pool with a stranger, going for a run as the sun was setting over Lira, with scores of people peddling past on their bicycles before darkness set in, and knowing that they would be safe in their homes because there was no longer the threat from the LRA. Life was passing all too quickly, and it was good to take in the enjoyable moments of life and appreciate how Uganda had changed for the better.

After Peace escaped from the LRA, she had also become part of our family. Robbie had a close relationship with her mother as she had followed her trials and tribulations throughout the years of Peace's captivity, and when peace escaped, Robbie travelled to Lira to meet her and her mum. On that first meeting Peace was withdrawn and quiet, and Robbie remembered her sitting bolt upright and saying nothing. During that meeting it was decided that Peace should come down to Kampala, where she could attend school and use our house as a home from home. She was years behind in her education, but she was keen to catch up and managed to adjust to being in class with students six years her junior. Over the next four years she stayed with us as she went to school, travelling back and forwards to Lira to see her mum, helping look after Joel and being a big sister to Joanne. When we spent time with

Peace we were all a little bit more enriched. I marvelled that this young lady could have gone through all that she did, yet preserved those characteristics of grace, beauty, humility and love, which she exhibited so naturally. There are people who have become dehumanized because they have gone through terrible experiences, while there were others whose inward strengths have been honed and refined, as they were in Peace.

After she finished secondary school, she had several months free before she was due to start University, and I asked if she would fill in as the administrator of a clinic in Pader in Northern Uganda. She willingly worked there for several months, and during that time demonstrated commonsense and wisdom beyond her years in how she handled staff issues. Most of the government staff with whom we worked were much older than she was, and when she tried to call them to account, they would tell her, 'But you are the same age as my daughter, you cannot tell me what to do.'

But she would reason with them and tell them that these were still requirements of the job and she managed to get more cooperation from the staff than other administrators who took a more confrontational approach.

Peace went on to do a diploma in public health and was also asked to speak at the UN in New York on human trafficking – she was someone who knew about this subject first hand. She sat beside Ban Ki-moon and spoke after his introductory remarks. Her speech was extraordinarily moving. We were so proud of her. As a result of her trip to the United States, some friends offered to arrange a scholarship to a university in Washington State to do nursing, so our daughter is now a student at an American University. It has been a long journey from the ordeals she endured in captivity to being an international nursing student, but she has succeeded.

In 2010 President Obama announced a bill to support reconstruction in Northern Uganda and the region which had been so adversely affected by the activities of the LRA. During

193

his speech he mentioned two examples of people who had been terribly affected by Kony. One was a young Sudanese social worker who lost his life, while the other was Angelina Atyam's daughter who had endured eight years of captivity. That daughter was Peace.

But I doubt if the President knows the subsequent story.

# Working practices

Uganda was a great country to live in: the weather was lovely, the vegetation beautiful, the people friendly and outgoing. Some foreigners came to work in Uganda and were at first enthralled by what they found, particularly by the social life and by how articulate people were, but they often got a rude awakening when it came to the work practices and work ethic. If people could talk their way into making things work, Uganda would have been the best developed country in the world. Donors were impressed with people's grasp of problems and understanding of the steps which should be taken in finding solutions, but then confused as to why so many basic issues on the ground remained unresolved. The problem lay in implementation: many public servants were good at analysing and talking about what should be done, as if the very talking was the same as doing it, but then nothing happened. This lack of implementation of simple things in the public domain was so common that it was accepted as the norm, and one only remarked when anything actually changed.

There were many occasions when there was a serious breach of discipline in terms of safety procedures or work practices, which went unchecked until things went dreadfully wrong. Lake Victoria, the largest inland Lake in Africa, has very little shipping traffic. But Uganda Railways have a couple of ferries which ply the waters between Kampala and Tanzania, mostly carrying cargo in railway carriages which are shunted off and on at either end. In all this great expanse of water, the two Ugandan ferries managed to do the impossible: they collided with each other, with the result that one sank and the other was badly damaged. Perhaps this accident should go down into the Guinness Book of Records as one of the most unlikely shipping disasters of all time.

The problem was that the route was usually so quiet and uneventful that as soon as the ships pulled out of port and set their direction, the crew went to sleep. In this case one ferry was on the return leg while another was outgoing, and both crews were, apparently, fast asleep. They had also both managed to pick the exact same route and had a head on collision since no-one was keeping watch. To make matters worse, someone then realised that they had forgotten to renew the insurance. This was obviously a comedy of errors, there being so little implementation of any basic code of practice, that it became possible for such an unlikely accident to take place.

Another tragedy befell a boarding school when a fire broke out in a dormitory, with the loss of the lives of nineteen children. In the subsequent inquiry it was found that neither the matron of the dormitory, nor the watchmen on duty, were at their posts at the time, so that when the fire broke out, some of the doors were locked, and there was no-one to guide the children to the means of escape. The watchmen were at the local trading centre, watching premier league football, while the matron was preparing her own supper.

We expatriates working in Uganda had different reactions to such poor work practices: many of us became understandably frustrated and ranted about 'these people' who could do nothing right and that such behaviour would not be accepted in other countries. When some of us found the watchman asleep, we would shout at him, or when the policeman stood by while gross traffic violations were committed under our very noses, we started honking the horn and gesticulating. When something didn't work properly, as was often the case, some people talked about 'these people' again. While this frustration was understandable in the face of some of the incidents which took place, one wondered if there was another way of dealing with it. Such levels of continuous frustration also left one wondering how some expatriates were able to work in Africa at all. It is true they had come from cultures where they could assume that basic services could be relied upon, but their frustration was not making any difference and only succeeding in alienating people. There were others who coped by saying 'this is Africa' because they did not expect anything to work in the first place. They appeared to have accommodated themselves to whatever was going on around them, without getting too bothered. Perhaps the balance lay along the path of the famous prayer: "God grant us the serenity to accept the things we cannot change, courage to change the things we can, and wisdom to know the difference."

There was no point in ranting and raving if it would not change the outcome of the situation and would only succeed in raising one's blood pressure. But on the other hand, if there were opportunities to change things for the better, one should get involved. The trick was in knowing what could be changed and what should be accepted.

While the poor implementation of projects in the public sector was definitely different from that of more developed countries, the work ethic in Kampala was, in certain ways, no different from that of any city in the world. As our own organization grew and was no longer a small intimate family, the number of staff multiplied and so did the usual ways of dodging work. After all, it was not as if all of the staff came to work because they loved it so much, though we did hope that we had a critical mass that were committed to our vision of making a difference to healthcare in Uganda.

As a generalization, workers in Kampala would set out on the journey to their place of employment on time, but the first obstacle in actually reaching their destination might simply be the weather conditions. If it was raining, a significant number of people would not venture out of the house until the rain had stopped. It never ceased to amaze me that a whole city could grind to a standstill when it rained; after all, it was not as if rain took us by surprise so that we did not have the opportunity to prepare for it. In the rainy season it could rain every day. But when there was heavy rain, everything still ground to a halt. Perhaps motorists were afraid to venture out on the roads because they had no way of gauging the depth of the potholes. Or perhaps there was no umbrella, so they could not get from their homes to the bus-stop. Or perhaps it was too dangerous to walk in the rain because the culverts and the roads were flooded, and one could accidentally step into a culvert and drown – this actually did happen on several occasions. Whatever the reason, no-one wanted to venture out during the rain, which meant that as soon as the rain was over, everyone came out at once, and there was an immediate traffic jam, with grid-lock all over Kampala. So on the rainy days, one expected a significant number of staff to be late, as a matter of course.

Work practices varied, depending on motivation and accountability, and although the following description does highlight certain aspects of working in Uganda, it should also be taken with a large pinch of salt.

For those who did manage to reach work after the rain, the first thing they were likely to do was to break themselves in gently by having a look at the day's newspapers, cup of coffee in hand – a very civilized way to start the day. Having read the newspapers and had a cup of coffee, there were those who felt there was still no necessity to engage in actual work since the day's gossip had to be gotten underway, and if, by some chance, there was no juicy gossip, it could be manufactured, or found in the *Red Pepper*, one of the local tabloids. Gossiping was a widely practiced and enjoyable pastime, and at work it was always possible to weave a good story round the comings and goings of the managers or bosses. And the beauty of gossip was that it did not need any factual basis, just the ability to be a good storyteller; people rated gossiping among their hobbies, such as listening to music or watching TV.

By the time the gossip had been dreamed up and passed around, tea-break would have arrived. This was an important part of the day since morning tea-break was actually breakfast, and one needed some food in the stomach to get down to work. After breakfast there were usually still some obstacles to that laudable ambition of working: the cartridge on the printer had run out, no-one had requisitioned the fuel allowance, the network was hung, or the equipment, or vehicle, which one had hoped to use, 'had refused'. Of course there was nothing that one could do about this state of affairs, since everyone in Uganda knew that computers, vehicles, and any form of inanimate object might simply decide to 'refuse' on a whim, and a mere human-being could only sit and wait until the thing decided to work again. At least the employee was able to use the time fruitfully to e-mail jokes, forward junk mail, or download music and pictures. Unfortunately, the system always seemed to be slow at this time of the morning – probably nothing to do with people using it to download junk and surf the net!

The good thing about this sort of activity, though, was that staff could actually be at their desk using the computer, with a document ready to be restored at the click of a button, should the boss walk in. However, this was considered unlikely because, finally, someone had delivered the boss's copy of the newspaper and another cup of coffee. When staff were gainfully occupied, e-mailing their friends or checking out Facebook, time passed quickly and in no time at all, it was lunchtime. There was more food to be consumed, and most of the staff had learned from bitter experience that they must not be late for lunch – having, at one time or another, arrived late when the food had all been consumed and not a scrap was left.

After lunch there was an actual physiological reason why the afternoon was slow, in that the heavy lunch of beans and *pocho* or *matoke* needed to be digested, so all the blood supply got diverted to the stomach, leaving precious little to run the brain. Hence, realistically, all one could do was to have a little doze. Fortunately, the boss had now gone out for lunch and it

199

was thought that he would not return for some time, so one could grab a quick nap and before one could say '*Matoke*', it was four o'clock and time to get ready to go home, though there was still a bit of photocopying to be done – for the evening classes.

There were of course many good reasons why people needed to go to their place of employment, other than simply to carry out work. The supply of electricity at home could sometimes be erratic, while the office generally had electricity which was necessary to carry out activities such as charging the phone, ironing clothes and making a hot cup of tea. Employment was also necessary so that one could eat breakfast and lunch, send e-mails, meet colleagues and generally be in touch with what was going on in the world. If, on top of all these benefits, one got paid regularly, then that was the icing on the cake.

Another common feature of employment in Uganda was nepotism. It is natural for people to be loyal to their relatives in any society, but in Uganda such loyalty was sometimes taken too far. The President, himself, recounted the story of his cousin, Columbus, who was found guilty of manslaughter, but even though the person had clearly committed a serious offence, the relatives were covering up for him and thought that the President should use his influence to get him off the hook. Fortunately, the President was of the opinion that Columbus should pay for his crimes, no matter who he was related to.

The cultural norms often meant that a person's loyalties lay first to himself, then to his family, then to his tribe, then the nation and lastly to his employer. There may not have been anything wrong with this hierarchy, except when these loyalties conflicted with the person's duties in upholding the law, or fulfilling his commitments at work.

In some western societies there was legislation against nepotism, and it was difficult for a person in a public organisation to give a close relative a job (unless it was a British Member of Parliament), the argument being that if relatives were working together, the relative might be favoured. In Uganda such constraints did not apply and it was common for those in authority to employ their own relatives. In fact it was difficult for a person in a position of influence not to employ his relatives, in that the cousins would arrive from the village expecting employment. It was a catch 22 dilemma – if the person employed his relatives, he was practicing nepotism, yet if he did not employ him he would be seen by the rest of the family as mean and self centred. While most people did not actually see anything wrong with nepotism, there were those who felt that the practice was so entrenched among the ruling elite that it gave the wrong signals and a carte blanche for people to look after themselves and their own family first, at the expense of their employer, the law, or the country.

Loyalty to the family cut both ways. Many Ugandans living abroad turned to their family who were resident in Uganda to implement projects in the home country – such as building a house – but discovered, to their cost, that family members were sometimes the least trustworthy. Houses which were supposed to have been built ended up being virtual houses, which only existed in the form of pictures sent over the internet, and the money vanished. Of course, the Ugandan living abroad was reluctant to prosecute his own family, and hence, all manner of embezzlement and theft took place within the family itself. But loyalty to the family was taken as a given when a family member was accused of a crime, such as the rape of the house-girl. In this case it was rare for the victim to go to anyone within the family for redress, since she would automatically be blamed for the incident and pressured to hush it up.

When it came to the hospitality industry in hotels and restaurants, the level of work practice varied greatly, with some hotels such as the Serena Hotel in Kampala leading the way in demonstrating that standards of excellence were possible; but high levels of service were hardly the norm in the more isolated areas of the country.

We were driving down from Lira and had crossed south of Karuma Falls, so we thought it was now safe to stop for a soda and a bite to eat. We spied a little place that looked better than average – though there was not a lot to choose from in that neck of the woods – and pulled off the road, relishing the thought of a cold coke and some food to counteract our low blood sugar levels. It was one of those places that are now ubiquitous all over Africa, with white plastic tables and chairs set out under a coloured plastic shade. Inside we could see what looked like a chiller packed full of cold sodas, so we were drawn in to escape from the thirty-degree heat. When we went to the counter, there was no one behind, but a young lady, who appeared to be a waitress, was seated in the restaurant eating a plate of sweet potatoes and ground-nut sauce. She did not rise, but since she was the only person to ask, we inquired what was on the menu.

'*Matoke* and goat's meat stew,' she replied, with a mouth full of sweet potato.

At that particular time, not being a good *Muganda* (who love *matoke* so much that they don't call anything else 'food'), I did not really feel the need for a plate of *matoke*, but the sweet potatoes and ground nuts looked quite appetizing.

'Could we have some of that?' I asked, pointing at her sweet potatoes.

'No,' was the reply, given without hesitation.

'Why not?' I rejoined,

'Because this food is for staff,' she replied.

I didn't actually want to take the food she was eating; I just wanted some similar food. From her attitude and demeanour,

202

she made it clear that I was just a passing customer and should know my place: there would be plenty more where I came from.

I had been in similar remote places many times and had usually found that a scrambled egg is a good fall-back, since there is generally nowhere so remote that there are not some chickens running around. So I changed my strategy and asked meekly for an egg.

'No,' was the reply.

'But why not?' I asked again, like an offended child.

'Eggs got finished,' came the response. There was just no answer to the 'got finished' line, so I decided to try to negotiate again on the sweet potatoes.

'Could we not have some sweet potatoes?' I asked another young man who had joined us, and who appeared to be part of the establishment. He didn't seem such a hardened case as the girl, so I reasoned that, if we were sufficiently humble, there was a chance of wheedling some other kind of food from him. Seeing our look of desperation, he went off to the nether regions of the establishment to look for some sweet potatoes, and our hopes rose. But they were dashed when he returned to tell us that there was definitely nothing on the menu today except *matoke* and goat stew. We finally accepted defeat and decided to settle for a cold soda on its own, but even that was not to be, because the electricity had been off for a few days, and the sodas were warm.

It was a reasonable supposition that Kiryadongo, as the place was called, had not had much exposure to modern theories of customer care, or been taught such epithets as 'the customer is king'. The waitress was not intentionally rude; she was just definite, she told us the truth bluntly. Of course this still left the question unanswered as to why we did not eat the *matoke* and goat stew. And in answer to this, one has to recognize that one's upbringing greatly influences one's taste. The *Baganda* living abroad would kill for a plate of *matoke*,

203

which is not readily available in London or New York, while the Irish are much more partial to a plate of potatoes. So when it comes to choosing between matoke and 'spuds', it just depends where you are brought up. I might have lived in Uganda for a long time, but I still like my Irish potatoes, as they are known in Africa. I am a Ugandan with Irish tastes.

# Providing healthcare for rural communities

Many companies which joined our IAA medical schemes had staff resident outside Kampala, where we did not have our own medical facilities. We made arrangements for other clinics to treat the IAA members, but some of these clinics were substandard and some could not be trusted in terms of their billing practices, so we decided to open our own facilities in centres outside Kampala, when there were a sufficient number of IAA members.

The first town we considered was Jinja, located at the source of the Nile, to the east of Kampala. Jinja had once been a flourishing industrial centre but now attracted tourists who wished to see the Source of the Nile, or to have near drowning experiences by white-water rafting the Bujagali rapids. I paid a visit to Jinja to look for suitable premises and located a large house, big enough to have a clinic on the ground floor with accommodation for staff upstairs. Renovations were carried out to create a reception area, consultation rooms, treatment room, laboratory and pharmacy, and the necessary staff recruited. For such clinics, the staff usually included a doctor, clinical officer, two nurses, lab technician, cook, guard, and cleaner, though the numbers varied according to the size.

At this point in our development, the organisation had grown big enough to have central corporate functions such as HR, IT, Finance, Training, Transport, Nursing and Medical Directorates, so we could call on these resources to help set up a clinic, recruit and train staff, and implement systems. The problem for doctors working up-country is that they become isolated and out of touch medically, hence bad habits creep in. As we developed several up-country clinics we were able to counteract this by having an active programme of training, with the trainers travelling round the clinics to mentor, train, and ensure that standards were kept high. We also developed a programme of continuing medical education through e-mails and on-line modules.

In a bygone era, Jinja had been the industrial centre of Uganda, with Entebbe as the government administrative headquarters and Kampala as a residential area. Jinja had once had a large population of Indians who were expelled during the rule of Idi Amin. Some of those who came back to claim their property were now crusty old men, who controlled extensive holdings and were as cantankerous as a basket of rattlesnakes.

However, most of the Indians who lived in Jinja were recent additions, having come from India to East Africa to seek their fortune. Many had started small businesses, such as hardware stores and supermarkets, which were staffed by cousins, brothers and family members. There were also two large sugar estates in the area, a textile works and a brewery, but much of the industry had seeped away, and Jinja had become a sleepy town, with wide potholed boulevards and large colonial houses in varying states of disintegration. Some of the houses had been rehabilitated into back-packers' hostels, or small hotels, and there were signs of life returning, with the construction of a new hydroelectric dam. Unlike Kampala, Jinja was well laid out in orderly symmetrical blocks, with the main street having the feel of an old African/Indian colonial town, which indeed it was.

I had been approached by a retired British Ugandan GP who wanted to settle back in Uganda, having worked in Birmingham under the British National Health Service for thirty years. George took up the position as the GP in charge of the unit in Jinja. He had a polished English accent and was enjoying being back in his country of birth, despite his long sojourn in the UK. He also appeared to have re-adapted to the African ways without a blip and had taken a young Ugandan wife. He had told me, when I employed him, that he had a wife and family back in Birmingham, and I only learned about the Ugandan wife when he brought her to hospital and mentioned shyly that he had brought a friend who was about to deliver a baby. The baby delivered safely, and George was a happy, though much older, father. He also enjoyed the Ugandan beverages, particularly the locally manufactured spirit known as Uganda Waragi, which was favoured by some over gin or vodka. UG, as it was fondly referred to, had one serious side effect (apart from rapid inebriation): its aroma hung on the breath for at least a further twelve hours. George liked to retire to the Jinja Golf Club in the evenings, and since it was dark, I assumed that he did not play much golf, but he did partake liberally of the UG spirit. The next day he would breathe alcohol fumes over his patients, which did not do much for their confidence that the doctor was of sober and sound mind. He was never actually drunk, but he certainly smelled strongly of alcohol, and his patients were worried that they would get drunk on the fumes.

Sadly, George did not have long to partake of the delights of his homeland in the form of the wine (or in his case the spirit), and the women, because he later went back to the UK for a visit and promptly died. We were all rather fond of him, and he himself had obviously loved coming home. Despite the loss of George, Jinja became the model for the network of International Medical centres which we established across the country.

I particularly wished to have clinics in the north of Uganda since the availability of medical services was limited in these areas, and the people had suffered greatly during the LRA war. Gulu was one of the main urban centres in the North, so once again I carried out a reconnoitre mission of the town in search of premises. There were no suitable premises to be found, but I noticed a building in a semi-completed state, which I thought would be ideal if we finished the work. I made inquiries as to the owner and found that the gentleman who owned the building was a certain Mr Oloya.

'Just call me Tourist,' he introduced himself, though I did not quite make the connection between the names, but later found out that in a past life he had owned a hotel called the Tourist Hotel. I negotiated that we would carry out the finishing work and in turn have a rent-free period of four years. We then sent our team of builders to Gulu, and they did a commendable job.

We found it difficult to achieve financial viability in up-country locations through purely cash paying patients; one reason was that our standard consultation charge was high for rural areas, and therefore, our clinics were expensive for the local population. Our consultation charge was relatively high because our business model was not geared to making money from selling drugs, but from the consultation itself. There was a built-in commercial incentive for over-prescription of drugs in many private clinics because patients were prepared to pay for drugs, but very little for the consultation. If people had to pay, they reckoned that they would rather pay for drugs since they were getting something tangible for their money – even if they did not need these drugs. Realistically, there was so little money in these areas that, no matter what the charges, it was hard to make rural clinics viable on a cash payment model.

From the IAA point of view, the reason for establishing an upcountry clinic was to use the clinic as a gatekeeper for the IAA members. Before we opened another clinic we usually reached tipping point, where the payments to other medical service providers was getting out of control, and there was a sufficient number of our own members to justify the cost of setting up our own clinic. There were also rural areas where there was a need for the service, but the contribution from IAA members was not sufficient to meet the overheads. This meant that a clinic would not be financially viable, and the IAA patients alone would not keep the doctors fully occupied. The answer was to use any surplus capacity for the treatment of charity patients. Clinic vouchers were distributed to the local schools, which were then given to children when they fell sick. The clinic recorded the number of charity patients treated and worked out a standard charge per treatment, which covered operating costs. A donor was identified to sponsor these treatments, the advantage to the donor being that the treatment was relatively inexpensive since there was no profit margin and no charge for the capital costs of setting up the clinic. The donor was also given a complete breakdown of the service provided and every patient treated. It was payment by results, but we were piggy-backing the service on the existing infrastructure. The advantage to our organisation was that the spare medical capacity was being used, which in turn resulted in better practice, and the potential deficit in running costs was also being met.

Uganda is a poor country, and even though the population stood at thirty-one million and was growing fast, there were less than one million people employed in the formal sector, which included 350,000 government workers. Like any developing country, there were great disparities between the rich and poor, with a tiny number of very rich people at the top of the pyramid, a relatively small number in the middle – including all the formally employed – and a large number at the bottom, hovering around the poverty line. Our organisation had deliberately targeted the middle income group – neither the very rich, nor the very poor – but even within this group, there were many who earned as little as one hundred dollars per month (or $3 – 4 per day), and healthcare was not high on their agenda in terms of expenditure. The cheapest way to pay for their healthcare was through the medical schemes of IAA, but these were geared mostly for large or medium sized groups because the risk was spread. These schemes could provide complete health coverage for the members at $12 per person per month, and for this the patient was covered for consultations, investigations, drugs, hospital admissions with full in-patient treatment and ambulance call-outs; it was a very comprehensive scheme. But this type of scheme was still benefiting only some tens of thousands of people in the formal sector, and different methods of payment needed to be found for those at the bottom of the pyramid.

In an urban setting there was generally more cash in circulation; hence, in theory, there was the ability to pay for essentials such as healthcare. Urban dwellers could be divided into the urban middle class, who had a job and a steady income, and the urban poor, who either worked in the informal sector or hustled for a living, existing in a hand to mouth manner. Unlike the rural poor, the urban poor had cash in hand, but it was used for the necessities of life, with a little for life's pleasures, such as alcohol and sex. But rarely was anything budgeted for medical expenses. Health was still not a priority, and it was not uncommon for relatives to be reluctant to part with money to treat a family member, but they would produce the cash for the funeral expenses when the person died. Personally, I would prefer that my relatives pay out the cash while I am still alive – nice and all as it might be to have a good funeral.

In the rural areas, the poor could exist in a cashless economy, since they grew their own food and lived off the land. Uganda had a forgiving climate, and with many areas having two growing seasons per year, there was usually some crop, either in the ground or ready to be harvested. Crops such as beans, ground nuts and maize grew well and intercropping was also carried out. So long as those living in rural areas could get into their *shambas* (small gardens) to plant, they rarely went hungry. While the rural poor did not need much money to survive, they had some need for cash to purchase small necessities such as soap, salt, clothing, and to pay for school fees and medical bills. These cash needs were met through the growing of cash crops such as coffee, cotton, maize and sunflowers

I was confronted by a Ugandan Professor of Medicine on the subject of people prioritizing medical expenses. We were talking about the struggles of the private health sector in getting patients to value medical services.

'A client will go to see a lawyer and fork out a large amount of money, just for the privilege of the consultation,' he pointed out. 'But in the case of a doctor, if the doctor simply examines the patient and makes a diagnosis which does not require any drugs, the patient will walk out without paying. He does not place any value on the doctor's time or professional expertise.' Then turning to me, he pointed his finger accusingly. 'And it is your fault.'

I was somewhat nonplussed by his accusation, since I was not aware that I was personally responsible for this bad attitude among patients.

'It was the likes of you – the missionaries,' he continued. 'You taught people to expect cheap, subsidized medical care.'

I could not disagree with him on that, but it had now become a catch 22 situation, with many of the mission hospitals more dependent on receiving a higher proportion of their income from fees, as their support from abroad dwindled. On the other hand, they still had to balance this with people's ability to pay, and the fact that they were humanitarian organisations.

## Capitation Schemes

There was certainly no easy answer to the question of how to make healthcare available to poor communities at a price they could afford. The mission hospitals themselves, by providing subsidies, contributed to the expectation of cheap healthcare and, therefore, the lack of prioritization of payment for healthcare. The scheme at the International Medical Centre in Lira demonstrated that excess capacity could be used to deliver service cost effectively to the most needy, but such schemes still needed some degree of donor funding. In essence,

211

rural healthcare, or healthcare to the poor, would always require subsidies; it was simply a question of which method was most effective in delivering the service. Oddly enough, the least effective method, that of putting money into the Ministry of Health – the least efficient organisation in the delivery of curative services in rural poor communities – was the method favoured by the large donors.

There was no simple answer regarding the payment of healthcare, but a first step was to educate the population that they should budget for their medical expenses in the same way that they did for education. In the case of the poor, if this amount were then paid into subsidized capitation schemes, where the service providers were paid a yearly fee per person for a defined deliverable service, then the provision of medical services to the poor, or those in rural areas, would become financially viable for the providers. There would also be an incentive for medical personnel to set up facilities at grassroots level. It would be possible to measure the impact, in terms of services delivered, such as numbers of safe deliveries, treatments for malaria, immunizations etc. And in turn, it would be possible to measure progress on the Millennium Development Goals, such as decrease in infant and maternal mortality. This model was being explored by Pham-access, a Dutch organization, with funding from the Netherlands Government, which was doing pilot projects in Nigeria and Tanzania.

This method of health financing was also being developed at community level by our own organization in collaboration with Bwindi Community Hospital. This small hospital was founded by a missionary and the work then consolidated by a young British GP by the name of Paul Williams. The hospital was situated a stone's throw from the tourist lodges for the mountain gorillas, and Paul had a well developed strategy for raising money, which involved hanging around the bars of these up-market lodges. Through the contacts he developed, he was able to attract financing for many of the hospital programmes, including the mother and child health programme, HIV, and safe motherhood. Paul was not only good at squeezing money out of well-heeled tourists, but he developed excellent statistics and reports, whereby he could demonstrate the effect of the projects. The missing piece was funding to sustain the treatment of adult patients, and he approached us to develop a community insurance scheme. The catchment for the hospital was sixty-five thousand people, all of whom were resident in the hills surrounding the impenetrable forest. They were poor people who could afford little, but through consultations with the leaders of the community, it was decided that they could contribute $3.00 per person per year to a medical scheme. He also did calculations to estimate the cost of providing adult services for sixty-five thousand people and came up with a figure of $6.00 per person per year to meet the shortfall in running the hospital.

Since Bwindi Hospital was the only hospital for the area, there was no need to have an insurance scheme which would be costly to administer, and at our suggestion, Paul was happy to have a capitation (or membership) scheme. We would act as intermediaries, collecting the $3.00 per person from the community; we would deduct only the small administrative cost of this and remit the rest on a monthly basis to the hospital. These fees could be collected through *Bataka* (funeral) community groups, making collections feasible. Paul had already secured funding (through more of his bar hopping), to register all the community members, so all that was required was a finger print ID reader at the hospital, and patients' ID, and the records would appear on the computer screen. The other aspect of the scheme was the quality assurance. It was possible for any hospital to receive money and then provide substandard service, so a set of indicators had been devised in order that the delivery of the service could be monitored and evaluated.

The other relevant factor was that we were only collecting half the funds necessary for the scheme from the community itself, and we needed to find a donor for the balance, but we reckoned that if we started the scheme anyway, we would attract more interest than if we were selling a theory. If all else failed, we would just leave Paul in the bar permanently!

Throughout Uganda there were many micro-finance organizations providing small loans to groups of people in rural areas, and these micro-finance groups could also be used as the membership base for such medical schemes. This would ensure pooling of risk and make the collection of fees and the issuance of membership ID feasible. In poor rural communities such schemes could not be self-sustaining without donor subsidies, and generally could not be run by the public sector because of the corruption and lack of accountability. The exception to this was Rwanda, where there was no corruption and government systems worked. Indeed Rwanda was developing a form of social health insurance which appeared to be working, where the members paid $2 per year and then 10% of the cost of the service.

As with micro-finance schemes, it was preferable that a medical scheme operating in a district should have a number of service providers competing for the business, but community medical capitation schemes would still need outside funding, while micro-finance schemes were self funding and, indeed, made handsome profits for the operators. If one were to measure results in terms of delivery of services, compared to what existed, the subsidies would be achieving measurable results and would not be thrown down the black hole of government ministries. Such schemes would not be actual insurance, where the insurer was collecting premiums, taking the risk, and paying out claims. The yearly membership fees would simply be collected by the scheme administrator and paid over to the relevant service providers, with only a small part being used to cover administration and quality assurance.

The service provider would provide the agreed services over the agreed period, usually one or two years and there would be no 'fee for service' payments, simply a small user fee to prevent abuse. In capitation, or membership schemes, the service provider takes the risk, while in the insurance scheme, the insurer takes the risk. The difficulty with insurance is that it is easily open to abuse and fraud since the clinic itself is generating the bills, and there is a built-in financial incentive to give the patient unnecessary treatment, or even to bill for treatment not given. Insurance is also more expensive since the operator has to re-insure to cover his risk, the scheme has to make a profit and also pay for administration costs. All this can be calculated through actuarial studies based on the claims ratio: the percentage of the premium used by the members. If the claims ratio rises too high, the insurer will lose money and will have to raise his premiums the following year.

In capitation or membership schemes, the service provider receives most of the money and signs a contract agreeing to provide defined services. These services can then be monitored by the administrator of the scheme to see that they are actually provided, but there is another incentive to the service provider to provide good service – competition. When a scheme is launched at district level, there is usually the choice of more than one clinic or hospital which could provide the service, so if a clinic delivers substandard services, that clinic would lose the business on renewal, as members are free to choose another service provider the following year. The advantage for the service providers is that they can predict their income based on the number of scheme members and can therefore budget to meet their fixed costs.

This was the model on which the IAA schemes were based, where we found that we could budget 85% of the membership fees received for the cost of the service provision within our own hospital and clinics. The only difference between this and community level capitation schemes was the price. Since we received no subsidies and offered a full tertiary level service, our schemes were more expensive than community schemes, where the services offered would be of a more basic level, and the government, or a donor organization, would also put in a subsidy.

# Security

There are few African countries where one does not have to deal with the demands of the police for some kind of bribe or '*chai* (tea) money'.

Ken, the Irish administrator working at Kiwoko Hospital, was driving through Kampala when he was stopped by the police for using his mobile phone. This was an offence, so when the policeman got into his car and told him to drive to Central Police Station, Ken took him at his word and started driving. After he had driven a short distance, the policeman seemed to change his mind and asked, 'But where are you going?'

'I'm driving to Central Police Station,' answered Kenneth, who was a bit perplexed since this was what the policeman had told him to do in the first place.

'Just pull over for a moment so that we can talk about this,' said the policeman as if there was some weighty decision to be made.

'Now, you have committed a grave offence,' he began, 'and the fine is 600,000 shillings.' Then, after a suitable pause, he added, 'So how can you help me to help you? After all, it is a very hot day, I have been standing here the whole day, and I am hungry and thirsty.'

Ken was a very straightforward kind of guy and had not lived in Africa long enough to take the bait. Instead he replied, 'I think you are being very harsh and unfair for picking on me to arrest. Today I have witnessed many people break the traffic laws in much more serious ways than I, and the police have done nothing.'

This was not the response that the policeman had expected, so by way of diverting the conversation, he asked where Ken worked, and on learning that he worked at a mission hospital, he adopted a more conciliatory tone. But he came back to the problem of the hot day and needing something to drink. The correct response would have been to give the guy a few thousand shillings to buy a soda, but Ken, taking the request at face value, apologised that he did not even have a bottle of water in the vehicle, and that he had nothing to give the policeman to drink. At that, the policeman decided that he was getting nowhere with this stupid *mzungu* and got out of the car, empty handed.

On another occasion one of our staff was stopped by the police because her road licence had expired. This policeman also got into the car and told her to drive to the Police Station. Off they went, but it quickly became evident that he also did not wish to actually reach his destination and asked her to pull over. Now she was the one who asked him, 'What are you doing? We just need to go to the station; I will fill in a fixed penalty fine and be on my way.'

'Madam, are you not a Ugandan, do you not know how to talk?' he replied. 'We Ugandans talk, we have ways of settling these matters.'

Once again, it appeared that he was hungry, and five thousand shillings would satisfy his basic needs. So, being a Ugandan, she gave him a couple of thousand shillings and he left.

On another occasion I got a call from our hospital truck driver.

'I have been stopped by the police,' he told me. 'They say the truck is not in good mechanical condition, and they are going to impound it.'

It appeared that the paint on the tail gate of the truck had worn off, and it was not the same colour as the rest of the truck! Since there was no real mechanical problem, there was no legitimate reason for stopping the truck, and no reason to pay a fine or a bribe. I spoke to the police officer on the phone and asked him to 'forgive' us for the poor paint job; he promised that he would let it go this time, and I thought the matter was settled. But when I spoke to the truck driver the next day, it transpired that he had paid the policeman, even though there was no offence. In this brief survey of people's negotiating power with the police, missionaries were too naive to understand what they were supposed to do; bright Ugandan females understood that Ugandans 'talk', but truck drivers just paid whatever they were asked. It was not much wonder we saw the police stopping trucks on a regular basis.

When we had first come to live in Uganda, I was acutely aware that the lack of security and the sense of law and order, which I had taken for granted in Britain, could not be assumed. But as time went on I no longer felt uneasy, though I did take sensible precautions, such as having security guards at the hospital and at our home.

Employing guards was a normal part of life since they were required as a deterrent. Some guards were armed with a bow and arrows, while others had a pump-action shotgun, a bolt-action rifle or an AK forty-seven. The theory was that the guards were supposed to be awake and do the guarding while we slept, but realistically, this was not always the case.

I had spent a sleepless night, not because I had a medical emergency, but because the guard was the one who was sleeping peacefully while everyone else was awake. The whole household slept until about three a.m. when I was gradually awakened by the sound of someone knocking at the gate. I tried in vain to block this sound out of my mind while waiting for the guard to investigate, but the knocking continued. Eventually, I had to acknowledge that I was losing the battle and got out of bed to look for the guard. I didn't have far to look because I practically fell over him sleeping on the couch on our front veranda. As I approached he managed to stand bolt upright.

'So you were sleeping,' I said, stating the obvious.

'No sir,' he replied, with little conviction.

'Then why are you standing in your socks?' I said, pointing to his boots sitting neatly beside the sofa he had just been lying on.

We both returned to the gate to investigate the knocking, and, as we parted, I told him not to leave in the morning until I had talked to him again. But since this desire to meet again was really one sided, by six-thirty the next morning he was nowhere to be seen. He was probably fresh as a daisy as he was the only one in the household who got any sleep while I was running around answering the gate. This guard did not earn much money and perhaps he reasoned that, since he was a low paid worker, he also deserved some sleep. Getting guards to do their job of guarding was more difficult than one would think, considering that all they had to do was to sit there, or occasionally open the gate – and of course, keep thieves out.

One night I was awakened in the dead of night by Robbie whispering, 'Ian get up, there is someone trying to break in.'

Being the fearless husband, I jumped out of bed like an automaton and ran down the corridor to find there was actually someone with his head stuck in the bars of our safety gate, located between the lounge and the bedroom section of the house. I didn't quite know what to do at this point, but my mind did register that this stranger should not be in our house at this particular time with his head stuck in the gate, so I decided to jump on the protruding head. Since I was in my bare feet this action did not inflict any great damage but had the effect of loosening the offending head from the bars. The owner of the head then pulled himself free and made a dash across the lounge and out the front door. I followed, all the time shouting for the guard, while the man made his escape by leaping clean over the wall of the compound.

Meantime, the guard came barrelling down our drive, running as fast as he could in the opposite direction – perhaps a trick of how the sound of my voice had carried, or else this was his normal response to an emergency. Suffice to say that by the time he got himself going in the right direction, the burglar was long gone. The funny thing was that the thief could have cleaned us out in the living room, but he must have thought there was something more interesting through the security gate, so he ended up with nothing. Fortunately, Robbie, being a light sleeper, heard him as he was trying to squeeze through and alerted her brave husband. After that incident we decided to weld more bars to the gate so that only a microcephalic could get through.

Like most African cities, Kampala may not have ranked among the safest cities in the world, but generally people did not feel insecure as they went about their normal business. In Moses Isagawa's book 'The Snake Pit', set in the time of Idi Amin, he described how people survived during that particular era. So many atrocities were committed, yet somehow people managed to go about their daily lives, keeping their heads down and ignoring what was going on around them, but when friends and relatives disappeared, it became very difficult. People working within government security organisations, such as the State Research Bureau, became so brutalised that they did not give a second thought to torturing and killing another human being if it happened to suit their purpose. But now as I moved around Uganda, I was not particularly worried when I was stopped by a police patrol, or at an army check point. There were also occasions when I encountered plain clothes policemen, or security operatives, but such people were not a common part of most people's daily lives, and one generally felt that they could be called to account.

Nairobi was a more dangerous city than Kampala. I sent one of my staff to Nairobi to collect some goods, and, when he arrived at the main Nairobi station at eight-thirty in the morning, he was approached by four men who appeared to be from the some security organisation. Although they were in plain clothes, they carried walkie-talkies and acted in an official manner. Having just arrived in another country, he was at his most vulnerable, being accosted by members of the security services. There is a natural tendency for all of us to feel uncertain at such times and wonder what we have done wrong: perhaps the visa was not completed properly, the yellow fever vaccination certificate wasn't presented, or we have brought some contraband food in our luggage. This reaction usually makes people more compliant to anyone who appears to represent authority.

The men asked Charles to come with them and moved towards a waiting car, but Charles hesitated, so one of them thought he would encourage him by giving him a slap. The passers-by pretended they had not seen anything and hurried on, since this must be an official arrest, but far from being intimidated, Charles had the feeling that there was something wrong and resisted. The men now tried to force him into the car, but he fought back, kicking and screaming and shouting for help. Still no-one came to his aid: perhaps people not wanting to get involved or assuming that this was a police operation. Fortunately, there were several uniformed police officers some distance away who began to notice the commotion and moved in the direction of the fracas. Although there were four assailants, Charles fought to prevent them forcing him into the car, and when the men realised that police officers were approaching, they let Charles go and took off.

The men with the walkie-talkies were not security operatives of any kind but were simply posing as such, to take advantage of the vulnerability of those who had just arrived in Kenya – a sort of welcoming committee. The police told Charles that he was a lucky man since they had not managed to force him into the car. Once in the vehicle, he would have been driven to a remote area, where he would have been robbed, stripped, and either thrown out of the car, or murdered. Charles escaped with only bruises and torn clothes, but otherwise he lost nothing. He phoned me a few minutes later from the doctor's office where he had been taken for a check-up. He was a good man who was obviously quick thinking and brave, the sort of guy whom I instinctively relied on and sent on these more challenging excursions. I could not imagine how I would have felt if, instead of getting a call to reassure me he was OK, I had gotten a call asking me to come and identify a body.

New-comers to Uganda were not usually accosted by men masquerading as security operatives, but there were other more subtle ways to be relieved of one's earthly possessions. Ugandans had the reputation of being friendly, and it was not uncommon for a Ugandan to sit down beside a foreigner and strike up a conversation. Of course tourists were happy when they were welcomed in this way because they wished to get to know the local culture. So a young English medical student, travelling from Kampala to the west of the country, was delighted when a gentleman took the seat beside him and engaged him in conversation. The medical student had been on a medical elective in Kiwoko Hospital where he had worked for the previous six weeks; he had enjoyed himself in the rural environment and even picked up a bit of *Luganda*. Before returning to London, he had decided to make a trip to Bwindi to see the fabled mountain gorillas, so he had secured a gorilla permit at the cost of several hundred dollars and boarded a bus. The person sitting beside him offered him a biscuit and he in turn shared his lunch with the stranger. He noticed that the biscuit was still in its original wrapper, so he wasn't worried about catching something from it; after all, this was not some dubious food, being sold along the side of the road.

And that was the last thing he remembered until he woke up in hospital. Some tourists saw that he didn't move when the bus reached its destination and strongly suspected that he had been drugged, so they managed to bring him to a nearby health-centre. All of his personal belongings had gone, including what he had in his pockets, since the gentleman had ample time to go through all his possessions. The poor guy was now stranded in the west in Uganda, with no money and suffering from the after-effects of an overdose of temazepam, with which the biscuit had been laced.

It was likely that the driver of the bus was aware of what was going on because he would have seen it all before and could have pointed out the person responsible, but he was probably paid to keep quiet. This was not a new scam and was administered through different forms of contact. Another visitor was given a can of coke which was sealed, so he thought there was no danger, but the drug had been smeared around the rim or injected into the tin in sufficient quantities to put him to sleep.

Although Nairobi was considered to be more dangerous than Kampala, it was all relative and people could die on the Kampala streets for the sake of a few shillings. Some Indians who owned a small supermarket near the hospital were travelling home at around nine p.m., but the fact that it was early evening and there were still many people on the streets did not stop a gang of thugs from staging a highway robbery. The Indians had been selected because it was assumed they were carrying the day's takings since they were reputed to dislike keeping their money in the safe. The robbers pulled their vehicle in front of the car, cutting off any means of escape; the driver kept his hand on the horn in an effort to alert passers-by, but the thieves were not intimidated and pulled him out of the car, while others went to the passenger's side and ordered the Indians to open the door. There were two cousins in the car and the doors on their side were locked, but when they realised that the man had a gun, they panicked, shouting,

'Wait wait,' as they fumbled with the door. But the thief was trigger-happy and shot through the window from only a couple of feet away. The window shattered, and the bullet hit the man in the chest; the thieves found the money and were gone. The driver drove straight to the hospital, but the man was dead, the bullet having gone through his heart.

When I arrived a few minutes later, I found the victim still seated in the car, as if he were sleeping. The only abnormality was a relatively small bloodstain on his shirt, but he had no pulse and was not breathing. His cousin was wandering around in a state of shock, while other relatives began arriving. The gunmen had taken this man's life for a relatively small sum – less than two million shillings ($1000); a life did not have much value. Perhaps it was because the victim was a foreigner, or that the murder was so pointless, that I felt so sad. He was just an ordinary guy trying to earn a living from running a small business. He was not rich by any standards; I knew the supermarket and their prices were cheap and profit margins small. I had met the various family members sitting behind the till and watched them patiently build up their business. The victim was married, with a wife and baby. That evening she was made a widow and the baby became fatherless because of some thieves who gained a few shilling but did not think of the consequences to others. This poor man had come all the way to Uganda in the hope of a better life, only to be shot down like a dog on the streets of Kampala.

A patient with gunshot wounds was brought to International Hospital in the middle of the night. The group of men accompanying him thought he had been critically injured and urged the hospital staff to do everything in their powers to save him. The doctor on duty assessed and stabilised the patient, did a number of X-rays and investigations to ascertain the extent of the injuries, and, over a period of several hours the patient was stabilised. The men therefore decided they would like to save money by moving their patient to the public hospital, where they could let the government shoulder the expense. They had not yet paid for the treatment received but demanded that the hospital provide an ambulance to take their patient to the government hospital. The driver, being aware of the non-payment, asked them to first settle the bill, but the group produced guns and became threatening, asking the driver if he had a family, and if he would like to continue to live to provide for them. The security guard was beaten up, and the driver was forced to take the patient to the government hospital.

When he had delivered his patient, he went to the police and reported the incident. The police came to the ward to follow up the complaint, but when they tried to question the men involved, the policemen themselves were surrounded, threatened at gunpoint and told to leave. The group claimed to be from CMI – the Chieftaincy of Military Intelligence – and obviously did not feel that they needed to comply with any hospital rules or regulations, nor that they were under the authority of the police – though they must have had some semblance of accountability since later someone came back and settled the bill.

There were people who carried guns, claimed to be under the authority of a state security organisation and felt that they were not subject to ordinary laws. One of the benefits which the government had brought was vastly improved security compared to former regimes, with the army and the police acting in a relatively disciplined manner. Gone were the days when ordinary citizens were harassed at army check-points and their possessions stolen, and although some policemen still asked for bribes, it was no longer at gunpoint. That a group of men could come into a hospital, hold a gun to the head of an ambulance driver, beat up the security guard, threaten the police and get away with it, was not acceptable. If state security operatives did not have sufficient respect for other people, to the point where they threatened them and beat them up, one wondered what sort of people we were dealing with and if these were the kind of people we needed to ensure State Security. My experience living in Uganda was that it was a largely peaceful country, but there were many others who still had memories of Amin's regime, when so called security personnel came into a hospital, pulled a doctor out of theatre, bundled him into the boot of a car and the doctor was never seen again. No-one wanted to go back to those bad old days.

In fairness to the government, when the Minister of Security heard about the incident, he came to see me personally and assured me that the men would be dealt with, though that was the last I heard from him.

# Motivating donors

Over the years while I was working to establish the International Medical Centres and International Hospital, Kiwoko continued to grow into a hospital of more than two hundred beds. It also developed a laboratory assistants' training school, a nursing school, a large HIV programme and an extensive community health programme. The funding for the running costs was largely met through Friends of Kiwoko Hospital. This foundation contributed around 60% of the hospital's running costs, without which it would have been impossible for the work to continue. It was probably the relatively direct linkage between those who donated and those who benefited which allowed this long term funding to continue. The absolute figure which Friends of Kiwoko contributed was around £20,000 per month, which would have been a mere drop in the bucket for the budget of a 200-bed hospital in a developed country, but it went a long way in rural Uganda.

The funding came mainly from ordinary people in Britain and Ireland who contributed on a regular basis, and one might wonder why people kept giving their hard earned cash to a hospital thousands of miles away. The answer was because they saw for themselves the difference that their contributions made; they could even visit the hospital and meet the patients, visit someone with AIDS in the community, or sponsor a student nurse who was being trained. In this case there was a very close connection between the donor and the recipient.

Many people give money because they feel guilty about living comfortable lives while others are suffering, but ordinary people have also been developing donor fatigue regarding support for poor countries. They see pictures of a malnourished child, or hear about a war or a famine, so from time to time they put money in an envelope or give their credit

228

card number, but usually they do not know what happens after that. And there are an increasing number of people who want to feel a sense of involvement with the project they are supporting. Some aid organizations have understood this and designed elaborate programmes to keep the donors in touch. Child sponsorship organizations, such as World Vision, are particularly successful because they keep the sponsor in touch with the child, but the infrastructure necessary to do this also costs money.

When I first went to Luweero, I worked closely with World Vision because of Janet. World Vision is one of the most experienced and successful development organizations in the world, with a budget of hundreds of millions of dollars, yet only a proportion of the donation actually gets through to the sponsored child. This is not because World Vision squanders the money but because it has many layers, all of which need to be financed. Such organizations have international offices and country offices which provide significant employment within developing countries, since they hire office staff, drivers, administrators, accountants, social workers and development workers to run their projects. When a sponsorship programme is run, they also need local people on the ground to send photographs and reports and to ensure that the school fees reach the school, all of which costs money. In order to demonstrate that the sponsor is getting value for money and that a large part of the sponsorship is contributing to programme costs, aid organizations also try to demonstrate that the majority of their budget is spent within the developing country itself.

The Irish organization, Fields of Life, spent practically no money on administration or programme costs, with all the money raised going to the specified projects. Fields of Life was started by an Irish farmer, turned clergyman, who lived in Uganda for several years, setting up a farming project to support orphans. During his time in Uganda, he became

229

involved in building a school, and when he returned to Ireland, he founded his own aid organization, specializing in building schools in the region. He became the administrator without pay, financing his personal needs through the sale of his family farm. Another part of his vision was to get Irish people to come to Uganda to experience the situation first hand; hence, he organized teams to visit and either physically build schools or get involved in church programmes.

His vision appealed to the Irish farming and business community because they saw him as man who was prepared to get his own hands dirty, and he was also making a huge sacrifice by not taking an income from his own organization. Also, the fruits of his work could easily be seen in the number of schools which were built in a remarkably short time – more than seventy in the course of a few years. The money kept pouring in – over one million pounds sterling in a single year – and it was practically all transformed into bricks and mortar: schools all over Uganda where people could physically see where their money had gone. The organization also paid school fees for some of the children attending the schools, in order to maintain an ongoing involvement. The project was so successful that they were invited by the President of Burundi to carry out a similar project in that country, and so it spread to Burundi.

Everyone was satisfied with what was going on, but there were some who asked the question: Now that you have erected many schools throughout Uganda, what is your ongoing responsibility for them? Fields of Life could answer this by showing that they were also sponsoring many of the pupils at those schools, so large numbers of children were attending school as a result. This was a measurable result since the number of children benefiting could easily be counted. The next question was about the quality of education the children were receiving. This made the organization look at another dimension: was it enough to build classrooms; was it enough even to sponsor kids; what was the measurable outcome of the money they were spending in terms of producing well educated children?

The government of Uganda itself had a schools building programme. The government had introduced UPE – universal primary education – through which every child was promised the opportunity to enrol in government primary schools, without paying fees. This meant a huge increase in numbers of children attending school and in the number of classrooms needed to accommodate them. These classrooms were duly built through grants to the various local district councils, but many of the classroom blocks were substandard, and on one notable occasion, a door fell off its hinges during the opening ceremony. Children were accommodated in government classrooms, but there was a shortage of qualified teachers which meant that the class sizes increased exponentially, and the standard of education actually fell. While Universal Primary Education was a noble aspiration, and there was certainly a far greater number of children in Uganda attending school than most other sub-Saharan countries, the end product was more children sitting in poorly built classrooms, getting a mediocre education.

If Fields of Life were to achieve measurable results, not just in terms of the numbers of schools built, or numbers of children in those classrooms, they would have to ensure that the teachers were qualified, that they were present in their classes, teaching the kids to an acceptable standard and that the children had education materials such as textbooks – to name but a few of the essential ingredients of achieving a good education. All this involves a programme for training teachers, supervision, school inspections etc, in other words a large administrative cost which would need substantial funding to ensure that the building of their schools made a real impact on education standards. While it might give an Irish businessman satisfaction that he had paid for the construction of a school in

231

Africa, that school would not be effective unless it was used to bring a sound education to the children. Building schools was an easy goal to define and measure, but there were those who realized that they would have to involve themselves in a substantial educational programme, which was not quite so visible, if they were to make a real impact on the lives of the children. Raising money for capital costs was the easy bit; it was meeting the recurrent costs of the programmes which was the hard part.

Putting up buildings was one way in which people could 'see' what their donations had achieved; another was to keep in touch with the child they had sponsored through letters and photos. Yet another way was to travel to the developing country itself and get involved with the programme being sponsored which seemed to be an increasingly popular trend among churches and aid organisations. One could be cynical and observe that if all the money spent on plane fares were sent to the project itself, much more would be achieved in financial terms, but human nature is such that people don't get motivated by sending the price of a virtual airfare to their favourite charity; there is no adventure in that.

Those who visit get their hands dirty: building something, working with the local people and seeing the everyday struggles that people go through. There is so much that is lost in a sanitised western civilisation; one can not readily understand what villagers go through in the struggles of everyday living, such as fetching water, getting wood for a fire, or even getting through the traffic, unless one has experienced it. There is something about the sights and smells of life or the resilience of the people that can never be understood from words or a picture. I met people who had hardly been away from their farms in Northern Ireland but found themselves in a village in Uganda, building a school with their own hands. One part of me reasoned that the local Ugandan builders were perfectly capable of doing this work, so why were these well meaning foreigners coming thousands of miles to take work away from Ugandans? But another part understood the need to engage with the society – even if it was only for two weeks and even if the person went back to his hotel in the evenings. The Irish farmer may have been bringing something to that village – another school building – but what was significant was what Uganda brought to him. If he had any sensitivity he left with a new understanding of the society, having seen how the people of that community lived. He left with some of that community having rubbed off on him. And if he was a thinking person, he left with fewer answers than he had come with, but with a greater understanding of his fellow man on the African continent.

# Dealing with the Banks

Since we had now established a hospital, a health maintenance organisation and a number of clinics, I felt that I was realising some of my goals, but that there was still a long way to go.

The hospital was providing a credible medical service, and we were also breaking new ground with some of the techniques we were using. I had purchased second-hand laporoscopic equipment for keyhole surgery and was keen to develop the expertise for this type of surgery within Uganda. As well as having the necessary equipment, I had made contact with a Ugandan laparoscopy surgeon working in South Africa who was prepared to come back home to carry out the surgery and teach the procedure. Many African countries had benefited from the brain-drain of Ugandan medics which started during the Idi Amin regime. Apart from South Africa, our neighbour, Kenya, also benefited, with many senior Ugandan specialists working just across the border. Some of these doctors expressed willingness to come back to build up the medical services within their own country, but it was difficult to leave hospitals where they were well facilitated, and well equipped, to come back to a country where the medical system was still largely dysfunctional.

Our first patient for the keyhole surgery happened to be a High Court Judge with gallstones. She was so busy that she did not wish to take the time off work to have the normal open surgery, as this would require several months of recuperation (some people are workaholics). When I let her know that she could have the gallbladder removed through keyhole surgery and that she would only have to take a few days off, she was happy to be our first patient. She realised that she was a guinea-pig, but was not in the least put off by this. The surgery was carried out successfully, and the next day Justice

234

Sebutinde was sitting up in bed, looking as if she were on holiday. She was a very well known judge, having taken part in several high level inquiries, and she insisted that she would like the media to interview her as the first patient in Uganda who had a gall bladder removal through keyhole surgery.

The story succeeded in stirring up controversy in the medical establishment because it was a small private hospital that had carried out keyhole surgery and not the main government hospital. It transpired that the government hospital actually had the necessary equipment, but it had been left in a store and never used. If my goal in starting a hospital was to make ripples, I was certainly making them. Those working in the government health sector had not taken the development of private hospitals in Uganda seriously. In fact some of the senior consultants referred dismissively to International Hospital as 'that *edwaliro*' (small clinic) or 'International Hotel', and when keyhole surgery was carried out, they thought we were treading in their space. As far as I was concerned, if we did something which pushed the government to improve services, then I was achieving what I had set out to do.

International Hospital had many shortcomings as a facility, but it was the best we could do, given the resources available. I had not borrowed money from the local banks and didn't have any company loans, and although I was not burdened by debt, this was not necessarily a good business strategy because I was always cash strapped. The reason I didn't have loans was that the rate of interest charged by the banks on the Uganda shilling was prohibitive, at the time 28%. One could borrow in dollars at a lower interest rate, but this was also a large risk since the shilling had depreciated by 100% over the previous seven years. The currency risk in dollars was high, while the interest rate on the shilling was prohibitive.

The lack of finance at reasonable interest rates was a hindrance for the growth of many small and medium sized enterprises in developing countries. There was some justification for the high interest rates, in terms of risk against currency fluctuations and risk in lending in a market where the borrower might vanish without trace, but banks in Africa were generally very profitable, due to high interest rates and high bank charges. The other factor which contributed to keeping interest rates high was government borrowing, since the government issued treasury bills at high interest rates. If a bank could lend money to the government for 12% per year, there was little incentive to lend at the same rate to a business venture or to ordinary people, who might fail to repay. This was obviously a chicken and egg situation.

Initially, the banks were neither highly regulated nor well capitalised, with the result that some local entrepreneurs owned banks where the customers' deposits got mixed up with their own personal finances. The combination of weak regulations, substantial defaults on loans from government controlled banks, plus local banks which were run with little accountability, was a recipe for disaster. Within a short period several banks went into liquidation, leaving their depositors high and dry, which forced the Bank of Uganda to step in and produce a much tougher regulatory framework. The government bank – the Uganda Commercial Bank – was sold off to a South African banking conglomerate, much to the annoyance of powerful local interest groups, who wished to keep it in Ugandan hands. Thus a number of banks closed, and international banks were able to become established in the marketplace.

While I was happy to see good banking practice, the management of many international banks was also being moved away from Uganda. Decisions were made in South Africa or Dubai as mergers occurred and larger international banks ate up smaller ones. Of course, this phenomenon was happening all over the world: it was now impossible to call in and see the local branch manager in person because he no longer existed. While the regulation of the banking sector was positive for the development of Uganda, I was also left wondering about the downside. In developing countries it was important that the banks were real partners in development. These were fragile economies where one was nursing relatively small projects into existence, and if decisions were made further and further away, local factors would not be taken into account, sometimes with disastrous consequences.

Barclays had a strong presence in Uganda in the colonial days, with a head office and a number of up-country branches. This network was essential for the facilitation of the trading of commodities, such as coffee and cotton, since having a branch network meant that the transfer of cash to the farmers was quick and efficient. After independence, there was a programme of nationalisation, and Barclays reduced the number of their branches, while the government opened the Uganda Commercial Bank with many upcountry branches – which quickly became dysfunctional. Barclays Uganda continued to serve expatriates and small corporate organisations, but had little presence in the marketplace. However, Absa Bank then merged with Barclays Africa, and the policy was reversed, with the result that Barclays opened an extensive retail branch network throughout the country.

By this point in our development we knew that, while the thirty bed hospital had been a good training ground and allowed us to develop the expertise in procedures such as laparoscopic surgery, it had many limitations. If I was going to fulfil my vision of developing a truly state of the art hospital, then I would need to build a new hospital on a green field site. The question was where was I going to get the money for such a project? Since I had chosen to do business in the private sector and was not in the aid world, I found myself dealing with banks, instead of aid agencies.

Many people in the west do not see banks as driving development, which they presume is the mandate of aid agencies, and names such as Barclays do not spring to mind as development agencies. But in development terms, the banks have an even greater role to play because they represent a means of sustainable development. I was banking with Barclays when they still had a local Corporate Director who knew his customers by name and could make decisions – or at least influence them.

The European Investment Bank had made a twenty-five million dollar development loan available to Uganda, and for the first time Barclays had a line of credit for long term loans for the health sector. The European Investment Bank lent the money to the Bank of Uganda at a nominal interest rate; the Central Bank then made this money available to retail banks at a wholesale rate. They, in turn, identified the projects and lent it out at a retail rate. There were several advantages with this particular loan which made borrowing attractive. The first was that the loan could be paid back in shillings at a fixed rate, so there was no currency risk; the second was that the interest rates were reasonable; the third was that it was long term.

I talked to Ben, the corporate director, about my idea of developing a new state of the art hospital, and he advised that the European Development Bank facility would be ideal. The bank assessed my project and approved the loan at an interest rate on the shilling of 7.2%, which was a low rate for Uganda. The loan could be repaid over a period of eight years, with a two year grace period. This was important for a long term project such as a hospital since loans in Africa were usually given over a short period of three to five years.

I borrowed one million dollars, which was the biggest loan I had ever taken but was still only a small portion of what I needed to fulfil my vision. It was, nonetheless, the start I needed.

I had raised money from donors to build Kiwoko Hospital, and I don't suppose it was normal for a doctor from Ireland to come to a developing country and then take the personal risk of borrowing money. But I had now been building this business for seven years, and I needed to take the next step. Also I reckoned that if the worst came to the worst and I lost everything, I still had my profession as a doctor to fall back on. Taking the loan gave access to a substantial tranche of funds, which made it possible to proceed with plans to buy land and start the process of planning a new hospital. The loan itself was insufficient for what I wished to achieve, but taken together with the income I was ploughing back into the business, we were able to take another step forwards.

Co-incidentally at this time we also won the contract to provide medical services for Barclays' staff. The two things were not related, but we were definitely development partners since I was borrowing from them and using the money to develop better medical facilities for their staff. Unfortunately, as Barclays grew the personal relationship was lost, and their organisation had no institutional memory, so they did not perceive any significance in the relationship. Barclays could have been proud of what we had achieved, but there was no one left in the organisation to relate to their client. Although the expansion of the branch network may have been good for the up-country customers, the change went with a loss of personal relationships. The consequence of this was that they lost many customers and there was a serious loss of profitability.

239

# Pioneering

As the next step towards the development of a purpose built hospital, I needed to look for a suitable site. Disputes over land ownership and titles were common in Uganda, and there was a term called 'selling air', whereby titles were forged, or registrations changed at the land office, and the same piece of land sold to several different people. I had an unfortunate patient who paid for a site on which she planned to build her home. One morning when she was surveying her property, she met two other people on her site doing the same thing – she had just been sold 'air'. The fact that there were different laws and registrations covering land made purchase complicated, and the disorganisation in the various land offices made it easy for conmen to collude with corrupt officials.

Confused land titles also tended to hamper investment since there was no clear policy or facilitation for large investors to acquire suitable land for development. Land was sometimes divided informally among families over a long period, with various family members having smallholdings with traditional rights but no actual title. Others simply squatted on available land, and the government eventually gave such people the legal rights over this land if they had been there for a sufficient period. An investor might wish to farm but find that squatters had settled on various parts, making it impossible for him to obtain a clear lease.

While it was good that peasants' rights were protected, land which was sub-divided again and again into small holdings was farmed in a less efficient way, such that it only produced enough food for subsistence, a situation which existed in large parts of Kenya. The problem in Uganda was not that there was insufficient land for everyone, but the manner in which the land was organised. Uganda could have been the breadbasket of the region, were it farmed properly. But each time land was required for a large commercial agro-processing business, it was difficult to identify an appropriate piece without inside connections. It was for this reason that prospective investors beat a path to the door of the President, in the hope that he could micromanage the problem and obtain a suitable site for their project. The people who facilitated this profited through their ability to obtain an appointment with His Excellency.

When I was planning to build the new hospital, one of the significant limiting factors was finding a piece of land close enough to the centre of Kampala, which was also big enough to allow for future development. I estimated that I would need around five acres. While it was not difficult to find such a site outside the city, I could not locate the hospital too far from the centre since patients would find it difficult to gain access. This was due in part to poor roads, poor city planning and traffic jams. While I was able to find many sites of one to two acres, there were few of five acres at a price I could afford. I asked Kampala City Council, but there was no help forthcoming, probably because there was nothing in it for any of their officials. Although there was an investment authority, they did not own land themselves and could only act as an agency to point me in the right direction. A combination of poor planning and insider dealing by councillors and politicians meant that various prime sites had been grabbed and other areas of the city were so haphazard that larger sites were at a premium. After a year of searching, I was fortunate to acquire a four and a half acre site which had no squatters, and without resorting to seeking political influence. It was situated on the border between a low cost and a high cost housing zone within three kilometres of the city centre. Now that I had acquired the land and the finance to start the project, I needed the services of an architectural firm. While there were several good architecture companies within Uganda, I decided to bring in some new blood and use a firm from South Africa.

My contact came through the husband of one of the partners who owned several cotton ginneries in Uganda. I had some fellow feeling with Bruce since he was an entrepreneur who had risked his shirt to develop a business within Uganda – and nearly lost it in the process. During his first year of trading, cotton prices were high on the world market and he made a healthy profit, but he ploughed the profits back into growers' organizations, giving the smallholders seeds, fertilizers and education, so that the small farmers could have more productive yields. Cotton was a major export of Uganda during the colonial period, but the export of cotton had almost ceased after the expulsion of the Asians, and it was now people such as Bruce who were endeavouring to revive this sector of the economy. Cotton was not grown on large estates, but by peasant farmers, and, if the world prices held and the weather was favourable, it was a significant cash crop for the rural poor.

Unfortunately, the following year the world market crashed, followed by drought and floods, and just about anything which could go wrong did go wrong, leaving Bruce's cotton operation insolvent. The only reason that the banks did not foreclose was that they could not find anyone to buy his ginneries, so they were forced to come to an arrangement that he would pay them a proportion of every bail of cotton that he sold in the future, until the debt was cleared.

'I owed the banks so much and this was their only hope of getting it back,' he told me, and he reckoned that it was sometimes better to owe a lot than a little because it gave more leverage. But Bruce was that kind of a pioneering entrepreneur who never gave up, and when things got tough, he would get going – by starting another business or even expanding. Over the years, he established cotton businesses in South Africa, Uganda, Malawi and Zimbabwe. When farmers were getting out of Zimbabwe, he was moving in. He stuck with his

Ugandan operation, and several years later he had paid off his borrowings and was making profit.

Those who were pioneers in the various sectors of the Ugandan economy faced the greatest challenges, and it was sometimes the people who came after them who reaped the benefits, unless the pioneers had the money and the determination to stick with it. One example of this was an Indian friend, Vipul Thakrar.

Vipul's family had been expelled by Idi Amin, but having arrived in the UK with very little, they built up a multimillion dollar business, growing, processing and selling basmati rice and other food products under the brand Tilda Rice. In a moment of nostalgia, Vipul bought a run-down rice farm, since Uganda was the land of his birth. The Kibimba Rice Development was not large by Tilda's own standards, consisting of only a few thousand hectares, but this particular investment proved to be one of its most troublesome. The problems ranged from crippling bureaucracy, local officials who deliberately tried to frustrate the development, adverse weather conditions, theft and even massive flocks of small birds. As well as rice, they planted corn to cater for the needs of their workers, and as Vipul drove past his healthy looking maize, he would admire the ripening husks, since at least that project seemed to be going well.

However, when it came time for harvesting, the only husks which remained were the ones on the perimeter of the field, all the maize in the centre having already been harvested by the local villagers. Between plagues of insects, birds, theft and unnecessary bureaucracy, Vipul was tearing his hair out, and the project was making a loss.

For my part I was very aware of the difficulties of pioneering a medical business and had also witnessed many hopeful investors come and then leave again, having lost their life's savings. Vipul and I understood the frustrations of doing

243

business in Uganda, even though we were both committed to the development of the country.

We were having dinner with the country representative of the International Monetary Fund and were discussing the merits of Uganda as an investment destination. The IMF representative waxed lyrical about Uganda's macroeconomic policy and how well the country was doing, while Vipul and I sat and listened. The IMF representative was the economic expert, but we were the people who had invested and understood the frustrations and difficulties on the ground.

'Give me 50 cents on the dollar and I am out of here,' Vipul finally declared.

'This place is difficult to do business in, and the only reason we are still here is that we have so much money invested we can't leave.'

I had heard that sentiment before.

Tilda's rice operation in Uganda did take several years to stabilize, but they stuck it out, became fully mechanized, and installed state-of-the-art rice grading and packaging equipment. After some years they were able to sell all the rice they could produce on the local market, and the project was making a profit. But it took time, guts and commitment to establish such a business – and access to a large amount of finance. When the President of the World Bank visited Uganda some ten years later, he wished to view a successful commercial farming project and was taken to Tilda's Kibimba Rice Estate as a shining example of good development. Vipul didn't bother to tell him the struggles he went through to make the project successful, nor did he tell him that at one stage he was at the point of pulling out.

I felt a kindred spirit with pioneers such as Vipul and Bruce, so when I found that Bruce's wife was a partner in a firm of Architects in South Africa I wanted to know her thoughts on designing a hospital in Uganda. One of the projects she had worked on had been the new South African Constitutional

Courts. Her company had also been involved in several exclusive game lodges in South Africa, but they had not yet designed a hospital. So one of the partners made a trip to Uganda to understand the climate, the soil and the local conditions, and I made a couple of trips to their office in Durban to discuss the details of the project. I made it clear from the outset that I did not have a big budget and, fortunately, although they were a prestigious firm, they were prepared to take on the work for a very reasonable fee. I needed to ensure that I made my cash stretch as far as possible.

In consultation with me, the architects designed a building which was functional, but simple, and which had good air currents so that we minimized the use of air conditioning and ensured optimal ventilation. The building was modular, in that it repeated itself on the different floors which then required only minor modifications for different uses. The ground floor accommodated the Accident and Emergency Unit, plus the outpatient consulting rooms, specialized facilities such as radiology, laboratory, central pharmacy, intensive care unit, central sterilization and theatre suites. The top three floors were designed for wards, but with flexibility in the design and functionality.

I planned to carry out the construction in several phases because I did not have enough cash to finish it all, endeavouring to make each phase self contained, so that we could expand into the next part of the building as soon as it was completed. This meant that the whole of the ground floor had to be completed first but that the tower for the wards could be completed floor by floor, with work going on at the upper levels while we occupied the lower floors. I reckoned that if I was able to complete at least half of the building, I would have a usable facility, and I would have taken a major step forwards, even if I didn't have the finances to complete the rest.

Although I had already been involved in many building projects, this was by far the largest, requiring detailed plans and structural engineering drawings, plus mechanical and electrical designs. The project was planned as a four storey building with several stairways, a ramp and a lift, and the building was designed with enough structural integrity, such that a further floor could be added in the future, should the need arise. We had agreed a design/build arrangement with the architects, in which they would supply the drawings as we got to that particular phase of building. But they were seldom more than one step ahead of us, and sometimes they got behind, though at such points we stopped and waited for them. We also had a local firm of architects whose role was in collaborating and obtaining the various local planning clearances. Since my strategy in carrying out any project was just to get on with it, I hired masons and porters and started the job, the first tasks being to level the site and build a perimeter wall. As the needs of the site grew, I employed a British ex-army supervisor, who had married a Ugandan girl and settled in the country. Jim had little experience of building, but knew how to handle money, organise and maintain discipline, and with several hundred workers on site, this was essential. Jim's favourite words were, 'Off my site!'

Subsequently a young Irish architect by the name of Angus – the architect, who had gone to University with Lauren – expressed interest in getting more experience through working in Uganda, so we gave him a job as our on-site architect where he got lots of experience and little pay. Not only had Angus to supervise the work on site, but we had to save money, where possible, without jeopardizing standards. He found that it was usually cheaper to manufacture items on site than to buy them ready made. For Angus this was the opposite of his experience in the US and the UK where labour was expensive and factory production was the way to go. In Uganda, labour was relatively inexpensive, while imports were expensive, and local sub-contractors could be costly due to inefficiencies and high margins. Hence, many items were made by our own workers;

we did the opposite of outsourcing: we in-sourced as much as possible.

Angus also saved money by going on to the internet and comparing prices. The quotation we received for hospital flooring was high, but eventually he found there were differential prices for the same product, depending on which part of the world it was purchased from. He scoured the world and bought from the cheapest region. I also visited the UK, where I had some contacts with dealers in second-hand hospital equipment, and was able to acquire items such as theatre lights, trolleys, etc.

I was on a trip to Northern Ireland, when someone told me that a large regional hospital was replacing their hydraulic beds with electric beds, and if I organized 40 ft containers to take the beds away, I could have them free. So I contacted a haulage firm and had four empty containers ready to receive the beds, which were loaded straight out the door of the hospital and shipped to Uganda. The beds arrived before the hospital was ready, but the containers themselves made useful stores and a site office.

# Rafting on the Nile

One afternoon while I was working at the IAA clinic, a young South African river guide walked into my office. Hendri had a proposal which I found intriguing.

'We have done some research and found that although the route of the Nile has been followed, there is no record that anyone has actually covered the course of the Nile on water from source to sea.' He paused and continued, 'We want to raft the Nile from Jinja to Alexandria.'

I was amazed that this had not been done before, but Hendri assured me that, although others had loosely followed the course of the Nile in the past, they had missed out large stretches because there was not the technology in the form of modern day rubber dinghies to enable them to follow the Nile on water. Of course there were a few rapids and falls, such as Murchison Falls, which were impossible to raft, but these could be portaged round and most of the rapids could now be handled by an expert white-water rafting team. This was all very interesting, but what had this to do with me?

'We need a doctor for the expedition,' he explained. 'We had someone lined up, but she dropped out and now we have come to you since you have lived in Uganda a long time and you know this country.'

So I wasn't their first choice, but I wouldn't have been my first choice either since I did not consider myself a natural adventurer, and come to think of it, I didn't like water all that much.

This was not a particularly convenient time for me to be considering going white-water rafting down the Nile, especially since Hendri reckoned that the trip could take them around three to four months in total. I told him that I was in the midst of building a new hospital, and it was impossible for me to leave.

'What about if you came for a few weeks when we are in the most remote parts with the least access to medical help?' he suggested.

'Where would that be?' I asked

The route would take them through northern Uganda and over the border into Southern Sudan where they would be travelling through a war zone, and there would certainly be nothing available by way of medical facilities. They would then be passing through the Sudd, a swamp the size of France, and there were definitely no clinics there either. Furthermore, it had been so long since anyone had made the trip through the Sudd that they did not really know how long it would take and should be prepared for the worst in this mosquito infested swamp. It sounded like a lovely trip and it was all very interesting, but I still had a hospital to build and several clinics to run, and I didn't feel that I could leave what I was doing.

I shared with the senior managers at the next management meeting that I had been approached to be the ship's doctor, as it were, on a rafting expedition down the Nile, but I felt that I could not go because there was too much going on. Rona responded that no-one was indispensable, and they would manage without me if I went on this little holiday for a few weeks. That was reassuring, but I still had my doubts, and Robbie was not very enthusiastic. This was understandable, since having survived cancer twice and subsequently continued to enlarge my entrepreneurial activities, I now had two hundred men digging a hole in the ground to build a hospital. So if I did not come back, she would have to dig her way out of all this – so to speak – no matter what Rona said about me not being indispensable. But the main thing that was niggling at the back of my mind was that this expedition was way beyond my comfort zone, and I really wondered if I could hack it.

I had developed the habit of making myself get out of my comfort zone every few years, in order to move on to the next season of life and just so that I would not get into too much of a rut. We had done it when I left my middle-class existence in Northern Ireland for the elephant grass of Luweero. I had done it again when I abandoned middle England and came back to Kampala to start over. I had done it when I poured all my income into remodelling an old building into a hospital, and I had been forced out of my comfort zone each time I got cancer. Although I was in the throes of developing the new hospital, I was an entrepreneur by nature, which meant I was actually still within my comfort zone, but I was not an adventurer. I had read the accounts of Speake, Baker, Pasha, Burton and Grant of the last century, but I was not of that ilk. I was not an explorer in Africa – that was a bygone generation – but I did live on a hill in Kampala overlooking Lake Victoria, the lake that flowed into the Nile, and I was fascinated by this whole area of the world: from Uganda through Sudan to Egypt. My own destiny was tied up with this part of East Africa, and I could not escape that fact.

I was being presented with a golden opportunity to get closely acquainted with the heart of the Nile in my adopted homeland. I could become 'Clarke of the Nile.' It had a certain ring to it!

The White Nile meandered through the territory from lake Victoria to Egypt, which had witnessed not only the trails of the legendary Victorian adventurers, but the suffering that the slave traders had inflicted on the local population as they shot their way up the Nile, killing the elephants, trading the ivory, and enslaving the natives. This was a particularly harsh part of Africa, which has hardly changed in over a hundred years. It witnessed the longest war in Africa, rumbling for fifty years in South Sudan and, more recently, the activities of Joseph Kony and the LRA, causing untold hardship and suffering for tens of thousands in Northern Uganda over the past two decades.

I decided that I would take this opportunity to travel the course of the Nile, experience the conditions of Northern Uganda, understand South Sudan and see for myself what Sir

Samuel and Lady Baker had endured in their passage through the Sudd, an area of swamp the size of France. I really wondered if I was up to it: could I manage sleeping on a raft or living in a mosquito infested swamp? I told Hendri that I would join them from Murchison Falls through Northern Uganda, South Sudan, Juba, the tribal lands and on through the Sudd, where I would get off and hitch a ride back to Uganda because there would be local medical help as they reached Khartoum and travelled on to Egypt.

Several weeks later I drove down to Jinja to be filmed with the rest of the team, launching the rafts at the source of the Nile and rowing down the river. But in my case it was all show, since I got off the raft about an hour later and headed back home. The other team members continued rowing down the Nile through Lake Kyoga and on towards Karuma Falls. The plan was to row all the way to the last area of dry land before the Sudd where the rafters would then be assisted by the fitting of small outboard motors to the two rafts to help them through the swamp. Otherwise, there was a whole lot of very boring rowing until that point was reached.

The expedition arrived safely at Karuma Falls where I joined them, but purely as an on-the-shore medical advisor. They were about to traverse a stretch of the Nile running from Karuma Falls to Murchison Falls, which was infested by numerous rapids, crocodiles and hippos. It seemed to me that if the rapids didn't get them, the hippos would, and I watched from the safety of the bridge as eight professional white-water rafters battled their way through the Karuma Rapids, avoiding a hippo pool, only to be tossed out in the surf as they plunged under the bridge.

This was roughly the area where Sir Samuel and Lady Baker were marooned for years under the control of the local tribal king. My role was to help set up camp and meet the team several miles down the river. We waited for hours and the team didn't appear until it was nearing nightfall. The reason for their

251

delay? The raft went over some submerged rocks and got a puncture. They had to pull off and repair it and then had to wait for the glue to dry. I had plenty of experience of punctures in Uganda, but never one on water. We arranged to meet again at Murchison Falls, and three days later they appeared at the head of the falls, having experienced a number of hairy moments. But they were alive and in good spirits.

I joined the team on water after Murchison in the relative calm of the river as it entered Lake Albert. They decided to take it easy and make camp that night in the Delta, and although I did not consider myself a great outdoors person, there was a certain beauty and peace as the sun set over the lake, and the experience was very pleasant. But during the night there were louder and closer animal noises than I had ever experienced, though the loudest noise was from my team-mate, Bingo, who was snoring in the next tent. He was so loud that he would have scared off any form of wildlife which ventured our way, but apart from Bingo, there were other animal sounds around the tents which discouraged me from going for a pee until the morning.

We paddled into Lake Albert and out the top end and managed to cause havoc to the local fishermen, who saw us come out of the mists early one morning and thought we were the fisheries patrol come to stop their illegal fishing; I have never seen dug-out canoes move so fast. We then entered an area where the Nile traversed through Northern Uganda and found we were in a mini-Sudd, surrounded by papyrus swamps. The shores of the Nile were so thick with papyrus that it was impossible to reach dry land, so we were forced to row without alighting from the boat. This meant that bodily functions had to be taken care of over the side – an experience quite lacking in privacy. Eventually, we found some dry land and stopped for a few hours rest, but the mosquitoes were so thick we were glad to start moving again; it was not a comfortable experience.

After a few days we were nearing the border with Sudan where there was a fishing lodge and where we had prearranged a rest stop. We were approaching the lodge early one morning, and everyone was dozing in the rafts, including those who had been allocated to row, but they had tied the rafts together and allowed us to drift with the current. Fortunately, someone awoke at the last moment as we were about to drift on top of a group of hippos and took diversionary action. Otherwise, we would have been history.

This was not to be our only close encounter with hippos. After we had rested at the fishing lodge, we set out for the Sudan border where another herd of hippos had formed a welcoming committee. The expedition had been organized mainly by Hendri, Pete and Natalie, with Hendri taking on the role as team leader. Perhaps because he was young, he felt he had something to prove, and his team mate, Pete, though he was an older, battle-hardened, ex-army type, had taken the decision to let Hendri lead.

Both Hendri and Pete were excellent rafters and, although I had complete confidence in their technical ability, I was beginning to wonder about the wisdom of this leadership arrangement. The doubts were reinforced when Hendri delayed leaving the lodge until the afternoon, and we found ourselves rowing again at night for no particular reason. This time we were looking for a landing site at the location of Gordon's Old Fort – or what was left of it – on the Uganda border. The problem was not so much the rowing at night – we had done that on many occasions – but the fact that we found ourselves in the middle of several groups of very antsy hippos that were hard to see in the dark. We had sat around most of the day doing nothing, and now we were in a precarious situation. The difference between these hippos and those near Murchison Falls was that they had been hunted by the local fishermen and did not much like human beings, while the Murchison Hippos were fat contented pigs. In theory, they should have been out of the water, grazing, but they weren't; they were watching us suspiciously, and we were much too close for comfort.

Hippos have been the cause of more deaths in Africa than any other animal and, sadly, one member of the professional rafters, who had completed the Karuma to Murchison section of the river, later died in a hippo attack on the Zambezi. That night there were a number of close encounters where we suddenly found hippos almost upon us – or we were almost upon them – but somehow we managed to avoid the hippos and stay in the boat. The next challenge was to find a landing site in the pitch dark, but we also accomplished this. This was either a tribute to Hendri and Pete's skills at navigation and seeing in the dark, or there was a certain amount of luck involved. It was with much relief that I put up my tent in the pitch dark because, of course, my torch stopped working at the crucial moment.

The next morning I awoke to find that I had pitched in someone's compound, though the person did not seem to be in the least phased when a strange *mzungu* unzipped his tent and appeared on his front lawn – like Dr Who emerging from the Tardis.

# South Sudan

After exploring Gordon's Fort – or at least the few mud bricks and bits of the iron ship that were left denoting the site – we headed down the river into Sudan. The problem with much of Africa's history is that it has disappeared back into the dust because it was built of mud bricks in the first place which, unlike the stone houses of the western civilizations, dissolves back to the dust within a few short years.

Our expedition was taking place while rebels from the south, who now constituted the Sudan People's Liberation Army, were still at war with the Khartoum-based Government of Sudan. South Sudan had been in some sort of a war for most of the past fifty years, though the combatants had taken a break for nine years in the middle. Fortunately, they were now having another short break since peace negotiations were taking place in Nairobi, and a ceasefire had been agreed. I suppose this was the reason that we had been given permission to travel this route in the first place since the opposing forces were not actually shooting at each other. This was not strictly true, as we found out later, but most of the time they were not shooting at each other.

As we approached the Sudan border, the current in the river became stronger, causing the dinghies to gain speed, and as we zoomed past a knot of people on the shore, we noticed that some of the men were waving at us, so we waved back, happily. It was only after we had passed that it dawned that they were border guards, and they had been flagging us down trying to get us to stop. Oops! At least they hadn't shot at us. Now that we had realized our mistake, our problem was that the current was so strong, since we were approaching the Fula Rapids, that we could not row back. We pulled into the opposite shore and tied our rafts to a bush on the bank. Hendri gathered together our passports and SPLA permit, jumped into the kayak we had towed along and headed for the other shore to make peace with the border guards, meantime telling us not to move from where we were moored.

Unfortunately, he had left us in the blazing sun and we were going to be fried eggs if we did not find some shade, so Pete took the initiative and we moved down the river to moor under cover of some trees. We made camp, and later that evening, Hendri returned with some Sudanese and the news that we were in trouble with the South Sudanese for running the border, and in trouble with him for disobeying his orders. We were all loaded onto a pickup, along with the usual quota of heavily armed Sudanese militia and headed for the customs post. It was the stereotypical African war scene: a battered double cabin pick-up, loaded down with ragged teenagers, toting AK47s, but in this case there were also half a dozen ragged *mzungus* riding along.

By morning some of the professional rafters on the expedition, Hendri, Pete and Bingo, had done a recce  and noted that we could not raft over the first rapid in the Fula Rapids. Apparently it was not so much that the rapid was big – though it looked enormous to me – it was the 'hole' at the bottom, which would suck us underwater, never to be seen again. We therefore carried our rafts and belongings round the first rapid and launched ourselves in at the foot. From thence we would go hurtling down a shoot of turbulent foaming water for about a mile or more until we reached calmer waters, after which there was another series of rapids which we would evaluate one by one to find a strategic line through.

The main purpose of this particular part of the expedition – unlike the usual white-water rafting for tourists – was to stay in the boat; it was not to have the thrill of being thrown out because if we landed in the drink, not only would we get wet, but so would all our supplies, including our camera equipment, laptops and GPS. We did have waterproof boxes in which we stored such equipment, but, despite this precaution, we would definitely be trying to keep everything afloat. With this in mind I was given the simple, though strategic, task of holding on, although I was told that I should also lean on command: left when I heard 'left' and right when I heard 'right'. I thought I could manage that.

We had now been joined by two SPLA soldiers who apparently did not know how to swim, but who showed no apprehension about sitting on a boat about to go through rapids which had been rafted only twice in known history. And one of the previous adventurers had never been seen again!

I climbed into my boat and did what I was told. I was apprehensive, but everyone else seemed to know what they were doing, so I reckoned that it was probably OK. We had a moment at the bottom of the first rapid where we had to come round twice to avoid being sucked into that large hole, but we eventually made it into the mainstream and went hurtling down the longest water-shoot in the world. From there we rafted all the way through the rest of the Fula Rapids, and, when it was over, the professional rafters declared that it was not all that dangerous, that they had rafted through worse spots. It had looked pretty hairy to me, but I was just a doctor who was happy to still be in the boat.

That evening we pulled in to the bank to camp, and Charles, one of the SPLA guys, took off, saying that he was going to shoot a gazelle, or some other living creature, for dinner. He was very trigger-happy and appeared to want to shoot anything that moved. He later told some inquisitive villagers that if they crossed a line he had drawn round our camp, he would shoot them. And I believed him. I think he was having withdrawal symptoms because of the ceasefire, since when Pete, in an unguarded moment, asked him how his AK47 worked, he immediately fired it off, making us all temporarily deaf. Fortunately for the wildlife that evening, they were not within shooting range, and we ate something reconstituted from powder.

Within a few days we were at the front-line of the SPLA and trigger-happy Charles said that he would have to leave us since we would be moving out of his jurisdiction. He told us, helpfully, that we would now be crossing no man's land where the LRA operated, and that we might be killed or captured, but that we would probably be safe if we made it to the forward base of the army of the Government of Sudan forces since he believed they were quite law abiding – if they were not shooting at the SPLA. This was reassuring.

But before we ventured across the lines, Hendri decided that we should pay a courtesy call to the commander of the SPLA front lines. The only problem was that the army camp was a six-hour track from where we had arrived. Hendri and Pete, spoiling for some real adventure, set out, leaving the rest of us in the tender care of Charles (and his line around the camp). We were not sure where they were going since they had made their decision within about a minute, and we were also somewhat concerned that we were camping on the front lines of a war zone, but they took off anyway and returned late that evening to say that they would like to take Dan, the cameraman, back to film the SPLA camp the next day. Wishing to experience what it was like to track through the bush in South Sudan, I volunteered to tag along. I'm glad that I went because it gave me some idea of what Alice and Peace must have gone through. The conditions were extremely harsh, and by the time we arrived back that evening, I had drunk all my water and was thirstier than I could ever remember, while Dan had a blister on his foot the size of a cricket ball. These were the conditions in which little children died, or in which they were killed, if they could not keep up.

When we reached the SPLA forward command, we found that it was in an abandoned village with light artillery set up round the perimeter. The place exuded heat and torpor, and the highlight of the afternoon was lunch in the officer's mess – a mud hut in the centre of which was a table with legs made of heavy artillery casings and top from a metal sheet. Lunch was some sort of stinking slop served in a large saucepan which arrived accompanied by all the chickens of the village and into which everyone communally dipped – including the chickens. It was the most disgusting food I had ever witnessed: the remains of a wild pig which had first been roasted and then boiled. The pot contained the bits which had been left over from previous feasts, including the intestines and other organs, floating in a thin soup. The SPLA soldiers appeared to be enjoying the meal, but they were enjoying even more the spectacle of these white guys trying to pretend they were eating. Hendri felt he had to show the stuff of which he was made and stuck a piece of intestine in his mouth. He then had the choice of puking, gagging, or swallowing the thing. He swallowed successfully, and in that moment I was proud of our fearless leader. The biggest challenge I could see for the SPLA was enduring the heat and the sheer boredom of doing nothing in the Sudanese bush, not to speak of the food. To compensate for this, they had beer made from sorghum, one of the locally grown crops which I suppose would help the time to pass more quickly if they drank enough of it. But I personally did not see how this was possible since it tasted like uncooked fermented flour.

When we arrived back at the river, we headed off quietly down the Nile, hoping that the LRA were not yet aware of our presence. I had come to appreciate the Nile by this time, as I could have a drink at any time I felt like it and did not have to suffer burning thirst. We just dipped our jerry-can into the water, strained it through a cloth and added a sterilization tablet. It was not very cold, but it kept us hydrated and, apart from one of the team members, we did not get gastroenteritis from the experience. When we reached the forward lines of the Government of Sudan army, we were very careful not to sail past this time, and the permission which had been given from the Khartoum government must have been transmitted to the

259

front lines because the soldiers appeared to be expecting us. Either that, or they were used to tourists rafting down the Nile as they did not show any surprise that we had appeared on their battle front. They invited us in, gave us drinks, which we shared from common cups, and, out of the corner of my eye, I saw some soldiers chase down a couple of scrawny chickens. An hour later, a platter of rice and roasted chicken appeared – the chickens must have lost the race – and we noticed that the government army kitchen was certainly better organized than that of the rebels.

# Juba

Later we were waved off by our new friends from the Sudanese army front lines and rowed on towards Juba, the garrison town held by the government in the midst of SPLA territory. The first thing I noticed as we neared Juba was a large church, and, in some ways, this represented what this war was about. The South Sudanese were Christian, while the northerners were Muslim. Bashir, the president of Northern Sudan had tried to impose Sharia law and the southerners were having none of it. After we crossed the border into Sudan, we had met a very fierce looking SPLA Dinka commander who explained: 'we are holding the line between Christianity and the spread of Islam southwards.' And many, including the American evangelicals, believed that this was the basis on which this war was being fought.

We were swept under Juba Bridge, the only bridge across the Nile after Pakwach, where the river left Lake Albert, and we moored below the Mango trees which lined the riverbanks around Juba. (Unfortunately, the Juba Bridge had not had any maintenance for many years, and several years' later part of it collapsed under the weight of an overloaded heavy vehicle.) A bus arrived to take us to the army post and they told us that our boats should be moored at their base on the other side of the river, so they tied the rafts to a police launch, and that was almost the end of our expedition. The police boats took off at such high speed that they almost swamped the rafts, but luckily Pete was aboard and managed to save them.

There is a culture of hospitality in the Moslem world and we were now the guests of the Northern Sudanese, so no matter what they really thought about us, they treated us well because we were their guests. But at the time we wondered what was going to happen to us because they did not speak English, we did not speak Arabic, and we were getting some rather mixed

261

signals. The first thing they did was to give us cold drinks; these drinks were not just cold, they were refrigerated and tasted heavenly. (When I returned from the expedition I used to wake up in the night just so that I could go to the fridge and have a cold drink because it was so sensuous.) This gesture was a promising start, but then we were left wondering what was going to happen because the army guys would not talk to us, except to bring up a problem: apparently we had one more person than they were expecting, and this was a big issue.

Eventually, they put us in a van and drove us round Juba for several hours, but when the van stopped, and we attempted to disembark because it was hot, they barked at us, 'you no move.' So we were somewhat intimidated and wondered if we were being taken for interrogation at the military camp.

After some time they drove us to a locked building and told us that we could now get out of the van. Someone unlocked and threw open the doors, revealing a small supermarket inside.

'Help yourselves, take what you want,' the army Major commanded us.

This was unexpected to say the least, and all the chain smokers in the team – everyone except me – made a beeline for the cigarettes. We were also given juice, biscuits and jam, whatever the supermarket was offering, which was not extensive, but looked like a lot, coming from where we had been.

Four years later, there was peace of a kind in South Sudan, and I was invited to set up some health-centres, one of which was in Juba. I had a meeting with a lawyer, and as I was waiting near his office, I realized that I was right outside the supermarket where we had been taken by the Sudanese army that first day. The whole regime had now changed, but the shop, the merchandise and the owners were still the same.

After stocking up with goodies, we were taken to the home of the Major, where we were put up for the next week. The place was hot and dusty, but for a few hours a day there was electricity, and the fans hummed overhead, giving some respite from the heat and the mosquitoes. There was a bathroom of sorts with a pit latrine which gave me the first opportunity to shave since leaving home. I did not have a razor, however, because Hendri had confiscated all excess baggage when we had reached Pakwach to reduce excess weight for the portage round Fula Rapids, so I had had to hand in my razor and my favourite pillow. Real explorers had beards and certainly did not have a pillow. What was available in the shops in Juba was some kind of lady-shave and was inadequate for the beard I was now sporting, but I hacked it off and appeared in what I thought was a clean shaven state. Bingo just looked up and said, 'Man, what did you do to your face?'

I didn't have a mirror, but when I acquired one to take a look, I saw a scratched chin with random clumps of hair attached. Bingo was right to be concerned.

Another problem I had was the soap, or rather holding onto it. We had a few small bits of soap, and I was relishing my shower from a basin, but for the sake of modesty, I was in the so-called bathroom, which had no windows and therefore little light. I was lathering down with the only precious bit of soap we possessed, when it slipped from my grasp, skittered across the floor, and disappeared down the hole in the floor which was the pit latrine. There was nothing I could do, short of rugby tackling the soap, before it made it to the hole, but I felt very guilty that I had lost the team's only bar of soap. But, instead of confessing my sin, I just kept quiet about it and no one seemed to notice.

On the evening before we left Juba, the Sudanese army laid on an official banquet in a park in the middle of the town. Being Muslim, they did not drink alcohol but compensated for this by eating. When I was sure that all the food had come and I had consumed everything that my gastrointestinal system could possibly cope with, the main course arrived. We were in a garrison town in South Sudan, surrounded by some of the most destitute and poorest people on earth, and we were eating like kings.

Several years later it was surreal to be in Juba again and to witness how it was changing. The banks of the Nile with the Mango trees, where we had landed, had been transformed into restaurants and bars where the night life of Juba unfolded. Where there had once been nothing in the way of women, except a few old hags who were covered up, there were girls in tight jeans, jiving to the music and swigging alcohol. Juba even had its own brewery, making beer which they named White Bull. It was as if the Southern Sudanese were giving the northerners the finger.

But we still had to get through the Sudd, much as we were enjoying the good life in Juba. The only traffic that traversed the Sudd at that time was the barges to re-supply the garrison, plus a few fishermen. These barges took weeks to come down the Nile, and there was lively debate among our army hosts as to how long it would take to get through the Sudd, with estimates ranging from three days to three weeks – rather a wide margin.

We were given a send-off by the army; they having bought us gifts to take with us, and waving us off on our way.

'Give that one to the *muzee* (the old man)' the commander shouted, as he threw across a hat into the raft. I was glad I had distinguished myself in some way. I was also happy to get on our way again because I was very aware that I still had a hospital to build and had now been away for several weeks.

# The Sudd

We paddled off down the Nile towards the area of the Gondakor settlement which had been a staging post south of the Sudd for expeditions into the interior at the time of Baker, Speke and Gordon. But the location of Gondakor Fort had apparently been lost without trace, and no-one seemed certain of exactly where it had been, except that it was somewhere north of Juba.

As evening approached, and we rowed on down the Nile, a great pall of smoke hung over the river, and we heard the lowing of hundreds of cattle. As we drew nearer, we saw that a cattle camp had been established on the bank of the Nile, with the cattle being tended by young people wearing nothing, or in the case of the girls, just a short skirt. Their faces were painted white and their hair was caked and stiff. These were the Mundari people, who lived with their cattle on the banks of the river. As we emerged out of the smoke, they ran along the banks to greet us, diving into the water, laughing and shouting. The army had given us a guide to translate, and that evening we were taken to an army camp on the opposite bank from the tribal peoples and given food and a bed for the night. The evening was hot, and beds, which consisted of string tied across rough wooden frames, were produced and laid out on the compound of the officer in charge. A goat was killed for supper, and a television was wheeled out which was broadcasting CNN; it appeared that satellite TV could reach anywhere in the world, and CNN had reached the remotest corners of the earth.

We were eating supper when we heard an announcement on CNN that there had been another massacre in Northern Uganda by the LRA. Scores of villagers had been rounded up and brutally burned and hacked to death. The news item lasted only seconds, and then CNN moved on to the main news of the day:

a gay marriage in California. Life was full of contradictions. I was enjoying the hospitality of the Government of Sudan, which was supporting the activities of the LRA who had just carried out a massacre in Uganda, my adopted homeland. One could not really make sense of it all, even the fact that I heard the news on CNN in the tribal lands of South Sudan, with the people of the Mundari Tribe just across the river, who still wore no clothes and slept with their cattle.

Life in Africa was sometimes confusing: the atrocities, the harshness and a way of life that had not changed in centuries, standing side by side with mobile phones, GPS and CNN. Unholy alliances facilitated the gruesome murders of ordinary villagers and innocent people, and I was enjoying the hospitality of those complicit in such massacres, because there was no doubt that the support of Khartoum was the main reason why the LRA was still active.

The next morning the army commander insisted that they slay a cow in our honour and send us on our way with some choice steaks. Dan, the cameraman, was worried about the amount of death we were causing, as both sides of this conflict wanted to kill something when we passed through.

Just across the Nile there were thousands of cattle, but none of them were in danger of being slaughtered, since the Mundari viewed them as symbols of prestige and power, and not as a source of food – apart from the small amount of milk which they yielded. We went back across the Nile to visit the tribe, and our army translator enabled us to engage in conversation with the young people, who explained that the elders were back in a village inland while they were looking after the livestock. They brought the cattle to the Nile for feeding and watering, and each of them was responsible for the cattle of their own family. The cattle represented wealth and changed hands for the payment of bride price. If a young man wished to marry, he would need, perhaps, fifty cattle, if the bride was considered strong and beautiful and not wilful or physically flawed. If the bride was imperfect in some way, the price would reduce to twenty or thirty cattle, but a bargain bride would mean some character flaw. The young men were given starter packs of cattle by their fathers and, when they had bred enough stock, they could then make the purchase of a bride. The tribe was polygamous and they could take as many wives as they wished, the only limiting factor being the number of cattle they possessed. This appeared to be a natural way of limiting the number of wives a man could support, and indeed, promiscuity was also contained, since sex outside marriage would ruin the reputation and the value of the potential bride.

As the young man to whom we were talking explained the intricacies of their cultural practices, I noticed that a boy was resting quite comfortably at the rear of a cow, with his hand up the cow's ass, in the manner of a vet carrying out artificial insemination.

'What is that boy doing?' I asked

'He is calming the cow,' was the reply. 'The cow likes it.'

I wondered how he knew that, but I let it pass. These people definitely loved their animals; they slept with them in the camp; they smelled like them, and they burned the dung on the campfires to create smoke to get rid of the flies. They used a mixture of urine and dye to do their hair and they drank the milk. But they would no more think of slaughtering a cow than of killing their own grandmother, and when an animal got old and frail, they took it to market and exchanged it for a goat. The cattle were their pets, and they knew each one of them by name and personality; cattle had never had it so good; the humans were there to meet their every need. This was a way of life which had not changed for generations and had actually been preserved because of the war, as, otherwise, there would have been boatloads of tourists just like us, peering at the spectacle of this tribal people and inevitably changing the culture in the process – as was the case with the Masai of Kenya.

As the Nile meandered on its way north, we were moving between territory held by the Government of Sudan and the SPLA or other militias, some of whom had not quite decided if they were sticking to the ceasefire. We had permits from both sides, but the government side appeared to be more informed that we were in the vicinity, and sometimes there were close encounters, such as the time when our boats became separated, and one boat went through a check-point without stopping, leaving the other rafters to grovel and apologise. But then this gave Pete and Hendri the opportunity to vent their spleens when they caught up.

At another time, someone fired warning shots – at least we assumed they were a warning, since none of us were actually hit. But maybe the guy on the bank with the gun (the one whom we thought had waved at us as we rowed past) was a bad shot. There was also the night when we drifted peacefully past a huge barge going the other way, but no-one appeared to notice since they were high above us in the water. But the next morning we were told that this was a dangerous flash point where active fighting between a government-backed militia and the SPLA was taking place. We had just fluked our way through. A few weeks later, full scale fighting broke out in that same area.

As we drew near the Sudd, the density of the mosquitoes intensified and, if we did not eat supper and get safely zipped in our mosquito-proof tents by nightfall, we became the main dish on the menu. There was also a problem for anyone who needed to leave their tent during the night for the call of nature, as in the morning the person's ass would look something like a baboon's where the mosquitoes had found unprotected raw flesh. Dan and I discovered a small hole in our tent through which mosquitoes were streaming, but which we cleverly repaired with toothpaste; we were real survival experts, challenging all that nature could throw at us!

When we reached Bor on the edge of the Sudd, we found that the outboard motors had arrived ahead of us, having been flown in on a UN plane, so we celebrated the end of our rowing days and could now motor our way through the Sudd, albeit slowly, since the outboard motors were only eight horsepower. They were bolted onto the back of the dinghies, jerry-cans of fuel were taken on board – there being no gas stations nearby – and we were on our way.

On the first night we found a small island of dry land in the middle of the swamp where the family of a fisherman had settled. We joined them on their island, pitched our tents and escaped inside to avoid the mosquitoes which had arrived en masse as darkness fell. As we were lying in our tents, we heard the most heavenly music: the family was singing prayers at the end of the day, and as we peeked out, we found that we were now part of a dense encampment, with dozens of fishermen having pitched their tents. In the morning, we discovered that the daughter of the fisherman, who was quite beautiful, was also deaf and dumb. I found the experience of spending the night with this family strangely haunting. They lived on the edge of the world, eking out an existence in the harshest of conditions, yet they were generous in spirit and marked by a quality of dignity and self-respect which I would not have expected to find in a fisherman's family living in a swamp in the middle of nowhere.

In the Sudd, the Nile spreads out into shallow lakes and waterways over a huge area, with large expanses of papyrus between. The important thing was to be able to navigate one's way through the plethora of confusing channels which, in our case, was greatly assisted by the GPS. There were also fishermen making their living in the Sudd, so from time to time we were able to ask directions. Unfortunately, they did not appear to have much of a sense of distance, since when they told us that something was just around the corner, they might mean several miles and many corners ahead. It was always a nail-biting experience, wondering if we had taken a wrong channel, until we found their landmark. One night, after refuelling, we set off again, when, fortunately, someone realized that we were going back in the direction we had come from; we had drifted around during the refuelling exercise without realizing it.

Not many white people had come through the Sudd, so on the few occasions when we stopped, we were the subject of intense curiosity and were not given much in the way of personal space. The villagers were studying us even more intently than we were studying them, though I found it fascinating meeting pipe smoking women. As we neared the northern end of the Sudd, we found an army encampment, where the main occupation of the soldiers was to make huge rafts of papyrus and float them down to Khartoum where the papyrus mats were sold. They had also collected all manner of dried crocodile skins, though we had met with no crocodiles and only one lone hippopotamus.

After exiting the Sudd, I realized that my part of the expedition was drawing to a close, and I felt the excitement growing that I would soon be on my way home. It had been an interesting expedition, but since it had also involved long periods of enforced inactivity, when I had simply to sit on a raft, it was not my normal style. I had done what I had set out to do, to be the medical person available on this particular part of the expedition, and now that I had fulfilled this commitment I was keen to leave.

Pete had organized a food drop by the UN and was bargaining with the pilot for me to hitch a ride out. The plane flew low over the Nile and dropped some plastic barrels of food to replenish our supplies, before landing at an airstrip several miles away, where they were picking up a security officer doing an assessment of the area. A friendly militia was organized to send some of their men to accompany me back to the airstrip. Several hours later, half a dozen men appeared, wearing nothing but their Y fronts and AK47s. These were my escort back to the airstrip.

After hurried goodbyes – because the militia made it clear that it was not safe to linger in this area – I was squelching through the mud on my way to a plane and back to civilization.

We had to cross several miles of swamp and water channels, sometimes wading up to our necks, and when it became too deep, the men put me in a dugout canoe together with my possessions and pushed me across, while they swam. I was happy there were no crocodiles, and we made it back to the village before nightfall.

The next day I was on the plane to Lokichokia in northern Kenya, the town from which the UN carried out its humanitarian operations into south Sudan, and the following day I was on a plane back to Nairobi and on to Entebbe. I was happy to be home. Much as I appreciated the experience I had gained on the expedition, I was eager to see how the building of the new hospital had progressed in my absence.

# Moving Hospitals

One of the first people who called me when I returned was Justine, a twenty-two year old student whom we had known since she was a child. Her Mother, Joyce, was a teacher in the local primary school in Luweero where Robbie had taught a class each week. Joyce had a hard life, bringing up four children without the support of a husband. Justine was somewhat younger than Lauren, but the two were good friends and played together as children.

One morning, while I was doing my ward rounds at Kiwoko Hospital, I found Joyce had been admitted with severe abdominal pain; she did not have any signs of appendicitis nor of any other condition which could cause peritonitis, yet she had an acute abdomen and was sinking before our eyes. Within a few hours she was dead, and the post-mortem showed that her abdomen was full of pus; she had primary ascending peritonitis, most likely caused by severe pelvic inflammatory disease. She must have been in pain for some time but had hidden it. We were still in a state of shock at the suddenness of Joyce's death, when her children appeared, having come to visit their mother at the hospital. Justine was ten and was carrying food for her mum, with her younger brother strapped on her back. I remember her blank look when we told her that her mother was dead; she could not comprehend that her mother was no longer with her and, in that moment, her life had changed forever.

Subsequently, Joyce's children were taken in by an orphanage beside Kiwoko Hospital, which was run by some American friends, Jay and Vickie Dangers, and after we left Kiwoko, we did not have much contact with Justine for years, except to hear that her brother had died of pneumonia. Then we received a phone call to say that Justine had been diagnosed with bone cancer. She had fibrosarcoma of the leg, an aggressive form of cancer, but the good news was that members of an American family, who were supporting the orphanage, were willing to pay for her treatment in South Africa.

After several months she came back to Uganda, and we understood that the treatment had been successful; she was enrolled at university, and it seemed that she was finally able to set out in life. We now saw her more frequently since she was in Kampala, and she looked to me as a friend and guardian. When she called and told me she had been waiting for me to come back from the expedition because she had developed pain in her chest, it did not ring any alarm bells at first. But when I saw her in person and listened to her chest, I could not hear any breath sounds on one side and diagnosed a pleural effusion.

In the light of her history, this was not good, and further investigations showed that she had a recurrence of the cancer. I contacted the doctor who had treated her in South Africa and consulted with colleagues in Northern Ireland, but their opinion was that any treatment would now only be palliative, and there was no hope of a cure. She went back to her home at the orphanage where a retired British nurse, Jill, had come to work a few months previously. Jill was literally a 'Godsend' who believed that it was her God given purpose at this point in her life to be there for this young girl who was going to die. She loved her and cared for her physical, emotional and spiritual needs over the next six months, as Justine slowly wasted away. During this time Justine never lost her sense of humour, even though she knew she was dying. It was heartbreaking to watch this lovely young girl on her journey to death.

When we received the call that she had died, we were also told that the burial would take place that same day, so we drove to the village and made our way in the rain through the banana plantation where she was to be buried. They were still digging her grave, while the body lay in a simple coffin inside a mud hut as the grave was prepared. Then they brought out the coffin and lowered it into the ground as they sang hymns. Joseph, who was her guardian at the orphanage, tried to say a few words, but he was too choked up; more songs were sung and prayers were offered, and then I was asked if I would say something. I was beyond grief, I could not speak, yet I felt that I owed it to Justine; I could not let her life go without marking her passing.

While I had been standing at her grave feeling the full impact of the sorrow and despair of losing this beautiful young woman, the necessity of hope became clear to me again. Then, slowly and deliberately because it was hard not to break down, I said, 'When we came to Luweero it was a place of skulls and bones, destroyed homes, hopelessness and despair. When we built Kiwoko Hospital, it became a symbol of hope rising out of the ashes. Kiwoko Hospital itself was built using the very stones from homes destroyed by the war. Our mission was to bring hope back, and Kiwoko Hospital became a place of hope where people were healed and new life was brought into the world. Today, as I am in the midst of such palpable despair when we have lost Justine, I realize again that without hope we are lost. Whether it is hope in the resurrection, or hope for a better future, we must never lose our sense of hope because that is what keeps us going. Justine would never have wanted us to lose hope.'

As I struggled to get those words out, I saw that the creation of hope had always been a large part of my own purpose in Uganda. We had been harbingers of hope, through a mission hospital in the bush, through training young people in healthcare, through trying to improve medical standards. And we still believed there was hope for the future, even when we lost the best, like Justine. I stood in the rain and felt my heart torn by sadness as the coffin was cemented into the grave, and at the same time, I understood that if I gave in to cynicism or

274

despair, there was nothing left. And despite the poverty, the unfairness of it all, the frustration and lack of progress in development, if I gave up, there was no meaning. Our role was to bring hope: for the patient, for the community, for the nurse, for our young people who are the future. I might get frustrated, I might get discouraged, I might get tired, I might even become cynical, but I should never give up.

Several years later, an American lady called me to say that she was the guardian of Justine's only surviving brother, Asaph, but she had to move back to the States. I told her to send Asaph to me in Kampala and, thereafter, I became his guardian. He still reminds me of Justine, with his cap of furry hair and his sense of humour. He is at University, doing a degree in health management, but after classes, or during the holidays, I find him working at our workshop, learning every skill he can. He is a truly remarkable boy, hardworking, smart and driven. Asaph is the hope that Justine left behind.

The first phase of the new hospital building was now nearing completion, and we felt that it would be possible to bring this section of the building into use while work continued on the rest of the project. In order for us to run a hospital, there were certain departments which had to be functional. We needed outpatients' and casualty departments, an operating theatre, X-ray, laboratory and wards, plus we needed to have our medical records system up and running. It was an advantage that we were already running a functional hospital, since we knew what was needed. On the other hand, we also had to continue managing our patients without a break. We commenced the process by ensuring that no new patients were admitted for elective or non emergency procedures until we had few patients left in the old hospital. There were still several in-patients whom we could not discharge, and these were transferred to the new hospital by ambulance.

Our staff worked all through the night transferring the patient records, the servers and hardware for the electronic data system, which meant that the least number of patients were inconvenienced, and by the following morning, we had a fully functional patients' record system. People worked tirelessly, transferring hospital furniture and equipment from the old to the new hospital, plus cleaning and scrubbing everything in preparation for the patients' arrival. The transfer went remarkably smoothly, primarily because of the devotion of some staff who did not sleep for forty-eight hours. In a country where there was often a serious lack of work ethic, there were also people who worked with extraordinary dedication and loyalty.

I had a great personal sense of achievement in moving to this purpose-built hospital, even if it was still far from completion, but I was not allowed to savour the moment for long because we found we were facing many new challenges. One of the primary differences between the old and the new hospitals was the sheer scale of things and the number of staff required. Where we had three security guards, we now needed three times that number; where we had thirty nurses, we now needed ninety, so our staff numbers and costs escalated, and although the numbers of patients rose, they did not shoot up overnight. On the other hand, since we now had a sparkling new facility, the patients' expectations and demands also rose. We were called International Hospital, so patients expected international levels of service, but sometimes we were still at local standards.

The standard of nursing in Uganda was not great and, although we had many dedicated nurses, there were problems with those who were poorly trained or had adopted bad work practices. In order to change such practice, many of the nurses had to be re-trained, and we thought it would be easier to train nurses from scratch than to have to reverse poor practice which had become ingrained. Hence, the idea of starting a nursing school was born. We still had a lease on the old hospital building and decided to transform it from a hospital into a nurse training school. The decision to start a nursing school was an expensive one as the tuition we could charge did not come near to meeting the real running costs, but, since we were driven by a vision of making a difference to healthcare rather than simply making money, we decided to push ahead despite the obvious commercial disadvantages.

Nurse training fell under the jurisdiction of the Nursing Council which was ruled by the Nursing Registrar. In nursing terms Rachel was next to God since she appeared to be answerable to no higher authority and, although she was personable, she was a nightmare as the professional in charge of nurse training and nursing standards.

Nurse training and practice in Uganda was lagging years behind modern nursing practices, with student nurses being required to do much bowing and scraping to the senior nursing hierarchy, but with many of the core values and the sense of vocation having been lost. One of the major problems was that nurses gained little practical experience during their training, so that even if they absorbed all they were taught in the classroom, they had no context in which to apply it. It was not uncommon to find nurses who were taking blood pressure readings, but did not appreciate the correlation between falling blood pressure, rising pulse and shock, and therefore did not know when to raise an alarm. Nurses might be taught the correct procedure for making beds, but, if there were no sheets on the beds (government hospitals did not normally provide bedding), they could get no practical experience. Nurses might be taught how to write nursing notes, but, if there was no paper, they would never get actual experience.

Rachel appeared to feel that the way to improve standards in Uganda was to raise the admission criteria for nursing schools so that prospective candidates would require 'O' and 'A' level science, but this had the immediate effect of excluding students from the rural areas, where science was not taught in the schools. Generally speaking, it was only the top schools in Uganda which taught science adequately, while the rural schools either did not offer it at all or taught it poorly. This was a case in which a government bureaucrat aimed for the ideal situation and regulated accordingly but ignored the reality on the ground. This practice could be likened to the story of the American tourist who stopped in the west of Ireland to ask an Irish farmer the way to Dublin. The Irish farmer scratched his head and then said, 'If I were you, I wouldn't start from here.'

But we were where we were in Uganda and had to start from that point. If there was very little adequate education in science, one could not ignore this and set entry requirements for 'A' level which were unrealistic for most students. The education system was interrelated and first needed to be overhauled, and then we could set the ideal standards.

As we prepared to set up the nursing school, we received some excellent news: Rose had finished her Master's programme and was preparing to come back home to join us. She had written asking what she would do when she came back home, and, without hesitation, I offered her the post of head of the school of nursing. So Rose had to meet the challenge of the entrenched bureaucracy of the nursing council. When she left Uganda she had the qualification of an enrolled nurse, almost the lowest qualification on the nursing scale. Now she was a registered board certified nurse from the States, plus she had her Masters in nursing. She had been offered high paying jobs in the US but had chosen to come back home to make a difference in her chosen profession.

The nursing council came for various inspection visits, for which we had to pay travel expenses and an allowance up-front, or else they would fail to turn up. Some of the inspectors were helpful while others were critical, putting up more hurdles, and the process moved at snail's pace. I told them that

278

there was no donor with deep pockets behind this project, and the delays were costing me money. I think this was difficult for them to appreciate, in that they were not used to dealing with a private individual who wanted to get things done quickly, but eventually, we were given a registration and allowed to recruit our first students. Our nursing school was providing more capacity to train nurses at no extra cost to the government, but it was difficult for those in the public sector to appreciate this. They were used to making the rules while the usual applicants, such as the mission hospitals and aid agencies, played the role of supplicants begging for favour. The fact that I had little patience for bureaucracy seemed to come as a surprise.

Instead of Rachel's unlimited powers being checked, the situation was left unresolved, until some unknown person became so frustrated they took the law into their own hands, and Rachel was assaulted and beaten up. This was obviously no way to settle such matters and was most unfortunate for Rachel herself, such that she feared for her personal safety and resigned. This practice of people taking the law into their own hands was not uncommon if they felt that the system was unfair and that the only way to deal with it was to make their own law.

Rose was an inspiration to her students, since she was a living demonstration that nursing was a worthy vocation. She did not just teach the academic subject matter, but befriended and mentored the students, with the result that the attitude of these new students was different. I was stopped in the street by the administrator of another hospital where our students had gone for practical experience.

'Your students are a breath of fresh air,' he told me. 'They remind me of how our nursing students used to be many years ago. They are keen and eager and take pride in what they are doing. Why are they so different?'

One of the goals we had was to give nurses a sense of vocation, and we appeared to be achieving it. It might be a small number of students we were training, but they were noticeably different and our nursing school was the seed of greater things to come.

# He has a gun

A couple of years after I had made my rafting trip down the Nile, the South Sudan Peace Accord was ratified, and the Northern Sudanese handed over control of South Sudan to the civilian arm of the SPLA. John Garang, the long time guerrilla leader of the SPLA, was named Deputy President of Sudan and President of South Sudan; a parliament of South Sudan was set up and sharing of the oil wealth agreed between the north and south. A federal arrangement was agreed for an interim period, at the end of which the South Sudanese would vote on either seceding or continuing to be part of greater Sudan. Flights from Entebbe to Juba were resumed so that it was now possible to make the journey to Juba in one and a half hours (as opposed to the six weeks it had taken by the Nile route).

I returned to Juba to explore setting up a health centre and found that it had not changed much, apart from the UN camps with scores of white Land-cruisers parked in compounds beside air conditioned prefabs. Tented camps had sprung up along the banks of the Nile to accommodate the contractors who descended on South Sudan as part of the planned massive reconstruction project. The price of a night in a tent ranged from $60 to $120, and the price for a prefab was over $200 per night; those who were in the hospitality business were making a fortune, as was the case in all war torn regions.

We decided to rent a prefab in one of the camps to set up a clinic, even though it cost $4,000 per month in rent, and sent a doctor, nurses, drugs and medical equipment from Kampala. There was immediate demand for the service, but since the prices in Juba were inflated by the influx of contractors and aid agencies, we had to charge relatively high rates, and the clinic served mainly the staff of these agencies and government workers. Hiring the prefab would only be a temporary expedient, and I began looking for a permanent building which we could lease at a more realistic rate.

I heard through the grapevine that an elderly gentleman had returned from Khartoum to rent out his house in Juba. We visited him and found him to be a gracious old man with many tales of life in Khartoum during the war. Twenty years ago he had been a minister in the previous South Sudanese government before that particular peace agreement broke down. Now his family were scattered all over the world, and he had not been back to Juba for over a decade. The house had a crack in the gable caused by heavy shelling during the war, and he was keen to have the crack repaired. I enjoyed hearing more of the history of Sudan first hand, and we amicably agreed a price and the terms of the lease under which we would also repair the crack and renovate the house. Within a few days we had visited a lawyer, signed the lease, and paid a year's rent in advance.

Within a couple of weeks, my men travelled to Juba with their building equipment to carry out the renovations. The only problem was that the gentleman had still not moved out, though he apparently had no objection to our builders getting on with the work. He had moved most of his furniture, and though he promised that he was moving, he stayed put; so I made another trip to Juba to talk to him and try to sort out the situation. The owner now seemed to have changed his mind and decided to stay on in the house, but our lawyer assured me that the contract was quite clear, and he had no right to be in the house at all, so on this basis, I decided that our only option was to continue working around him and hope that he would leave. Unfortunately, he appeared to have hardened his attitude and told us unceremoniously to get out – perhaps on the basis that the crack in the gable had been repaired by this time.

Since we had reached a stalemate, the other option was that he would give us our money back and we would cut our losses and go, but he flatly refused, saying dismissively that the money had already been spent. He seemed to believe that, as we were foreigners, we did not have much in the way of redress in South Sudan and that, as a Sudanese, he could handle the situation as he pleased. The Sudanese had a saying 'Sudan for the Sudanese', and although they needed help from foreigners to rebuild their country, they were diffident towards outsiders.

The ex-minister was a tall, heavily built Dinka who carried a stout stick which he was not afraid to use, and when he commanded the workers to leave, he backed this up by lashing out with the stick. I happened to be there at the time and witnessed his actions, but I didn't quite realize he also had another weapon concealed in the house. As I looked on, he reached for a pouch and started loading a gun. It was time to leave rather fast; we were not about to argue with a man with a gun – even if he was old.

This was not the first time someone had pulled a gun on me, but on the previous occasion it had been thieves and not a seventy year old ex-government minister, and I didn't really know how to react to this situation. I had paid ten thousand dollars, we had repaired his house, all our building equipment and supplies were still there, and he had ordered us off the premises at gunpoint. I later realized that many of the Sudanese were quick to resort to violence to settle disputes, but at the time I had no idea how things were normally handled, and I just hoped that there was some higher authority to which he was answerable. We went straight to the police and reported that we had been threatened at gunpoint, to which the police responded that we would need to write a letter through a lawyer, then go to the Chief Prosecutor's office and get an order from this office for the police to take action. At that point they could open a case, and we could file our complaint.

'But he threatened us with a gun,' I remonstrated, 'Is that not an offence in itself?' since even in Uganda it was an offence for which the police would make an arrest. But apparently this was not enough, and I needed to follow their system.

The process of making the complaint took all day, and calling the old gentleman before the police and the chief prosecutor took several weeks, but eventually, he was instructed to pay back the ten thousand dollars and to give us our equipment and supplies. The fact that we had already spent several thousand dollars repairing his house was our loss, and the last we heard was that he was in negotiations with other foreigners to rent out the house again. He probably planned to get the renovations completely finished before he kicked them out. We felt that we had got off lightly – at least we got our money and our equipment back.

I was not about to let an old man with a gun put me off, and we continued to search for a permanent site on which to build a clinic. Eventually I found a suitable plot, the arrangement this time being that we would lease the plot for ten years and build our health centre which would then revert to the owner at the end of the lease. Like many war torn areas such as Kabul or Darfur, rents were inflated and very favourable to any local property owner. After ten years, the owner would not only have received rent for the period but would also own the building – not a bad deal. With this arrangement in place, we were able to construct a purpose built health-centre.

One of the main grass-roots organizations in South Sudan is the church. The Episcopal Church of Sudan was running a small clinic in Yei to the west of Juba which was being supported by Church Mission Society Ireland. CMSI requested me to build and equip a new clinic for the church in Yei and train clinic health workers. They had obtained funding from Irish Aid for a tripartite arrangement between CMSI, The Church of Sudan and International Medical Group. Hence, we constructed and equipped the clinic and trained the Sudanese health-workers at IHK in Kampala. There were two English volunteers, John and Poppy Spens, supervising the project and, thanks to their commitment and the collaboration of the various bodies, this clinic became very busy, with two and a half thousand patients being seen every month. As a result, we were asked to repeat the arrangement in Lanya, a small town between Juba and Yei, where we also constructed a health centre and trained Sudanese health workers.

I returned to South Sudan after a gap of eighteen months to inspect the new buildings in Lanya and Juba, flying into Juba, and then travelling by road (more correctly dirt track) for several hours to this very rural area. We drove back to Juba the same evening where I found that the main roads in the town had been paved since my last visit. It may have been only a few kilometres of tarmac road in the whole of South Sudan, but since it was in the centre of the town, it made a great difference to the feel of the city.

Juba had grown rapidly, and there was now tangible evidence of development. Among other changes, the night life was throbbing, and Ugandans had even come to Juba for the weekend to party – interesting choice of locations. As I stood on the banks of the Nile, chatting to a Sudanese who had recently returned from Australia to help rebuild his country, I felt hopeful that South Sudan had a chance of a good future. However, there would be many preconditions to be met if this piece of dusty earth were to become a functional jurisdiction: if the various tribes could be at peace with themselves, if the peace accord between North and South held, if South Sudan benefited from the oil revenues, and if the infrastructure could be rebuilt with adequate roads, hospitals and schools.

If all these things were to happen, then South Sudan might emerge as a real country. Rwanda was in worse shape after the genocide but managed to pull itself back together as a country, but Somalia had disintegrated into warring factions and anarchy. I did not yet know which fate would befall South Sudan, but I could only hope for a good future; the people certainly deserved better.

There were many challenges which South Sudan would need to overcome if it were to develop as a country, one of which was simply the fact that it was landlocked like Uganda, Rwanda and Eastern Congo, which made the cost of getting goods into the country high. The paradox was that in countries such as Uganda, Congo and South Sudan, some of the poorest countries in the world, the cost of doing business was often astronomical. The reason was due to inefficiencies, lack of frugality, wasteful public expenditure and poor value for money for public contracts. I was brought up in a farming community in which farmers had a philosophy that they could not spend the money they made in a good year in case the following year was lean. Uganda was poor, but most times any sense of frugality was lacking, plus many of the commodities which were imported were expensive, due to unnecessarily high added costs.

Most goods came into this region through the port of Mombasa, but containers often stayed in Mombasa for a month or more before they were released, and the longer a container stayed, the higher the charges. The system of goods coming through Kenya may have been beyond South Sudan or Uganda's control, but the government could have lobbied for the swiftest and cheapest means of transit for its goods since all extra costs were added to the purchase price. There was practically no functional East African railway network, yet rail transport was far cheaper than road, and the further inland one travelled the more the roads were broken up and, at times, impassable. When eventually goods did make it to Kampala, which was a hub for the region, they were stored at an inland container depot, and the paperwork was begun, but the system was so slow that at one point there was a strike by the clearance agents themselves because they were so frustrated by the speed at which the Revenue Authority moved – or rather didn't move. These were the very agents who gave the URA officials 'facilitation' to move their particular paperwork to the top of the pile, but despite this, very little moved anywhere, and the goods accumulated demurrage charges which were added to the final price for the consumer.

All goods which came into the region, not only had taxes added, but had charges for storage, customs clearance, port charges, transport charges and handling charges. Also bureaucrats appeared to feel that time was free and did not think anything of having an agent wait around for days, or even weeks, while they slowly did their paperwork. Goods were made unnecessarily expensive by adding these extra costs through obvious inefficiencies and bureaucratic hurdles. All of the countries in the region would have done better by making their systems flow faster and more smoothly, and reducing additional costs on goods entering, but there appeared to be vested interests in keeping the status quo. Those who owned the port facilities were collecting extra charges through delays; road transporters were making money because the railways were in a state of collapse; tax officials would lose the 'facilitation' if it was a simple system; internal container depots were getting extra storage charges because of delays; and there was much employment for agents, middle men and gofers who helped expedite the whole process.

While all these vested interests were in control, it was unlikely that things would change much, and the land locked countries would continue to pay over the odds just to get merchandise onto their soil and into the hands of the consumer. And this was just one small challenge among so many others which faced South Sudan on its journey to become a functional state.

# Flouting the rules

As we opened the new hospital, established the nursing school and set up a clinic in South Sudan, we were absorbed in what we were doing, but apart from work there was also the normal buzz about life in Kampala: the state of permanent chaos and unpredictability which pertained to the business of ordinary living. Activities, such as driving or getting to work, were a challenge in themselves. Dealing with the police was an art, and learning how to protect oneself from petty thieving was part of everyday life.

The rule about living in Uganda was to expect no one to obey the rules because everyone thought he was the exception. Many people thought they could get away with taking huge risks and live to tell the tale. It was an everyday occurrence to see taxi drivers pass on blind corners, but by the time one of them had learned that the odds were not always with him, he was dead and had caused the death of his passengers. Breaking the rules also included breaking the laws of human decency. People justified this on the basis of need and reasoned that if they did not take an opportunity when it presented itself, someone else would and they would lose out. This rationale was applied irrespective of the effect on others, often with tragic consequences.

A fuel tanker crashed on the Trans-Africa highway – not an unusual occurrence – and some people thought they saw an opportunity to improve their lives. There was free fuel in the overturned tanker that had careered off the road, and all they had to do was get along with their jerry-cans and take it. These people had seen reports of such accidents in the past when the oil tankers burst into flames, incinerating everyone, but the opportunity was just too tempting, so they rushed along regardless of risk. Unfortunately for those poor souls, this tanker also burst into flames, and everyone within a radius of fifty feet went up in smoke, but this was not the end of the tragedy. Along came a speeding taxi, the driver anxious to finish his journey and pick up another load of fare-paying passengers. He saw the billowing smoke but did not slow down and so barbequed himself and his passengers. Next there came another tanker, which the survivors frantically tried to warn, but it was going too fast, so the driver added his tanker and himself to the conflagration.

An Asian gentleman was crossing the road to the main post office in Kampala. He was a visitor and wished to purchase an airtime card, but he was struck by a car as he crossed. Fortunately, he was not critically injured and the driver stopped, put him in his car and drove him to hospital, like a good Samaritan. When he arrived at the hospital, the driver took the injured man to the casualty department and removed his valuables for safekeeping. Then he left, taking his victim's money and valuables with him, and that was the last he was ever seen. Whether the temptation was just too much, or whether he had planned to rob the man is an open question, but he left the patient with nothing. It was common practice that the first thing a passer-by did when he came upon a road accident was to rob the victim. A friend of mine was involved in an accident and realized that the passer-by had not come to help, but to steal his mobile phone, and he pleaded with him to first call an ambulance. When Angus, the architect, came upon an accident and was phoning for an ambulance while bending over the victim, trying to get some details, someone snatched the phone out of his hand. As a result the ambulance crew could not find the patient. The goal of gaining some immediate benefit drove people both to take great risks and show extreme callousness.

Moses was the doctor who ran the clinic in Lira. He liked to work up-country and opted to go to Lira when we opened that clinic. This was unusual and gratifying, in that most doctors wanted to stick around Kampala, and it was more difficult to get good medical personnel to work up-country. He was the key man at the clinic, providing the leadership, expertise, and the organizational capability to keep things running smoothly. His home was in Kisoro in the far west of the country near the Congo border, and he took leave at Christmas to visit his grandmother. He boarded the night bus in Kampala for the journey of at least ten hours and went to sleep in the back of the bus. Thieving was always worse during the Christmas season. Whether the thieves had a need to provide presents for their families, or they reckoned that people had more money, Christmas was high season for burglaries, thefts and hold-ups. Highway robbery was common, with the thieves employing various tricks to get the motorist to stop. One was to throw an egg at the windscreen, and when the driver stopped to clear the mess, the robbers were lying in wait. Another was to pretend to be injured and then rob the victims when they stopped to help. Buses were a common target since the thieves could net the belongings of more than fifty people at a go.

While Moses was asleep, thieves were planning a highway robbery. They obstructed the main road with big stones so that the bus would have to stop, but it was in the dead of night, the visibility was poor, and the bus was travelling fast, so the driver crashed into the stones, overturning the bus. Half a dozen people were killed instantly and many more injured. The thieves were not put off by the disaster and loss of life, but entered the bus and stripped the dead and dying of their possessions. The dead were later identified and their names published in the newspaper, apart from one unknown man. But Moses failed to arrive at his grandmother's home, and the unidentified man was later identified as Moses. We had lost one of our best men. At the end-of-year meeting, which was supposed to be a recognition of the year's achievements, a pall hung over the proceedings, and afterwards little knots of staff hung around, with people fighting back the tears. We had lost a family member. The best in Uganda had been lost because of the worst.

The carnage on the roads was so bad that the Ministry of Transport introduced a law forcing all minibuses, buses and trucks to have speed governors fitted. The governors cost between 600,000 and 800,000 shillings ($300 - $400) and the cost was borne by the owner. The vehicles which traversed the roads at exceptionally high speeds were the buses because they were powerful, but light, and the worst accidents involved speeding buses, so a law which enforced a reduction of their speed was desirable.

Subsequently, I was travelling on the road which linked Uganda to Sudan and found several buses bearing down on me at great speed. The usual technique was for the bus to come right up behind the vehicle in front and then give a blast of the air-horn, scaring the driver off the road. None of the buses which passed me could have been using speed governors because they were low flying planes. Since speed governors had recently been introduced, one would have thought that serious action would have been taken by the police to ensure compliance, but this was not the case. The police were stopping buses and checking that they had speed governors, but so long as the device was seen, it was passed, and the fact that buses were still death-on-wheels did not appear to register with the police. Speed governors were introduced for the purpose of achieving a reduction in speed, but the result was never achieved because the speed governors had been disconnected.

New traffic laws were made fairly regularly, but new and ingenious ways of breaking these laws were conceived so that the introduction of the laws was meaningless. The wearing of crash-helmets by *boda boda* riders was made compulsory – very commendable. However, in order to ensure his safety, it was necessary for the motorcyclist to actually *wear* the helmet on his head, but *boda boda* cyclists had a tendency to ride with the helmet over their arm, or fastened to the handlebars, and this was acceptable to the police so long as a helmet was in sight. Was I missing something here? Was the helmet supposed to be protecting the handlebars or the arm?

Since the government had gone to all the trouble to draft these laws and pass them through cabinet and parliament, what was the point unless they were enforced? Either the law should be enforced in a manner that worked, or we should stop going through the motions – unless the reason for such laws was to generate business for those who sold speed governors or helmets, but I would never have been so cynical as to think such a thing.

Having lived in Uganda for many years and witnessed first-hand how the laws were universally flouted, I was interested in how other countries ensured their citizens complied with the law. The story is told that men from Mars were studying the earth, trying to understand which creatures were in charge, and decided that dogs were in charge. The reason was that they saw people taking their dogs for walks, but when the dog did a poo, the person cleaned up after it. Their rationale was that if human beings were cleaning up after dogs, then dogs must be in charge. When I used to jog on the streets and parks of Northern Ireland, before I came to settle in Uganda, I would have to watch where I put my feet, but since that time, laws have been passed, making dog owners responsible for cleaning up the mess. This dealt with the problem of the dudu on the pavements, but also resulted in dog lovers walking round with little bags of dog poo in their pockets.

What surprised me was that 90% of dog owners conform to the law. If I made the obvious comparison with Uganda, where laws were passed and then ignored, what was the difference? A law was introduced, requiring everyone riding *boda bodas* to wear crash helmets, but few riders and almost no passengers wore crash helmets. The reason given by the passengers for failing to comply with the law was that they might get their

292

heads dirty, yet in Rwanda, everyone on a *boda boda* wore a helmet, including the passengers. So why could the English get people to pick up dog poo and the Rwandans get passengers to wear crash helmets, but in Uganda any law that was not convenient was ignored. The reason appeared to be that authorities in other jurisdictions were consistent in their enforcement so that people got into the habit of obeying. In Uganda, laws were not enforced consistently: the police were either too harsh or too lenient, or were happy to take a bribe to look the other way.

The public transport system in Uganda not only had buses but *matatus* (minibuses), plying the roads. Fortunately, we were generally in the position of having our own vehicle, but there were occasions when we had to resort to public transport. On one such occasion we had driven from Pader and were just approaching Karuma Falls, when our vehicle lost power, despite the fact that we were going downhill, and then the car came to a complete standstill. This was not a good sign, and there was also another problem with the place where we had chosen to break down. There was absolute silence in the car as I looked out the window and twelve pairs of eyes stared back at us. Their expressions were deadpan and they did not appear particularly interested in our fate. As if to emphasis the point, they turned and mooned us, their pink inflamed backsides shining in the sunlight.

'What will we do now?' I asked out loud,

'Don't get out of the car,' Robbie warned. 'Those things are dangerous.'

Of all the places between Pader and Kampala where we could have broken down, we had come to a standstill in the midst of a family of baboons. As we sat there pondering, we heard the sound of another car approaching. Help was on the way, the people in the car would see that we had broken down and would give me a lift to the nearest trading centre. But the occupants of the car just waved at us as we tried to flag them down. They made the assumption that we had stopped to look at the baboons, and I could not get out to tell them differently.

'Now we are cooked,' I thought. 'Everyone who approaches will just wave at us and drive past.'

I desperately tried the ignition again and again and finally the car spluttered to life, amidst a cloud of thick black smoke. It was not a healthy sound, but the vehicle inched forwards and we made it through the baboons and on to the Karuma Falls trading centre, where the car died completely. The consensus of opinion was that the local mechanics would not be up to the job, and the owner of a local lodge kindly offered to allow us to park the vehicle in his yard until a mechanic could be summoned from Kampala. It was now around six p.m., and since the accommodation in Karuma was limited, we opted to travel to the next town of Masindi.

Within a remarkably short space of time we were loaded into a taxi, heading towards Kampala. This was one of those local taxis – the variety that has a push start – the driver jumps out and pushes. There were several windows covered in plastic sheeting, since the glass had gone missing, the back door was tied with rope, and the shock absorbers were a thing of distant memory. Despite the less than pristine mechanical condition, the vehicle moved along smartly – particularly down the hills. We made frequent stops to allow various passengers to disembark, and, since we had to clamber out several times, the remaining passengers suggested that the *bassungu* (white people) move to the very back seat, where we would be out of the way. The occupants of the taxi were friendly, striking up conversations, and there was an air of camaraderie and shared hardship. When we reached the next main trading centre, the driver decided that he didn't want to go any further and threw everyone out. We didn't mind since he put us on another taxi bound for Masindi, but there was much haggling with other passengers who had paid their money and were getting short changed.

Our Masindi taxi seemed to be of a higher quality since it started with a key, and all the windows were intact. But against these gains our seat was not properly bolted down, hence, when we accelerated, we were tilted back, and when we braked, we shot forward, so we had to anchor ourselves firmly by holding on to the bar in front.

The taxi set off at a leisurely pace; we were not fully loaded and the driver beeped his horn at every passing stranger, dog, tree, or random object, in the hope of another fare. Darkness was falling as we turned off the main road on to the gravel road to Masindi, and as the roads and the visibility got worse, the driving got faster and more reckless. Fortunately, I could not see much from where I was sitting, but Robbie, seated in the front, was having a white knuckle ride. The driver overtook on blind corners and put on his main beam to blind oncoming vehicles as a matter of course. We gratefully disembarked in Masindi, still in one piece, but this random sample of *matatu* driving confirmed my opinion: riding a *matatu* might be a very efficient way to travel, but was the Ugandan equivalent of Russian roulette.

The inconsistency of enforcement of the law meant that some people paid heavily for minor infractions, while others broke the law with impunity and got away with it. In some cases, people literally got away with murder, while others paid heavily for minor offences.

A wife found her husband in bed with another woman and threw sulphuric acid over them both. It was not what one would call a crime of passion; it must have been premeditated, since she happened to be carrying acid with her in a plastic jerry-can at the time. She was charged with assault and might be charged with attempted murder, depending on the extent of the injuries, because there was no specific law in Uganda to deter would-be acid throwers. Some got off with six months, others never went to jail at all, so there was little deterrent in the mind of an acid thrower, but the victims were often blinded, disfigured and suffered horribly.

A man committed a traffic offence and then tried to escape the police by driving away from the 999 patrol. He was unsuccessful, and when they caught up with him, they beat him up and threw him in the back of the pick-up under their feet. By the time they arrived at the police station, he was found to be dead – he had suffocated. Whatever his traffic offence, he paid with his life.

A woman borrowed some money but failed to pay it back, so the debt collector impounded one of her vehicles; the dispute escalated and the woman wished to get the man off her back, so she hired some men to persuade him to leave her alone. The men she hired ensured that he never bothered her again – he was found dead the next day. He paid a high price for seeking to retrieve the money he was owed.

A policeman's wife died in mysterious circumstances, and the policeman was arrested since the crime was witnessed by a relative, and the evidence pointed to the husband. But by the time the case was due in court, the relative had disappeared, so the case was dropped, amidst emotional scenes by the policeman and his supporters. Stories later appeared in the press that the relative had been picked up on a motorcycle and spirited away after the crime. Oddly, the police did not bother to find out what had happened to their witness, nor did they appear to feel it was suspicious that she had gone missing at this crucial time. It was only when the story reached the press, and there was a public outcry, that the police reopened the case and the officer was re-arrested.

An employee was caught red handed, stealing, and admitted her guilt, but by the time she was taken to the police she had found a clever lawyer who told her to deny everything. The magistrate was bribed and released her immediately, so she did not serve a single night in the cells. Later the file went missing, the police officer in charge of the case was transferred several times, the magistrate went on a course, and the authorities showed little interest in pursuing the case – so it was dropped.

Uganda was a relatively free society; it was not the same state as it had been under Idi Amin, when people disappeared in the boots of cars never to be seen again. It was true that those classified as posing a national security risk could find themselves held in police cells or in a safe house, and at times there seemed to be a fine line between 'national security threat' and 'political threat'. Therefore Uganda was not perceived as an egalitarian society, but a society of elites, where some were punished harshly, while others escaped without penalty. The downside of checks and balances was that the law was so often contested, debated, and inconsistently enforced, that it often failed to be a deterrent.

In Rwanda, a minister, or senior public servant, might find himself languishing in jail on corruption charges at the behest of the President, but in Uganda pursuing corruption was under the jurisdiction of the DPP and the courts. There was an independent judiciary and various courts of appeal right up to the constitutional court. And the educational system produced ten times more lawyers than doctors – perhaps to ensure that the letter of the law was adhered to! The law in Uganda was based on the British system of justice and had the same high standards of proof, such that a person was deemed innocent until proven guilty. Unfortunately, the police and the Department of Public Prosecution seldom brought the necessary proof to meet the standards and fulfil the chain of evidence. So it was the norm for witnesses to go missing, documents to be mislaid, the police to lose interest, or the magistrate to be influenced. There was also the constitutional right to bail and of appeal, and hardly any time was served behind bars by those who had money to hire a good lawyer or grease the system. Only the poor, the unrepresented, or the severely politically impaired languished in jail.

The Ugandan system was based on the view that it was better that 99 guilty men go free than one innocent person be condemned, but the result of all this freedom was that few people had confidence in the process of governance or the fairness of the law. Therefore, Uganda was not perceived to be an egalitarian society but a society of elites, where some were punished harshly, while others escaped without penalty. This resulted in increasing lawlessness, evidenced by the flouting of traffic laws, the growth of mob justice, and theft on a widespread scale. From such behaviour it was a small step to throwing acid, or organising an assassination. We had freedom, but we did not have the competence or the systems to police that freedom, with the result that law and order in the society was slowly breaking down.

# Recycling

Robbie's car was getting a bit long in the tooth, so I had bought a second-hand vehicle in Dubai and organised for it to be shipped to Uganda. When I was notified that the car was on its way, I asked Charles to go to Mombasa to drive it back to Kampala, and knowing how rife thieving was in Mombasa Port, Charles decided to get there before the ship docked. Part of the appeal of this particular vehicle had been that it came with a small TV screen, which could show DVDs, or even television, and being a parochial boy, I was very taken with this gadget.

Charles arrived to find that the vehicle was completely dead and could not even be driven off the ship because the computer, which was necessary to get any life into the car, had been stolen. Naturally, the electric window switches had also been stolen. He scoured the whole of Mombasa to find a replacement computer and eventually found one at an inflated price. This at least enabled him to get the car started, which was when he discovered that there was no TV screen either. Thieves had stripped out any electrical item of value, while the vehicle was still on the ship, so I could not even blame the usual suspects from the Mombasa Port. Such thefts seemed to happen to me constantly, and I wondered if I was a special case but decided that I was no different from anyone else who happened to live in Africa. Everyone experienced the same kind of thing and our reaction was often TIA – 'This is Africa.' Then we had a laugh, because what else could we do.

I had left my car around six in the evening, when it was still light, and returned at eight, after it was dark, to find that the guard was still there, and everything appeared normal – except that someone had shattered the back window, reached in and stolen my laptop. I had been jogging at the regular Monday evening *Hash* at which over one hundred of us got together for a jog and some social activities afterwards. It was a good way to start the week and blow away the stresses of a Monday, through hard physical exertion, though all the good we did was immediately undone by the liberal amounts of beer which were consumed.

*The Hash* was a worldwide fraternity and was referred to as a drinking club with a running problem. Generally speaking, hashers were expatriates working in a foreign country, but the Kampala *Hash* was unique, having been largely taken over by Ugandans, with a smattering of expatriates. It was a great social leveller because it did not matter if one was a managing director, a student, or whether one came from an embassy or a slum – we all smelled equally disgusting after a run. The alarm in my car had not gone off, and the guard swore he had seen and heard nothing. Unfortunately for him, the police didn't believe him and he then spent the next few weeks in jail. Something else which bothered me was how the thieves knew I had a laptop in the car in the first place, since the windows were tinted and no-one could see what was inside. I had probably been trailed by the thieves who saw me leave the hospital with the laptop and followed me to the hotel. A syndicate, it was believed, was stealing laptops and selling them in the neighbouring countries, so there had been an epidemic of laptop thefts. For example, an office worker left his laptop on his desk while he went to the door to greet a colleague and returned to find that the laptop was gone; someone had reached through the open window and stolen it.

I had lived in Africa long enough to know not to leave any valuables in a vehicle, but I thought I had taken the necessary precautions. I had been lulled into a sense of complacency because the car had a very loud alarm, was parked in an enclosed hotel car park, with an armed guard standing ten feet away, so how could anyone possible steal from such a secure location?

Thieving was a business, with different specialist professionals serving the demands of a free market economy. One particular business which was self-perpetuating was the demand for vehicle spare-parts, with the supply chain itself creating more demand. This type of business was not new and had apparently been going since colonial times. A friend working in Kampala told me that his parents, who had lived in Uganda in the sixties, had a hubcap stolen from their Volvo. They visited the spare-parts market, where they inquired if anyone could supply the hubcap. The dealer asked them to wait, while he sent his boy out to bring one from the store, and to their delight, he returned with the exact type of hubcap they needed. But when they returned to their vehicle they realised that they still had only three hubcaps – they had bought their own hubcap, stolen while they waited!

It was common to see vehicles with gaping holes where the sidelights should be because these were a favourite item to recycle in the used auto-parts industry. Preferred items were sidelights, electric window switches, and wing-mirrors, all of which could be stolen in the twinkling of an eye. The sidelights and wing-mirrors could even be stolen while the person was still sitting in the car. I went through a difficult period of not being able to keep the lights on the car, having three sidelights stolen within the space of two days. I replaced the first one, and no sooner was it replaced than it was stolen again, but this time they took the other one as well to make it a set. To add insult to injury, I was then stopped by the police who threatened to book me for not having sidelights. I was not a happy man since I blamed the police in the first place for my misfortune, who instead of being out trying to catch the criminals, were trying to arrest me.

In order to replace the stolen parts, one had to buy from the very market that dealt in the stolen parts, so one might be buying back one's own lights, thus creating a cycle of demand. It was the perfect business model. Motorists resorted to all kinds of devices to retain their sidelights and switches. Sometimes they marked them with the car number, but this had little effect. They tried gluing them, but, in the case of the switches, the upholstery was then ripped out along with the switches, making the damage worse. Cementing round the screws helped delay things, but the thieves burrowed through the cement.

As well as the businessmen in the car parts recycling trade, Kampala had its share of conmen, fake goods, and people pretending to be something they were not. I was amused by a letter in the daily newspaper where someone complained that he had bought fake water. How could water be fake, I wondered. People complained about fake electronic goods, fake drugs and fake hardware supplies. Young Ugandans use the word 'fake' commonly, and when I asked them to define a fake person, they were somewhat unclear, but assured me that many people were fake. The terminology summed up their view of society, which reflected cynicism about the accepted value systems where image was more important than substance. The clothes someone wore or the car he drove was what impressed people and, unfortunately, these accepted values did not promote hard work, good character, or high moral attributes.

Image was seen as important and many men strove to have the right clothes or to drive the latest car, but in the case of women it was not necessarily the western stereotype of image or beauty which was appreciated, though the western perception of beauty was also percolating through the society. There were many African women who had a certain curvaceousness and fullness of figure, which was seen as more attractive than the skinny western models. The 'akabina kanene' (big bum) was still appreciated, and in the case of men with increasing girth, they were perceived to be prospering.

Many African chiefs and leaders are literally big men and their sheer bulk contributes to their presence, Idi Amin being one notable example, so my own lack of flesh was taken to reflect poorly on my wife who must not be feeding me properly. Presence was important, and, on meeting a well known politician, I commented that he had put on weight. He fondly patted his stomach and good-humouredly remarked that this was his 'patriotic front' and that, as a politician, he needed to show that he was a man of substance. Some men had potbellies as evidence of their prosperity, and it was said that one could gauge how long a traffic policeman had been in that job by the size of his stomach.

There was so much unemployment in Kampala that the majority of people had to hustle for a living. Some masqueraded as businessmen or security officials, but were actually thieves and conmen. I was at an Irish embassy function when I happened to strike up a conversation with a well dressed gentleman seated next to me.

'What is your connection with Ireland?' I asked him.

He was happily partaking of the free food, and, between mouthfuls, he told me that he had gone to Dublin University.

'Which one?' I asked. With this question the guy became extremely vague and appeared to lose his appetite. Putting down his plate he muttered an excuse and headed for the door. He was a conman who had managed to con his way into the ambassador's home as an Irish university alumni and was having some supper, as he sized the place up. Had he stayed, phones, cameras and anything valuable would have gone missing.

White collar crime was commonplace as the perpetrators knew there was little possibility of serious consequences, and IT crimes were growing. It simply took someone to approach a couple of insiders in a bank, or the Ministry of Finance, and bribe them to make some adjustments in the system. From there it was a matter of stealing someone's password and transferring the money between various accounts, so that the trail was difficult to follow, and the money disappeared. In such scams it was unusual that the end user would ever be found, and certainly he would not be waiting in the bank to collect his cash; but this did happen on one occasion. The bank became suspicious, and the police were alerted so that they surrounded the bank and the person was caught. But he was not that bothered by his arrest because he knew the police did not have the technical ability to follow the money trail and bring a successful prosecution. The laws were weak, and there was enough money to spread around to ensure that files got misplaced, court hearings were delayed until people forgot what had happened, and the thief was released. None of these criminals ever spent more than a few nights in prison, yet large amounts of money were stolen from banks, ministries and private companies. It appeared that white collar crime did pay, and the thieves felt that it was really no-one's money – it was only a ministry, a donor, or a suspension account and no-one was really hurt.

Despite the assumption that white collar crime was non-violent, and no-one really got hurt, several people did pay with their lives. These were internal auditors and whistle-blowers who were seen as a threat. An internal auditor was murdered at the gate of her home because she had uncovered an accounting fraud in the aid organisation where she worked. She was a young mother with two children. Large sums of money were involved in these crimes, and the criminals did not shy away from protecting their interests, even if it meant assassination. Murder was easy because it was a matter of paying someone a few hundred dollars to hide near the entrance of the victim's home and shoot him when they arrived at his gate. There were spates of such assassinations and, although various culprits were picked up from time to time by the police, there were very few successful prosecutions.

# Why not start a university?

Since we now had a nursing school, we began to ponder the possibility of expanding the training programme to include other health professionals. Uganda was training less than 200 doctors per year for a population of over 30,000,000 people. This was woefully inadequate, especially when the number of medical graduates was compared to the number of law graduates, which exceeded one thousand per year. Not only were insufficient doctors trained, but those who were trained quickly moved out of clinical practice, particularly in rural areas, to work for aid agencies, or went abroad for post-graduate studies.

There is a general awareness of the external brain drain in which doctors from Africa leave to find work abroad. One can not really blame these doctors because many of them find that their speciality is poorly facilitated within their own country. Also the terms and conditions for doctors working abroad are much superior to those in most sub-Saharan African countries.

But there was also another kind of internal brain drain within Uganda itself, which resulted in doctors moving away from hands-on clinical practice and also made it very difficult to attract doctors to work up-country. Logically, medical workers should have been posted to the rural areas where 80% of the population resided, but it was much more likely to find them clustered in the urban centres and Kampala, in particular. The Ministry of Health posted doctors up-country, but many of the positions remained vacant. Even among the posts which were filled on paper, many of the health workers reported only erratically and it was hard to find the staff at their posts. There was little accountability within the ministry itself. The mission hospitals in rural areas also struggled to attract doctors.

After completing internship, many doctors did not even consider an up-country posting and would opt to work in

Kampala. They would then be offered jobs in projects run by aid agencies or research organisations, usually funded by American donors – USAID, CDC, Johns Hopkins University, being some of the big names. These jobs were generally in fields such as HIV which were favoured by donors, and the pay was twice what the government or private sector could afford. Some of the jobs had a clinical component, but generally this was only in a narrow field. Such projects also offered good opportunities for training, such as funding for a Master's degree at an American university, and when the doctor had obtained his Master's degree, he might go into project management and no longer have much clinical involvement.

Some doctors stayed in the clinical specialities, such as surgery or cardiology, but comparing the numbers of specialists to the needs of the population, these numbers were woefully inadequate. The result was that there was far less medical activity than one would have expected compared to a developed country, the reason being that patients could not access the service of the appropriate specialist when needed.

Although treatment for minor illnesses was usually accessible, many of the more complex problems were left untreated. Mulago Hospital, the large government teaching hospital, had a bed capacity of fifteen hundred, and since it was always full, the assumption was that it must be a very busy hospital, but this was not necessarily the case. Activity of a hospital can be measured, not only in bed occupancy, which was high in Mulago, but in turnaround time, number of procedures carried out, number of lab tests etc., and if these indicators were measured they were comparatively low. One reason was there were not enough specialists, for example not enough anaesthetists, so operations could not be performed on time. There were not enough cancer specialists, surgeons, or metabolic physicians. The average length of stay for patients was very long because they occupied a bed waiting for something to happen. This was due partly to the shortage of specialists and partly to other shortages and inefficiencies, resulting in critical gaps in supply.

In terms of priorities to meet the healthcare needs of the population, we seemed to have got things the wrong way round: we had the fewest doctors in the rural areas where the largest numbers of Ugandans resided. We did not facilitate the practice of specialities such as interventional cardiology, or oncology; hence, those doctors who trained in such specialities continued to work abroad. Grant funded HIV or research projects attracted the lion's share of the cash, so many doctors were becoming project managers and researchers instead of clinicians. Therefore, there were few doctors in clinical practice, and many of those doctors stayed for relatively short periods. One would have to conclude that there was a disconnect between the various actors working in healthcare and the glaring needs which were not being met.

There was a general recognition, however, that there was a deepening human resource for health crises in sub-Saharan Africa. With this in mind, we began to think about broadening our strategy from nurse education to the training of other health professionals, including doctors. Apart from the nursing school, we were also training our own staff in management procedures, customer care, financial management and human resource management, so we felt we could formalize this training and offer courses to other institutions. There was still a very old-fashioned approach to medical management in Uganda, where the management of hospitals was placed in the hands of a doctor, who usually had little relevant training, but since no-one else knew how to run hospitals either, the job went to the doctor by default. Doctors were also loath to take orders from professional managers, whom they considered beneath them in terms of seniority. Hence, medical professionals were pulled out of clinical duties and given managerial and financial responsibility, for which they were ill equipped. The result was double jeopardy – a valuable doctor was lost to clinical practice and placed in an administrative job which he did badly.

As a doctor myself, I had no formal training in finances and management and had to learn on the job, but it was this very sense of my own inadequacy which made me hungry to learn and develop such skills. The fact that we were successful provoked me to pass on what we had learned. Our strength was that we had learned from experience and not just theory, and knew what worked in the Ugandan context. So we set up Uganda Health Management Institute and offered short courses and modules in subjects such as financial management in healthcare, customer care and communication skills for health-workers, among others. Other medical institutions sent their staff for training, and we shared what we had learned.

Uganda Health Management Institute and International Hospital School of Nursing became the seeds for another idea which at first we thought was beyond us.

'Why not start a university?' someone suggested in a management meeting.

There were many good reasons why we could not start a university – chief among them being that we had no money and no knowledge of how to go about it. One doesn't just wake up one morning and start a university. There must be processes and procedures, academic requirements, academic staff, premises, and of course the finance to do it all. We were in a strategic planning session, reviewing where we wanted to get to. I was surrounded by young Ugandan professionals who were not afraid to dream, and I had certainly never shied away from the big idea. That year we had already expanded to Sudan, but Rose and Dr Moses were promoting the idea of starting a University. We were not very ambitious; we just wanted a small niche university, specializing in the training of healthcare professionals, with the ultimate goal of starting a Medical School. One practical stimulus was that we were spending so much running the nursing school that it would be more sustainable to train nurses to degree level, because degree courses were non-residential and cheaper to run. This would allow us to train nurses to the highest standards in a course that would be self-sustaining.

By this time we had finished half of the hospital block, with work on the other half still continuing. The last floor had reached the shell stage, which meant that the roof and frame of the building were complete, but nothing else. There was enough potential bed capacity on the ground, first and second floors to meet our needs, leaving the last floor free for future development.

'What about using the top level as a teaching floor?' someone suggested. 'It could become our new university.'

This was not a bad idea, and though we had not set out to build a hospital with a teaching floor, we realized this was the best use for this spare capacity.

Having sorted out where we would accommodate the university, we needed someone to run it and we needed a name for the institution. I had heard about an Irish lady who had been involved in setting up a catholic university on the equator, so I made inquiries and found that her contract with that university had finished, and she was thinking of going back to Ireland. Although we were both from Northern Ireland and had both worked in Uganda for over a decade, our paths had never crossed, and I discovered that Deidre Carabine, or Dee, as she was known to her friends, had not one but two PHDs.

'We are thinking of setting up a university, specializing in teaching subjects related to health. Would you be interested in helping us?'

Dee was definitely interested, since she could either go back to cold, wet Ireland and teach Medieval Religion, or stay in Kampala and help set up another university. I'm not sure if it was purely on the basis of weather conditions, but she chose to stay and lead the project.

The name was easy, since we were a university specializing in health sciences, so it became the International Health Science University.

Dee worked for eighteen months to get all the paperwork sorted out for the registration, which included the business plan, proposed faculties, courses to be offered, financing, staffing and facilities, while I worked with the building team to complete the top floor. We solicited books from friends in the Mater Hospital in Perth, Australia; the Irish embassy gave us a grant towards transporting computers, which were supplied from computer aid; we made chairs and tables in our own workshops, and the computer cabling and networking was carried out by our boys from the IT department.

The National Council for Higher Education had a mandate to regulate the development of tertiary education establishments. Uganda has an extremely young population and historically a good reputation within East Africa for high standards of education. Whether this was merited is a moot point, but perhaps it reflected that standards were lower in the surrounding countries or that education was cheaper within Uganda; thus, there was a proliferation of schools, colleges and universities within Uganda. Some of the institutions which called themselves universities were disorganized and chaotic, and were universities in name only. The government, therefore, gave the Higher Educational Council powers to regulate and deregulate institutions which did not meet the required standards. This began to create benchmarks and accepted norms.

The regulations of the Higher Education Council covered everything from governance to the necessary physical structure and, of course, academic standards. There was even a regulation about how many toilets should be provided. Our proposal to start a university, which specialized in the teaching of health sciences, was warmly received by the council, as they were aware of the tremendous shortfall of health-workers in the region. In the process of registration, we were first given an interim license, which gave us the green light to make our preparations to reach university status. This involved developing a business plan, outlines of courses to be offered, faculties with which we would commence the teaching programme, organizational structure, governance and physical structure.

Although the university was owned by the hospital, and, therefore, I was technically the owner, the university was governed by accepted university structures, with a chancellor, a vice chancellor, a university council and senate. The board of International Medical Group appointed the chancellor and the vice chancellor, and representatives to the council,

Over the following eighteen months various inspections were carried out, meetings held, reports and submissions made, until one day a letter arrived, informing us that we had a provisional license. We had written to other universities and health related bodies inviting them to send representatives for the university council and also invited Justice Julia Sebutinde, who was currently sitting as a Judge in The Hague on the trial of Charles Taylor, to be our chancellor. Dee, our vice chancellor designate and our registrar also happened to be female, so we were the first university in Uganda with an all female team of chancellor, vice-chancellor and registrar.

Justice Julia Sebutinde had the first laparoscopic gallbladder removal in Uganda at the old hospital, and she had been a strong supporter of our development from our first clinic in Kampala to the establishment of the university. We were required to hold a ceremony installing the chancellor and the vice-chancellor, with full pomp and ceremony, including a procession, the wearing of robes and a mace. It was all a little surreal, but within a few months we had over two hundred students enrolled in various courses, including nursing, health management and public health; the following year there were over four hundred, and the next year six hundred. We

311

developed the first remote learning course in Uganda, which could be accessed on the internet and had students studying in far flung corners of the country. Our dream had certainly taken roots and our next project was to start a medical school.

# Looking for good fortune

Uganda was full of contradictions, and while there was a thirst for learning and the schools and universities were full, reasoning and the scientific belief had still not displaced the traditional beliefs, but rather appeared to sit comfortably alongside them. The majority of Ugandans were poor and uneducated, and many turned to witchcraft for solutions to the problems they faced in their everyday lives.

When I was living in rural Luweero, I was not surprised that people sought out the witch-doctor before coming to the hospital; we were, after all, the destination of last resort. The villagers had seen people die at the hospital, and it was only when all else failed that they were forced to try western medicine. The traditional healer provided them with a simple understandable solution, which was culturally appropriate and cost effective. He also had a track record of one hundred percent success because none of his patients died on his premises. By the time they became moribund, he had sent them on to the hospital.

There was certainly no doubt that some of these herbal remedies worked, though the quantitative measurement of dosage was always a bit of a guess. I once had one patient who availed himself of the traditional healer's herbal treatment to increase his 'strength'. When we referred to 'strength' we were generally referring to erectile function, and my patient felt that his sexual experiences had been pleasant, but rather short, which was not surprising since he was still in his early twenties. However, he wished to prolong the experience, and after taking the appropriate herbs, he found that he was indeed erect for many hours – he had priapism which took some days to deflate.

For painful conditions the witchdoctor would often make small incisions on the skin over the area of the pain and rub in herbs. This made sense to the patient because the medicine was getting straight to the root of the problem, while swallowing pills seemed to be taking the long way round. What was surprising was that many educated people were prone to seeking solutions from witchdoctors and traditional healers, not just remedies for sickness, but also for good fortune. There was a widely held belief that blessings would not be forthcoming unless some form of sacrifice was made, and it was commonplace for those embarking on large projects to make a sacrifice at the outset. These sacrifices could be harmless enough – a goat or a chicken – but the use of body parts was becoming disturbingly common. There was a brisk trade in human skulls, some of which were exhumed from graves, but even more macabre was the use of severed heads. A young man was arrested, walking along the street carrying a plastic bag, containing a fresh human head. The boy had cut the head off his friend because the witchdoctor had told him that, in order for him to obtain riches, he must supply a head for the rituals.

This demand for human sacrifice resulted in the disappearance of many children, to the extent that it was difficult to quantify the magnitude of the problem. But hundreds of children disappeared each year. The witchdoctor generally demanded a perfect specimen without any blemishes or scars, which prompted parents to have their children's ears pierced, since the child was then likely to be rejected.

These practices involving human sacrifice might not have been so remarkable among jungle tribes in some remote part of Africa, but they were taking place in Kampala which was a modern city, and where people had the opportunity of a western education. One such person was a failed medical student who, despite his lack of qualifications, set up a clinic and worked as a 'doctor' – a fairly loose term in Uganda. He ran his clinic for several years on the outskirts of Kampala but was frustrated that he was not making his fortune, and that the success he wished for eluded him. It did not seem to twig with him that his lack of success could have anything to do him being an unqualified quack. He was advised that, in order to become wealthy, he should make a sacrifice, and, if he really wished for guaranteed success, the sacrifice should be a child. A small family lived near his clinic, and he watched the children play under the tree every day. Thus, he began to study the movements of the children and managed to waylay and kidnap one of them. Using chloroform, he suffocated the boy, and then slit his throat and hid the body. He went back to work as if nothing had happened, even though he was living beside the family who were distraught by the disappearance of their child. He was only apprehended because his accomplice was picked up by the police, confessed to the killing, and led the police to where the body was hidden.

Many people were led into such practices because they believed there was some secret formula to success. This belief was nurtured by the evidence that a few people in Uganda were fabulously wealthy, but they were not perceived as having attained their wealth through honest endeavour. People therefore justified witchcraft and theft as legitimate means to get out of poverty.

Apart from this, apparently respectable people got involved in activities such as embezzlement or bribery, with the justification that everyone else was doing it. The sad thing was that if someone did achieve their ambitions of becoming rich through theft or embezzlement, it made no difference to their standing in society; so long as they were rich, they were considered to be a success. It was a case of the end justifying the means.

Many people saw their lack of good fortune as a failure to appease the spirits rather than any failure of their business plan or lack of hard work. This type of rationalisation, and the resulting widespread practice of witchcraft, spawned a thriving, though macabre, service industry, with middlemen willing to supply the particular body ordered for the ritual. The least harmful in this supply chain were the grave robbers, since the person was already dead, though some of the grave robbers also indulged in a form of cannibalism and ate parts of the freshly buried bodies. There were also those who specialised in abductions, taking orders for a particular type of human being: perhaps a young woman thought to be a virgin, or a child. They filled the order and delivered it for an agreed fee.

The teenage daughter of a nursing tutor at the university was waiting for a *matatu* in the late afternoon on a busy street. The taxis would stop randomly when the driver spied a potential passenger, so one did not have to be at a recognised stage, and this young lady was picked up by what she assumed was a normal taxi. Nothing seemed abnormal until they started going in the wrong direction and were not making any further stops. The girl expressed alarm, but she was quickly overpowered and warned not to cry out. The kidnappers drove out of town for several hours and delivered her to an empty store, where she was confined that evening. The following day a man came to view her – to inspect the merchandise he had purchased – but he was not happy because she had pierced ears and she was shoved back in the store. While the haggling had been going on, she had noticed several other young girls who appeared drugged. Her pierced ears had saved her life. That night the guard was drunk and she was able to make her escape. Her kidnappers probably had no use for her anyway. She made her way to the nearest town and called her mother who came and picked her up.

The incident was never reported to the police, and no search of the area was ever made, so no-one knows the fate of the other girls. This may seem bizarre, but people had little confidence in the police, and once they had solved their own problem, they did not want any more involvement. For the kidnappers, she was just a commodity, and since they had failed to bring an unblemished item, they may not have been paid. If the merchandise had been satisfactory, they would probably have received a couple of hundred thousand shillings ($100). The kidnappers would not have felt any conscience about their trade since they did not consider it their responsibility what happened subsequently. In the case of girls being kidnapped for the purposes of rituals, they were usually drugged and raped, but both adults and children were sacrificed for body parts – often the tongue and the genitals. There were thousands of unsolved disappearances of children and young people in Uganda, and there were many unsolved murders where the victims were found with their genitals and tongues cut out.

While some people turned to witchcraft, another group turned to the church. On the face of it, this was a more acceptable approach, but some unscrupulous pastors saw an opportunity and made a business from people's desire for blessing and good fortune. The twist was based on the American prosperity gospel, which taught that if people wanted to prosper, they should first give an offering. They called it sowing – you sowed your own wealth and then it would germinate and bring forth a plentiful harvest.

There was nothing wrong with this lesson in agriculture, and there are many people whose generosity has apparently been blessed with more abundant riches. However, a number of church leaders in Kampala saw the opportunity for blessing themselves through this prosperity gospel and went about it aggressively. Some were extremely successful at reaping personal benefits because, although their flock was sowing to God, someone had to act as a caretaker. The 'sowing' was honed to a fine art: if someone wanted a visa for the US, he would be advised that since he was going to walk far, he had better start by 'sowing' his shoes. The shoes would be placed on the altar, and the person would walk home barefoot. Others would be told they needed to learn how to sacrifice, and they should give up their mobile phones. Others were encouraged to bring their car keys, leave their cars, and walk home. It was not only those who were seeking riches who were conned, but also the sick. One lady was told to give up her car and she would be healed of AIDS. Several months later she had the courage to go to the newspapers and tell them the story, exposing the fraudulent pastor.

Other pastors were in such demand that they simply charged a consultation fee for which they laid hands on the person and prophesied that their needs would be met. At least this transaction was straightforward. One pastor decided to add value to his prayers by administering an electric shock when he laid hands on the supplicant. He had a contraption concealed up his sleeve which delivered a shock, so that people were slain by 'the power of the spirit' – or at least the power of the electricity.

No matter how one looked at it, whether a person turned to a witchdoctor or a crooked pastor, he was getting a raw deal. On the one hand he paid to become involved in ritualism, involving sex and human sacrifice, while on the other hand he got fleeced by the pastor, and in neither case did he achieve good fortune.

I also witnessed amazing examples of genuine faith, probably because it was such a raw society where people had great needs, which brought out the best or the worst in them. People had incredible challenges to handle everyday and it was not surprising that they turned to a higher authority for solace, or the strength to deal with them. I witnessed faith and inner strength in many of my patients who were HIV positive and who were living with a death sentence, young mothers who were not only facing death but were desperately worried about the future of their children. But faith was a delicate balance since the act of faith itself meant that there was no certainty of the outcome.

In this context, I was uneasy about the large American evangelical machines which rolled into town and staged

318

miracle crusades. Benny Hinn conducted a crusade at the national stadium, during which people fell down 'under the influence of the Holy Spirit', and there were many miraculous healings. All of these were, of course, captured on video for broadcast on his TV station. These large miracle crusades played well to the viewers back home, because although the faithful of the Midwest might never have witnessed the blind see, or the lame walk, in North Dakota, they could see that it happened in Africa on a gospel TV channel. Africa apparently had loads of miracles. But the vast majority of these miracles were never substantiated with any scientific evidence. So did these monster miracle campaigns really make a difference to the lives of ordinary Ugandans? There was certainly the danger of diverting people in real need from the rational approach to the 'I am believing in a miracle' approach. Too often I had seen people fail to take treatment because they 'were believing' for a miracle. I have to say that, as a doctor, I remained cynical about the value of such healing crusades which could sometimes do more harm than good.

# Corruption and politics

As our organization grew and we became recognised for the work we were doing, I was often invited to gatherings where I met the movers and shakers of Uganda. Although Uganda had a population of over thirty million, it was a relatively small group who controlled things at the centre, and it was not that hard to rub shoulders with them.

I was at a New Years Eve party and was having a conversation with a senior government minister. He had been a politician and a minister in Uganda for eighteen years and was one of only three people who had kept his parliamentary seat over that whole period. This piece of information was something that surprised me, as I had not realised that each new parliament brought a whole slew of fresh backbenchers, though the balance of power had not shifted from the ruling party. Perhaps this explained why the level of debate in parliament was often so low. He had been in the cabinet in various positions during that period but had served longest as a full minister over works and transport, with his ministry having enormous powers in awarding tenders. Since so much shoddy work was carried out in the roads sector, people held him personally responsible for the poor state of the roads and particularly in Kampala, where some roads had more potholes than tarmac.

'But Kampala is not under my jurisdiction,' he protested. 'It falls under Kampala City Council whose politically elected head is the Mayor; it is not central government that is responsible for repairing the roads in Kampala.'

According to him central government had no authority over how Kampala was run, and we all had to suffer as a result. As the evening wore on, and the conversation became more animated, he gave me another key piece of the jigsaw.

'And the second thing is, I have very little power to control my own civil servants; they are not actually accountable to me in terms of disciplinary measures, but to the Public Service Commission.'

These same conditions existed within the Ministry of Health, where doctors were not answerable to the managers of the hospital, but to the Department of Local Government or to the Health Service Commission, which were disconnected, both geographically and functionally. This system was created to ensure security of tenure for those working in the public service but now appeared to be ludicrous because it was very difficult to call people to account. If the minister had a problem with one of his civil servants, he could make a complaint, but the worst thing which could happen was that the person was moved to another position.

'I would have sacked seventy-five percent of the upper echelon of staff by this time if I had the power,' he added, and then, to emphasise his disgruntlement, he went on, 'I have had enough of politics, I want to get out and work within my home constituency, setting up a vocational training institute.'

'Why not stay within politics and do the same thing?' I asked. 'Do you not have more influence as a politician?'

'But one is blackmailed by one's constituents,' he replied.

The political equation in many African countries was simple: what can you give me so that I will vote for you? This was not in terms of reform programmes, better education or anything esoteric, but how much sugar, or salt you could provide for my vote. This was what made elections expensive and politicians susceptible to corruption: the aspiring politician was making a heavy financial investment and banking on being elected in order to recoup his money. So, according to the Minister, the life of a politician in a third world country was fairly frustrating; the political head was always blamed for any misadventure, but he often had little control over it. Most people made the assumption that all politicians were corrupt, and if a politician claimed that he was hostage to the system, no-one was inclined to believe him. This minister was being blamed for not looking after the roads in Kampala, but they were not under his jurisdiction. He was also being blamed for the inflated prices and shoddy contracts being awarded by his ministry, but it also was possible that it was his engineers who were colluding with the contractors to receive bribes and inflate prices. On the other hand, these same engineers and procurement officers told the contractors that the reason for the sizeable bribes was because there were many people to pay off in the chain, up to the minister himself.

There was a well publicised scandal involving the embezzlement of Global Fund cash within the Ministry of Health, where an inquiry showed that the concerned minister simply instructed the Permanent Secretary to write cheques when he needed them, and the PS meekly obeyed. In theory, there were many checks and balances to ensure that government funds were properly accounted for, but the minister paid scant regard to any accepted accounting practice. When an inquiry was set up, there was no convoluted paper trail to follow because he had not bothered to cover anything up. It was seen as the accepted norm that a 'big man' would use his position for personal gain. There were also other parties who had a finger in the pie of corruption: people working in such organisations as the World Bank and the EU in particular, where systems could be manipulated to ensure contracts were awarded to companies colluding with insiders. The web of corruption had spread throughout all levels of society.

An independent audit of the National Social Security Fund showed that the managing director had used his position to take large advances in his salary, including a housing allowance and expenses way beyond what he was entitled to. This was another example of someone who had been given authority in a public body and used his position for personal benefit. People in these positions confused stewardship with ownership and did not make the distinction between personal finances and public money, as long as they had the authority to sign the cheque. Politicians and public servants were taking money as if it was their own, without any sense that they would ever be called to account.

'I am not corrupt because of conviction,' the minister continued to reassure me. He was keen that I should know he was one of the good guys. It was certainly a fact that if a politician or public servant did not have a strong and honest character, he would quickly fall prey to inducements since they were so widespread within the system.

The situation was different just across the border in Rwanda, which was gaining a reputation for zero tolerance of corruption. They had a very straightforward method of dealing with the problem: people went to jail, and the government refused to pay for contracts which were judged to be substandard. There was one instance where the President wished some trees to be planted in a city park, and a foreign investor claimed that he had a certain variety of fast growing trees which would grow tall within a year. So, on the basis of his claim, he was given the contract. The trees, however, did not take to the Rwandan soil conditions and did not grow well. A year later the President passed the park and noticed that the trees were stunted, so he left instructions that the investor should take the trees out and refund the money. The investor had to do what he was told, or he would have been kicked out of the country. If this incident had happened in Uganda, the President would probably have noticed that the trees had not grown, but excuses and promises would have been made and no further action taken.

The Rwandan method may have been somewhat draconian and a number of Rwandans fled the country because a business deal went sour. There was also a sense that everyone was watching their backs, which tended to delay processes because no-one wanted to step out of line. The difference between Rwanda and Uganda lay in the fact that the President of Rwanda was able to rule without fear of offending his political constituency, while in Uganda there was much balancing: inclusiveness, forgiveness, bartering, and buying off the various interest groups; such were the consequences of democracy. President Kagame had summarily dealt with any dissenting voices, and did not have to worry about causing offence to the political establishment. Thus, having warned his ministers and civil servants about abuse of office, he was able to put his money where his mouth was and take action.

There was one incident in which Kagame warned his ministers and public servants that the vehicles they were driving were too large, and they should only drive vehicles below a certain cubic capacity to save on running costs. But many officials were still driving their oversized vehicles, so one morning he had the police set up roadblocks and confiscate the vehicles, leaving the officials to walk to work. If this had happened in Uganda, there would have been an outcry from within the party and threats to form splinter groups, but the Rwandan President did not have to worry about such a backlash. In Uganda it was almost a pattern that if any stalwart government supporter found himself being pursued by the law, he then changed his party allegiance, and was welcomed by the other side who then started supporting his case. Therefore, the ruling party was slow to call its own to account since they would have to deal with the political fallout. Political loyalty was often coupled to personal gain, and such people did not expect any adverse consequences for breaking the law as long as they were loyal to their political masters.

Corruption in Uganda resulted in much shoddy work, but since there were usually no serious consequences, things did not improve. The two neighbouring countries sent out different signals. In Uganda the worst that could happen was a suspension or perhaps a night in jail, while in Rwanda one could end up in jail for a considerable period. In Uganda there was much talk and little action; we talked about all the offices that had been set up to deal with the problem: the Inspector General of Government, the CID, the Department of Public Disposals and Acquisitions and the one with the best name, The Ministry of Ethics and Integrity. Uganda also hosted international conferences to discuss corruption and talked incessantly about the problem in State House, in parliament, in the newspapers, in public inquiries, but all the talk had little measurable effect.

It transpired that there was also a regulation in Uganda about the recommended engine size for government vehicles, which detailed the size of engine which certain grades of politician and public servants were entitled to. Within weeks of passing this statute, half a dozen ministers and officials were shown to have purchased new vehicles, well outside of the regulations, a favourite being the new VX Land cruiser. The story was published in the newspapers, but what action was taken? Were the cars confiscated from the offenders? Were they disciplined in any way? Were they reprimanded? None of the above. Precisely nothing happened, except talk.

To make matters worse, there were obvious double standards and contradictions concerning the people who were supposed to be involved in the fight against corruption. The Ministry of Ethics and Integrity published a double page spread in the New Vision about the actions which were being taken to stem corruption, while on the next page there was a column criticizing the Minister himself for dubious accounting practices when he had been the Minister of Information. It seemed inexplicable that the same newspaper could carry a large piece by the anti-corruption Minister, while the Minister's failure to account for 3,000,000 shillings, plus another $20,000 were highlighted on the next page. In a western democracy there would have been strident calls for his resignation, but he just 'brassed' it out and nothing happened.

It was not that there was no action against corruption; it was just that it seemed to be selective and only the little people got caught, sometimes because their accountability was so pathetic that there was no possible defence. In an inquiry into the siphoning of Global Fund money, it was found that one lady had submitted receipts as proof of expenditure for a conference at a hotel. The receipts might have been acceptable but for the fact that the hotel had burned down before the date of her conference. If she had forged the receipts from a hotel which was still standing, she would have got away with the scam. What puzzled me was that in many of these cases of embezzlement and corruption, following procedures and giving accountability was completely lacking, yet I had personally been told by senior public servants that correct procedures must be followed at all times. One Permanent Secretary reassured me that the processes of government might be slow, but they produced accountability. Nonsense.

The other issue was the courts themselves. While it was commendable that some action had been taken, most prosecutions in the courts dragged on forever and were not brought to a successful completion. A clever lawyer could argue that his client's constitutional rights had been violated, that the IGG did not follow proper procedure, or that the trial was politically motivated. It seemed that, although a number of prominent people were arrested over the years and spent a couple of nights in Luzira Prison, while waiting for bail (apparently a constitutional right for everyone in Uganda), very few people were actually sentenced to a jail term, and once a person had been released on bail, it was the last we heard of him.

There was a groundswell of approval when a case was brought against the Minister of Health in the Global Fund and GAVI Funds scandals, as it seemed to demonstrate that there was one law for all. But true to form, the minister went to the highest court in the land and appealed the constitutionality of his indictment, which included questioning the jurisdiction of the Inspector General of Government and the 'political interference' of his former boss, the President. There was never a shortage of lawyers to argue the minutiae of the law, and after several years, the case still dragged on with no serious consequences.

I met many interesting and influential people at the various events to which I was invited, but I also had to put up with the usual idiosyncrasies of such public functions. I found that the ability of people to talk was exacerbated when someone was let loose in front of a microphone. I had observed, having attended many such functions, that when people stood before a microphone, hearing the sound of their own voice made them lose control. Pentecostal evangelists were severely afflicted and were propelled into making long and loud prayers and sermons, with much repetition. They were also not entirely sure if God was a bit deaf, so, just in case, they shouted into the microphone. It was likely that if God was in the heavens, this increase in volume did the trick, since everyone within a range of half a mile had no trouble being involuntary members of their congregation.

Next to evangelists, politicians had the malady, and when they got control of a microphone they were incapable of relinquishing it. They were like a car going down a hill with no brakes; their own momentum just kept them going. The Master of Ceremonies was also susceptible to this disease and felt constrained to make numerous introductions and recognitions, all of which were accompanied by the person standing up and waving to the crowd.

What was it about recognizing 'big people' at such events? While it was only natural for people to want recognition, I thought some of them could manage on a bit less. Politicians were starving for it, but could they not have gotten their satisfaction from representing their own people? If there was an Honourable Member of Parliament, it was mandatory that he or she stood up to be recognized. Large amounts of time were taken up giving the correct titles and observing correct protocol. In Britain the title 'Honourable', from the British parliamentary system, was only used on the floor of the House, while outside Parliament the person reverted to being plain 'Mr', but in Uganda MPs were referred to as Honourables on every occasion – a bit of a mouthful. My own view was that it was still possible to be respectful if we got rid of all the titles and ceremony. But that was how it was in an African country. The funny thing was that although people shortened my title to 'Doc', I never heard any of the 'Honourables' being referred to as 'Hon'.

Though corruption was endemic in the society, not everyone was corrupt, nor was everyone corruptible. A friend of mine, Zac, who also happened to be a bishop, was appointed as the chairman of the committee which audited governance as part of a self appraisal mechanism under the Africa Union – The African Peer Review Mechanism. Because of his position, there were those who wished to influence his findings positively, but they did not know how to leverage him; he was not a businessman, therefore, he was not looking for any contracts or deals; he had no interest in any prime position which could be gifted to him, nor did he want money. He, therefore, created a problem, and someone was heard to remark in frustration, 'Ah that one, we don't know what he wants.'

Obviously there were some who thought that everything could be managed as long as one knew what benefit the person needed. Most people appeared to work on the assumption, like the Mafia, that everyone had his price, but what happened when it was a moral person who could not be bought? The most difficult person was someone who said and did what he believed was right. Unfortunately, there were few in this category and most people could be influenced in some way.

Finding an honest man was a rare thing and put the bishop in a strong position.

The cabinet minister wanted the best for his country, but through a combination of factors, his ministry had developed one of the worst reputations for delivering shoddy work. Politicians became hostage to their own politics: if they wanted to be re-elected they had to please the party and their constituents. They became compromised by the political horse trading to keep themselves in power, and when this was taken in conjunction with the lack of accountability of the public sector, they might be puppet kings. An African politician was definitely not a CEO, who had a clear line of reporting, accountability and discipline, and could therefore control what happened. I sometimes wondered why politicians did not take a common sense approach to getting things done, but then I was not a politician; I was the head of a private organisation and did not have to work under the conditions that applied to them. The other alternative was to have an autocrat such as Paul Kagame as Head of State, who did not have to worry about the politics of keeping himself in power and just did what he felt was good for the country. But how many such leaders did we have, and what happened when they went wrong?

When the next election came around I paid attention to whether the minister would stand down to pursue his dream of working at the grass roots among the community, but I noticed that he stood again as the party candidate. Perhaps the benefits of being an important part of the system were too hard to forsake.

# Reaching out

Over the years we were involved in various emergencies, such as the time when several bombs went off in a Kampala suburb, when Robbie and I were only a hundred metres from the scene. We heard a dull thump and saw people scatter in all directions and, with our experience from Northern Ireland, realised that these were bombs. We turned the car around and drove home, where there was an ambulance parked, and within minutes, we were back at the scene. Several people lay dead and a score were injured. We collected those whom we could fit in the ambulance and deposited them at various hospitals, since this incident happened before we had developed our own hospital. Those who did not need hospital admission were taken back to our clinic where we stitched up lacerations and dressed the wounds.

Several years later we were driving back home on a Sunday afternoon, after having had lunch, when we came upon an accident where a pedestrian had walked straight in front of a car. The body was lying in a crumpled heap on the road, so I pulled in and ran across to see if the person was still alive. She was still breathing, but was unconscious and obviously badly injured.

'I will call an ambulance,' I said to those who were gathering at the scene and ran back to get my phone, but when I looked behind, the people had picked up the body and were following me, so I laid the girl in the back of the car. Since they had already moved the patient, there was no point in waiting for the ambulance, and it would be quicker to drive straight to the hospital.

I put on the warning lights and drove to the hospital as fast as I could, meanwhile calling Dr Moses to meet me there. Everyone arrived at the same time and the patient was examined, stabilised, x-rayed and taken to theatre within thirty minutes. She had a head injury, internal abdominal injuries, a fractured pelvis, and an enormous laceration of the back. Her hospital treatment required several weeks' stay, but, eventually, she made a complete recovery. We later found she was deaf which accounted for why she had walked in front of the vehicle. Her parents were so grateful for what we had done, but, tragically, within two weeks her father was killed in another road accident.

During the time I was building the first hospital, the LRA activities were continuing to cause suffering in the north, and we wished to offer some help to the victims. Els de Temmerman was a journalist who had reported from many of the hotspots in Africa and had seen the worst, but despite this she still had a love for Africa and had settled in Uganda. She had seen the Rwandan massacre and the LRA war, and had written a book narrating the harrowing tale of the abduction of the Aboke girls, including Peace and Alice. She subsequently toured the Netherlands, giving lectures at schools and raising money to pay school fees for hundreds of children in Northern Uganda. Her commitment and energy were enormous, and she constantly drove herself to the limit.

The first trip that I made with Els to the north of Uganda was not the most comfortable. She was taking some visitors from Belgium who wished to see what was going on, plus transporting donated medicines, and when I volunteered to go, she immediately organised a clinic just so that I would not be idle.

Early that morning I was squeezed in a small space among the boxes of medicines in the back of her vehicle, with my chin resting on my knees, and we set out on the five hour journey. By the time we reached Lira, I had seized up and was walking in a crablike position; I was sore and tired and wanted something to eat, but before I could massage my muscles, Els had already started work, registering children for school, getting the biography of each child and paying their school fees.

'They are waiting for you at the clinic,' she said. Low blood sugar was not a problem for a journalist on a mission to save the world, so off I went to do the clinic, grumbling that no-one seemed to have any need for normal things like food.

At the clinic there were about eighty formerly abducted children, who had been held by the LRA for periods from a few months to ten years. They had old shrapnel wounds, bullet wounds, and general muscular aches and pains, resulting from constant beatings. Osteomyelitis – infection of the bones from old gunshot wounds – was one of the more serious conditions from which they suffered. One boy had such bad infection that his hip joints had melted away, and his femurs were fused with his pelvis, so that he no longer had any joints and walked bent over. The problem with osteomyelitis is that it grumbles on for years, destroying the bones, while new bone forms over the dead bone, with pus leaking from various sinuses. Unless the bone is opened and the dead bone taken out, there is no chance of cure. One girl had a fracture of her arm which had never healed, so that the arm hung uselessly by her side. She was a small quiet girl who had been held for ten years and witnessed ghastly killings and beatings. Her job had been to induct the children when they were new, which was when they were most likely to be beaten or killed; she had no expression and no reactions. I organised for those with chronic osteomyelitis, plus the girl with the non-united fracture, to be brought down to International Hospital for surgery.

When she came to the hospital, she was frightened because she had never been to Kampala before, she had never been in a hospital, and no one spoke her language. We found one of the staff who could communicate with her and reassured her that nothing bad would happen, and we could fix her arm. We put in a plate and some screws, and I met her the following year when she had a functional arm. On this occasion I was rewarded with a smile, but sadly the young lady died due to AIDS which she had contracted in captivity.

After I had finished seeing the patients, I returned to the hotel where Els was still registering children. She was interviewing a child called Joanne who was the sister of one of the Aboke girls. Joanne's sister was in captivity and she had also recently lost her father. She was a gangly fourteen year old who wished to complete her schooling in Kampala, but Els's programme did not stretch to paying for boarding school fees in Kampala.

'Could you help?' Els asked me. I decided to reach out by sponsoring this child, and thus Joanne became part of our extended family.

After that trip I made many more visits to the north, and during one such excursion I visited a poor village in an impoverished district that had been begotten from another poor district. The first district had cloned itself, creating a second district with a government administration and jobs for a few of the privileged, but no noticeable difference to the lives of the ordinary peasants. The district was Pader, and the name of the village was Acholibur, and within the regions of Acholibur there resided 18,000 people, since Acholibur was not only a village but the location for an Internally Displaced People (IDP) camp.

By this time there had been measurable development in the rest of Uganda, such that many people had a decent lifestyle, but Pader and Acholibur had been by-passed by development. Instead the area had been terrorized by Kony since the early nineties, and those who lived in the IDP camps had less than nothing. In Luweero I had been living among a peasant population who had very little; some of them lived in mud huts, had a few cooking utensils and a sleeping mat, but they still survived and had a passable lifestyle. In the IDP camps, though it was much the same picture, there was one immense difference: the peasants in Luweero had their

333

shambas in which they could tend their crops; they had cassava, groundnuts, beans and matoke, and they never went hungry. But the people in Acholibur could not even get to the fields to plant because of the activities of the LRA and the army. In Africa people have lived in mud huts for generations, and there is no shame in it. Such a person can still provide for himself and his family from the land, but it was a whole different story when the mud hut was one of a thousand, clustered together in the middle of a barren land. The occupants depended on the World Food Programme to bring them a few cups of maize every month. They had become beggars in their own land, and all dignity of life was gone.

Within Acholibur there was not a single carpentry workshop, there were no small scale welding workshops, such as one witnessed along the sides of the road in Kampala. It was impossible to buy a cold soda since there was no electricity, but one could see the bullet holes in the buildings and be entertained by stories of numerous attacks on the village by the LRA. I saw all this for myself, but in the midst of this I experienced something else that touched me deeply; I found someone who still had a generous spirit and wanted to give to others, even though she had nothing herself. It happened to be a market day and despite everything, there was life and colour in the market, with what meagre produce there was available being laid out on the ground for sale.

'What is this?' I asked Richard, the social worker with whom I had travelled

'Dried potato,' he responded. 'Sweet potato that has been cut in strips and dried in the sun.'

I tasted it and wondered if it would ever find its way onto the shelves of Marks and Spencer's. There was also millet, yeast, dried cucumber, maize flour and sorghum.

'In a few months,' explained Richard, 'there will be no market here since there will be no surplus food to sell.'

As we were leaving, Margaret came to greet us. She had only one arm, as she had lost the other during her escape when she was shot by the LRA. She had been abducted and held in Sudan for three years, but had made her bid for freedom during a raid in Kitgum and was shot in the process. She spoke to Richard who turned to me.

'She wants to give you a chicken,' he said.

Hospitality was a tradition in Uganda, and it was not the first time I had been given a chicken, but this was different. This was a person who had suffered terribly, someone who lived in one of the poorest places on earth and had practically nothing, yet she still wished to give me from the little she possessed. I had helped Margaret by buying her a sewing machine, and now she wanted to express her thanks. Although I did not wish to take from the little that she had, she insisted, and I felt it would have been an insult to refuse. So I accepted the gift and that night we ate roast chicken.

International Hospital was involved not only in helping some of the individual victims of the war in the north, but had also embarked on a number of charitable projects, one of which was making AIDS treatment available in Kasesse, far in the west of Uganda. We had been approached by the HR Manager of the Hima Cement factory to run a factory clinic. The cement factory was located in Kasesse District and had recently been taken over by the international construction company, Lafarge.

USAID were funding a programme in which they were seeking to get commercial organisations to take responsibility for the management of HIV for their staff and the surrounding community. This USAID initiative was headed up by a fast-talking American doctor, known as Pete Cowley, who had obviously missed his calling, since he was a born salesman who could have made his fortune selling sub-prime mortgages. He abandoned clinical practice and gravitated to an organisation where he could sell ideas; in this case he wanted to get our organisation and Lafarge to work together and provide HIV care not only for their staff, but for the local community. He had the advantage of being well connected with the USAID programmes which provided free anti-AIDS drugs, so was able to put all the key components of the programme together. Thus we commenced a community outreach programme for HIV: Hima Cement put in some money, we put in money and staff, Pete's organisation put in some money and ensured that the programme was registered to receive the ARV drugs, and our project in Kasese became a model for other community HIV projects associated with factories and farms.

When the new International Hospital was under construction, I decided that we should include a charitable ward as part of the overall plan. We were assisted in completing this through funds received in memory of Paresh. His father and his cousin, Sudhir, gave $125,000 towards charitable medical work which we used towards Hope Ward, the name we adopted for this ward. Since we were developing relatively sophisticated facilities at the new hospital, Hope Ward focused on offering complex treatment for the destitute. Such treatment was varied in nature, but included treating children with AIDS, patients with cancer, those from the LRA conflict who needed reconstructive or orthopaedic surgery, or those with congenital heart conditions.

Hope Ward was launched with the help of sponsorship from a number of corporate companies in Uganda: Hwan Sung industries, several banks, including Stanbic, Barclays, Crane Bank, East African Breweries, Coca Cola, Everett Aviation and several charitable organisations, including Bead for Life and Mvule Trust. It was good to see that local companies were interested in doing something for their own community, and this sponsorship allowed us to meet a portion of the running costs, though the largest sponsor was International Hospital itself.

One of our first patients was a little boy who was run over by a train. People do not usually survive if they are hit by a locomotive, but in this boy's case it was one of his legs which had been run over, and he was found crawling away from the track, spurting blood. If one of our own staff had not come upon the scene and quickly got the boy to hospital, he would have died of shock. As it was, the surgeons were able to save him, although he lost his lower leg. It was not so much that the surgeons had to amputate as to tidy up the job since the train had already done most of the work. In a remarkably short time the young man was jumping around the ward on crutches and was discharged to the care of an organisation which worked with street children.

Another patient had a hole in her bladder. This condition was the result of prolonged obstructed labour, where the head of the baby pressed down on the bladder, cutting off the blood supply and causing necrosis. The outcome was not only a dead baby, but a mother who was totally incontinent. This condition is now well known and goes under the term vesico-vaginal fistula or VVF, and there are several international organisations dedicated to the training of surgeons in the repair of VVF. In our case one of our general surgeons was already proficient at repairing these conditions and carried out the procedure for a nominal fee. The lady was in her forties and had been incontinent for twenty years. Since the condition had persisted for such a long time, she also had several other complications, but Dr Owori repaired all her defects and she left the hospital dry. She came to my office to thank me and could not contain her joy, having lived with this condition for so many years that she never thought she would be normal again.

Since we were carrying out various charitable projects, yet we were still a private hospital, this caused some confusion as to whether we were a charitable or a profit-making organisation. So in order to define the various activities, we set up a foundation under which we could group all our charitable activities. Naturally, the name we chose was International Medical Foundation or IMF, not to be confused with the other IMF. IMF was a useful vehicle under which we could then organise what was 'not for profit' and what was commercial. It also became the vehicle through which we could set up various charitable and community projects, each with its own stream of funding.

International Medical Foundation had one big advantage over other stand-alone aid organisations involved in medical work since it could use the infrastructure, systems, corporate functions, and organisation of the whole of International Medical Group. This meant that money did not have to be raised for infrastructure, and funds raised could go directly to the various programmes. The setting up of IMF also helped define the actual amounts in monetary terms which the projects cost and to which donors were contributing. This structure allowed full accountability and made it appropriate for IMF to solicit funds from other sources. Local fund-raising events were also carried out, such as a concert and a fashion show, at which I was one of the models! Personally, I thought that, with a bit of practice, I could have a promising career in this field and did not really understand why people laughed at me when I strutted my stuff on the catwalk. Some well known local artists contributed paintings for sale and fashion designers donated clothes for auction; local artists also turned up to paint murals in the hospital and on Hope Ward.

# A public private partnership

As part of our efforts to help the people of northern Uganda, we had set up a medical centre in Lira and were exploring ways in which we could bring medical services to Pader. So Easter Monday found me in the north of Uganda, driving from Lira to Pader. I had set out early, since I had many miles to travel that day, but had been on the road for only half an hour when we were flagged down by some local people.

'It is not safe to travel any further. There is a gunman further on, stopping vehicles.'

The villagers thought he was the bandit who had been terrorising the community for several weeks, having killed four people and stolen several head of cattle. A few miles back we had passed an army patrol, so we decided to drive back and get them to deal with the situation. We quickly found the patrol and explained to the soldiers what was happening, suggesting that they could ride back with us. Several of them scrambled into the car, fully armed, while others perched on the door sill, and off we sped. The army had been scouring the area for this renegade and were keen to catch him. On reaching the trading centre, there was an animated discussion on how to catch this dangerous criminal. Their plan was that I could drive along the road with them, concealed in the back of the car; the terrorist would assume that I was an ordinary civilian when he flagged me down, and the soldiers would jump out and shoot him. Strangely enough, I was not so keen on this plan, so they opted for plan B, which was to ride on the back of a pick-up and go and look for him. The soldiers jumped on to the back of the pick-up, slapping and cocking their guns, Rambo style, and with tires screeching, they sped off.

In a surprisingly short time the pick-up appeared on the horizon again, travelling at breakneck speed; it skidded to a stop and the soldiers tumbled out, together with their quarry. I was in awe that the army had apprehended their man in such record time and brought him back alive. I noticed that he had been disarmed, and they had removed his footwear, but that he appeared to be wearing a new army uniform. However, knowing that at times the rebels had better uniforms than the army, I let it pass. By this time a crowd of villagers had gathered to gawk; the soldiers said nothing, and we all stared at the bandit. I could not help wondering what was going on in the mind of such a person, and when I realised that he could speak English, my curiosity got the better of me and I decided to strike up a conversation.

Not knowing how to make small talk with a dangerous rebel, I asked, as an opening gambit, 'Why did you kill those people?' as one does in a conversation with a murderer. But he immediately fired back at me, 'I have not killed anyone.'

Now I was the one who was confused.

'I am a soldier,' he went on, 'and last night there was a disagreement between me and some other soldiers, so I packed my things and set off to walk back to headquarters.'

In short, he was not the person who had been terrorising the community, he was just a disgruntled soldier who had left his unit, but because he was armed and had tried to stop some motorists to beg a cigarette, the local people thought he was a bandit.

Having gleaned this invaluable piece of intelligence, I thought I should pass it on to the army.

'This is not the man you have been looking for, he is one of you.'

'Yes, we know,' they replied nonchalantly; they were obviously a bit disappointed.

I wondered what would have happened if the soldiers had been more trigger happy and had shot first and asked questions later, as often happened. By this time the District Executive Security Officer had been called, and he reassured me by phone that everything was now under control, and I could go on my way peacefully.

We travelled on to a place called Patongo. Simon, a property developer from the UK was travelling with us because he wished to donate some money for a project in the north of Uganda. He had twenty thousand pounds of his own money and felt that he could raise more if we identified a small project where such funds could be used effectively. We had known Simon when he worked in Luweero as a volunteer twenty year previously, and his interest in Uganda had not waned.

On the way to Patongo we passed three villages where there had been massacres within the previous four years. In one incident, the LRA had cut off their victims' legs and boiled them in a pot; the survivors were instructed to eat the legs, only being saved from this gruesome cannibalism by the arrival of the army. In another incident, over two hundred people were slaughtered. Patongo had been the location of one of the biggest IDP camps in the north, but now that the LRA had departed, the numbers living in the camp had reduced, though it was still a busy trading centre with over thirty thousand inhabitants. During the war Médecins Sans Frontières operated a health centre, but as soon as the emergency was over, they pulled out and handed the health centre back to the government.

When we visited, there was evidence of previous medical activity, with a large waiting area for patients, but the area was now inhabited by only a couple of calves, and there were no patients. In the children's ward there were a few mothers with sick babies, attended by the sole health professional at the centre – a young nursing aid. Apparently the other staff had not reported, or had gone home for the weekend. In the medical ward there was a single patient who was dehydrated and wasted from TB. The nursing assistant had managed to give him some IV fluids, but otherwise he was in a pathetic condition.

We also visited an orphanage nearby, where we found thirty-six children below the age of four, all seated under a tree. They stared at us without reaction, and the staff told us that these were the most destitute – those who had no relatives – but they could have taken in six times that number if they had the resources. The people of Patongo had suffered much, and now that there was peace the situation had actually deteriorated because the relief agencies had pulled out, and the government health service was worse. A health centre which had a full complement of staff and drugs became a ghost centre, populated only by animals and a few pathetically sick people who could not gather the strength to go further. This was the reward for those who had managed to survive the war, those who were not boiled in a pot by the LRA, those who had kept body and soul together in an IDP camp – they were given fewer services and less healthcare.

Money which should have gone to support healthcare had been diverted. Was there not something strange about this order of priorities? In Pader there were thousands of people who were trying to put their lives back together and what priority had the government given to them? A twenty-eight year old man should not be dying alone from TB, and thirty-six children should not be huddled under a tree with no stimulation. My own children grew up with all kinds of inputs, so why were these children any different? Pader felt like the end of the world, but in reality it was only six hours drive from Kampala, but the people there could be forgiven for thinking that other Ugandans really did not care.

Twenty thousand pounds was not enough to set up a medical facility, and neither did I wish to work independently in that part of the country. I felt that the most productive way to use our limited resources was to work with a larger organisation such as UNICEF, or the government itself. We approached UNICEF, but after some months of trying – making complex project proposals and contacting officials at all levels – we were informed that UNICEF were no longer putting resources into this particular geographical area. UNICEF appeared to be a bureaucratic organisation, where it was unclear who the final decision makers were, or what were the priorities of the organisation.

We made contact with the Ministry of Health to try to understand their programme and spoke to the District Health Officer who promised that she would get back to us, but after several months we realised that we were getting nowhere. It was hard to understand why no-one wanted our help in an area which had been devastated by a war and where the existing medical services were clearly so inadequate.

Finally, one of my own managers, Patricia, told me that her family was from the north and her grandfather had been the Chief of the whole of Karamoja, which then included Pader. Her uncle was the head of the army battalion which was disarming the Karamajong warriors, and she felt that he would know someone in the hierarchy of Pader District. This went to prove that it was not what you knew, it was who you knew that counted – even if one wished to give away money. She recalled how her grandfather had gone big game hunting in the only Land rover in the whole district, and that he had a large compound with several wives, each with her own hut. When she visited as a child, she had made the mistake of eating her fill at the first grandmother's hut, since she then had four other dinners to get through to show equal respect for the other grandmothers. Patricia arranged a meeting with her uncle, a tall striking army officer, who told me that the site of the district headquarters in Pader was their family land, and he would arrange a meeting with the Head of the District.

We made another visit to Pader and found that the District Chairman was a lovely old gentleman, who was keen to work with us, and, in his position as chairman, he was also the boss of the various government health centres. He suggested that we work in the main government health centre in Pader town itself; hence our first public/private partnership was born. We appointed an administrator, a laboratory assistant, a nurse and a clinical officer and later a doctor, and we earmarked a supply of drugs to supplement the government drugs. There was a Ministry of Health budget for drugs and for supporting this health centre, but it was sometimes difficult to see where the money went, in that staff received their pay late, and drugs did not materialise. There were also other small things which were not budgeted for, with the result that vital equipment became non-functional. This was the case with the small Suzuki Jeep which could be used as an ambulance, but the tires were worn out and needed to be replaced, so we provided the funds and, as a result, had a functional ambulance. We also painted and refurbished the health centre, providing a better ambience and more privacy for patients and purchased equipment for the laboratory.

Initially, this collaboration was viewed with suspicion by the other clinic staff and it was like treading through treacle to get anything done, but gradually attitudes changed, and the government staff became more cooperative. At first there was a problem with getting people to come to work on time, but even that changed, and the staff started reporting regularly. The big change took place when we sent a doctor who provided leadership and motivation. Everyone began to take pride in their work, success bred success, and Simon was able to raise more funds to finance the programme – there was nothing like people knowing that their money was being effective to motivate them to give more.

Sadly, the momentum was lost when the government appointed another clinical officer as the 'in-charge' of the centre. This gentleman had an entirely different attitude and refused to co-operate. The result was that the project became paralysed, and after many promises that things would be different, we had to admit defeat and pull out. It was a poor reflection on public sector workers that the systems were so complex that people could not be called to account. It appeared that some of the government workers wished to get rid of us so that they could steal the drugs, and indeed, no sooner had we left than the senior sister from the health centre was caught stealing two large cartons of Septrin tablets. This was all a sad reflection on the ability of the government to provide even the most basic of health services to one of the neediest districts in Uganda. I felt that in the twenty years in which I had lived in Uganda, the delivery of health services by the government, in certain rural areas, had become worse not better.

# Engaging in Africa

One of the events which impacted me most was the Rwanda genocide.

Kiwoko Hospital was located in the Luweero Triangle, which had become known at the time as 'the killing fields of Africa' since many thousands of people perished there during the eighties. By the time we arrived there was peace, but there was ample evidence of the killings, with thousands of unburied skulls and human bones. Someone who fought in this war alongside Museveni was Colonel Fred Rwigyema who was born in Uganda but whose parents had fled from Rwanda in the conflict of the 1960s. By 1990 Colonel Fred was one of the leaders of the Rwanda Patriotic Front which invaded Rwanda. They represented stateless Rwandan Tutsis whom the Rwandan government would not acknowledge and who were no longer welcome in their own country. Colonel Fred died in the first days of the insurgency, but this marked the beginning of the war which sparked the Rwandan genocide and eventually resulted in the Rwanda Patriotic Front taking power.

Rwanda was our neighbouring country; many Ugandans and Rwandans shared common roots, and I knew and worked with the Banyarwanda, the name given to the Rwandese who lived in Uganda. Many were well educated professionals, such as nurses and administrators with whom it was easy to relate. At the time of the massacre I was studying in London at the School of Hygiene and Tropical Medicine, and as I listened to the news, I saw that the whole disaster that had befallen Luweero was being played out all over again while the world stood by doing nothing. The picture which was portrayed in London was of African tribes massacring each other again, but nothing could have been further from the truth. The people who were being killed were educated, intelligent people with families and friends who had, until that point, been living normal lives. And then they were mown down on the basis of which identity card they held.

I stopped trying to find any answers to Africa in terms of spiritual meaning, or answers about development, or understanding any big picture at all. I thought that such genocide had belonged to previous generations, but now it had happened twice within a few years, right on my own doorstep. At the time when rationally I should have given up on Africa because I no longer had any answers, the opposite happened. I felt that I could not walk away nor become an observer from afar; I could only engage with it. I knew that the tragedies would probably continue, but I could not just stand by. It was easier to engage than to observe and, being a doctor, my engagement was in medicine. Even if I could not understand the malaise of Africa, I could at the very least help individuals through my medical skills.

There is a rather overused story about a boy who was walking along the beach, throwing back starfish which had become marooned in the sand. A passer-by came upon him and, noting that there were thousands of starfish on the sands, asked why he was bothering, as it appeared to be a futile exercise. The boy thought about what the stranger said and then picked up another starfish and tossed it back in the water.

'But it is not futile to this one,' he observed.

I had not been back in Kampala for long when I met Miriam. I could not miss her: when she walked into the waiting room she lit it up; she was one of the most beautiful girls I have ever seen. She had come to consult me about what appeared to be a simple illness – a sore throat – but when I examined her, I found that she had oral thrush, a fungal throat infection which occurs in adults when their immune system is compromised. When I looked at the white plaques, I was pretty sure of the underlying disease – AIDS.

347

'How long have you had the sore throat?' I asked.

'For a few days,' she answered, and flashed one of her beautiful smiles.

'Have you ever had any other problems with your health?' I asked, trying to establish how long the illness had run. However, she was ignorant of other symptoms, and therefore, when I suggested an AIDS test, she replied, 'Why not?'

She had not really thought of the possibility that she could go to the doctor with a sore throat and be told that she had AIDS. But then, after reflection, she had second thoughts and asked for time to think about it. Hence, I treated the thrush and she went on her way, but a few weeks later she was back, and this time she was ready for the AIDS test. It was positive, as I was almost certain it would be.

'Are you in a relationship?' I asked. She told me that she was and that she also thought that I knew her boyfriend because he was a doctor.

'Please talk to him and tell him,' she pleaded with me.

When I went to see him, her boyfriend was blissfully unaware that anything was wrong and greeted me warmly. He had just been in theatre and was still in his scrubs,

'To what do I owe this pleasure?' he asked, as we settled down for a chat.

'I'm afraid I have some bad news,' I told him. 'Miriam has AIDS.'

Steve was in a state of complete shock. For some reason he had not even thought it was a possibility. His second reaction was that he wanted an AIDS test himself, immediately. I carried out the test which turned out to be negative. He made me do a whole series of tests over the next few months, but all the results were negative – they were a discordant couple – and although she was in late stage AIDS, she had failed to transmit the virus.

This was at the time when mono and dual anti-retroviral therapy were becoming available, but not yet triple therapy.

348

Miriam's boyfriend took her to the United States for treatment, but in her case the treatment slowed the progress of the disease hardly at all. She wasted away to skeletal proportions and there was nothing that we could do, except try to give her some comfort as we watched her die. Steve looked haunted as he saw Miriam shrivel up before his eyes. He would hold her in his arms and comfort her – just being a presence with her in the last weeks and days of her life – but none of us could stop what was happening, and when she cried and said, 'Why is this happening to me?' we all cried with her because we had no answers.

Rose was with me when we visited Miriam and Steve in their home, and it was a tough experience for all of us, mostly because, even though we were all medical professionals, there were none of us who were not touched in our soul by Miriam's plight. She was an innocent girl, who should have had so much living to do, but she was dying before our eyes, and we were powerless to do anything. We felt guilty – guilty that we could do nothing, and guilty that we were going on with life but she was not.

A twenty-four year old girl who had a spinal tumour was treated in my hospital. By the time of her treatment we had developed International Hospital to the level where it had an intensive care unit, and we were able to give sophisticated medical treatment, including life support on a ventilator. The tumour was an astrocytoma which had progressed rapidly and was pressing on her vital centres, but it was inoperable, and the outlook was hopeless.

However, we were able to add a few more weeks to her life and give her love and care in her last days. Africa can be a harsh environment in which to die, and there are many who do not die with dignity. At least we gave Diana some degree of dignity and the knowledge that there were people caring for her in her last hours. It was hard to watch a twenty-four year old die; she was paralysed apart from her right leg, but she could smile, and I was rewarded on several occasions by her weak smile. I would touch her arm and then, remembering that she might not feel that, I would touch her foot, and she would smile at me. She could not talk because she had a tracheostomy, but we had made a connection. A few days later, she became semi-conscious and died. I had thought she might rally and I would see her smile again, but it was not to be, and although I hardly knew Diana, she touched my life.

The following week we had a foreign patient admitted to the same ICU. He was a gentleman in his seventies who was in chronic heart failure. He had come to Uganda on a long flight, and the travel and altitude had compromised his oxygen circulation, putting more strain on the heart. The journey tipped him into acute heart failure, so he was brought from the airport straight to the hospital. The doctor in charge of ICU told the relatives that the outlook was poor, and we also had a cardiologist assess his condition which confirmed the poor prognosis. As had been predicted, in the early hours of the morning the patient deteriorated, and he died, but the staff on duty made a poor attempt at resuscitation. It was a case in which resuscitation should not even have been attempted, but the relatives were furious because they had been present during the abortive attempt and thought that those involved were incompetent.

In their grief and frustration, they made all kinds of derogatory statements about how bad the staff were, how bad the hospital was, and finished by saying that it should be closed down. While I understood their grief, and was myself disappointed by the poor performance, I knew that the outcome would have been the same. But I was also hurt that someone could walk into a country and, within a few hours, write off what we had been building for many years. Our work was a long term attempt to mitigate suffering and bring professionalism and hope to the community. No part of it had been easy, and there had been many frustrations along the way, but did that mean that one should just write off our attempts as futile?

There was no way that we could change the fate of any of these patients. At the time the drugs were not available to change the course of Miriam's AIDS, but we were at least able to be with her. Diana was beyond hope, but we could bring some comfort and dignity to her passing. Even the gentleman had received care that would not have been available in Uganda a few years previously.

Africa is not an easy place in which to work, and for people with a superficial involvement the effort might appear futile. What one can do may appear so little and so fragile that some feel it is not even worth trying, but there are those who work here because it is more difficult to stand by and do nothing. Engaging in the society, trying to make a difference, training people, making a system work, can be difficult and often discouraging, but on the other hand, a smile from someone like Diana can make it worthwhile. When I look back on Miriam and the pain she went through, I wish we could have done more, but if we were treating her today, we could stop the disease in its tracks, not simply because of the progress of medical research, but because we ourselves have progressed in the development of the facilities and professionalism.

My own experience of having cancer and the knowledge that without the professional treatment I received I would not be here today drove me to keep trying. It is often an accident of birth which is the deciding factor whether one lives or dies, and there is the mentality that places like sub-Saharan Africa are basket cases where the population is condemned to suffer from conditions which the developed world has long since conquered. But someone struggled to understand and research the drug which saved my life. Someone trained as a doctor to give the latest regime in chemotherapy, and another person

351

trained as a nurse to administer the drugs, and I am alive as a result. I have benefited from the dedication and professionalism of others. Do we not owe the same debt to our fellow man in Africa?

The situation may well be like the boy throwing the starfish back into the sea, but we will have engaged with lives, brought hope and made a difference to some. And even if at times it all appears futile, I would rather be engaged than to stand on the sidelines looking on, as the world did while hundreds of thousands of Rwandans perished.

# Open Heart surgery

We had now developed six divisions of International Medical Group: International Hospital Kampala, International Medical Centres, International Air Ambulance (IAA Healthcare), International Health Science University, IMG Construction and International Medical Foundation, and we employed over six hundred people. We had come a long way since treating patients under a tree or in the vestibule of the church in Kiwoko, but this had not been in an effort to build an empire, it was because there was always more to do. The various parts of the organisation promoted each other in terms of building capacity and developing infrastructure.

It was still not possible to concentrate on one activity like running the hospital without taking care of the other parts of the equation, such as healthcare financing, nursing standards or primary healthcare; thus, we were developing our own complete solution. Besides those patients who paid cash, IAA provided an affordable method of financing and contributed about 60% of our total income. The hospital was developing the capacity to handle complex and sophisticated procedures, the university was training nurses and health professionals, and the clinics were providing primary care. The Foundation, in turn, was using the primary healthcare facilities for community and charitable programmes, plus the capacity of the hospital for complex treatment of the destitute. The construction division provided the necessary expertise to build the hospital, was instrumental in adding value, and was continually called upon to build and renovate more clinics. And all parts of the organisation benefited from the corporate functions of Finance, HR, IT, Transport, Executive management and corporate governance.

When I moved to Kampala, I had set in motion a programme to bring development through a commercially-driven, self-sustaining model, and we were demonstrating that it was possible. But like any other fast growing business, we were under pressure to find more capital for expansion. We had not borrowed heavily nor been the recipient of private equity or grant funding, and there never seemed to be enough resources to fulfil our vision. It was a very different model from the usual developing country, aid-funded project, where one put in a proposal, the budget was approved and the programme carried out accordingly. Also, despite being relatively large and well managed along accepted corporate lines, we were still entrepreneurial in that I was prepared to take risks and push the boat out for an ideal, even if there was not a clear budget or money in the bank. If we felt it was right to embark on a certain project, such as the nursing school, we would go ahead, even though it put us under financial pressure. This was not a business strategy to be recommended, as it was highly risky, but on the other hand, had we concentrated solely on the profitable aspects of the organisation, we would have simply been a private hospital, treating those at the top of the pyramid. We had a larger vision to build the capacity to deliver healthcare in Uganda at the top, middle and base of the pyramid.

Our vision of making a difference to healthcare through developing local capacity had many facets, one of which was to expose Ugandan professionals to accepted international standards, but one problem with sending health professionals abroad was that many never returned. Another aspect of our vision was to provide affordable quality healthcare within Uganda itself. Patients tended to look to South Africa as having the best healthcare, but the cost of private medical treatment in South Africa was high compared to the earning power of East Africans. The other option for good medical care was in Nairobi, but the doctors in the private Nairobi Hospitals had modelled their charges on South Africa, making the cost of medical treatment in Nairobi exceedingly expensive. As a result, East Africans were increasingly turning to India, and hospitals such as the Apollo Group were capitalising on this trend in medical tourism. I wanted to grow our own capacity to enable us to offer medical care up to the standards of Nairobi or South Africa, but on the Indian pricing model so that the treatment costs would be commensurate with East African purchasing power.

I reckoned that if I formed collaborations with Indian hospitals for the treatment of patients who were beyond our capacity, but also made an arrangement for these hospitals to train our nurses and doctors, this would help us to build up our own capacity. Another advantage of sending medical staff to India was that they were likely to return because the climate and working conditions in Uganda were more attractive than India.

Co-incidentally, I was approached by an executive from Apollo Hospitals with a proposal for a joint venture with IHK. Apollo Hospitals are the largest hospital group in India, worth over seven hundred and fifty million dollars, and were interested in exploring opportunities for expansion in Africa. They had a joint venture in Mauritius and had been working with several other African governments in consultancy roles. I was flattered that such a large hospital group had even noticed our existence and realised that a collaboration would have many tangible benefits for IHK. I was invited to visit their hospital in Ahmedabad and to travel to Chennai to meet the chairman. The Ahmedabad hospital was impressive, but had not been doing well in the local market and was looking to develop medical tourism in order to boost its business.

The chairman of the group, Dr Reddy, was seventy-five years old, but still held the majority shareholding and was very much in control. He expressed his desire to form a joint venture with IHK; we shook hands and I left, leaving his development and financial team to work out the details. Surprisingly, nothing happened, and I wondered how their team was organising their due diligence and moving the project forward. Then I received a phone call to say that they wished to have an MOU ready for signing within a week because the Chief Minister of Gujarat State was travelling to Uganda with an Apollo Hospital Director. Their approach appeared to be heavily influenced by a desire to make the right political connections, though this was not the way I worked. Perhaps this consideration was dictating their stop/start approach because, within another week, I had yet another message saying that the trip had been cancelled, and they were rethinking their expansion programme in the light of global financial considerations. The collaboration with their Hospital in Ahmedabad did go ahead, with training of staff, consultants visiting from their hospital, and referral of patients for tertiary care, particularly for cancer treatment. We sent nurses for practical training in specialties such as ICU, operating room, renal dialysis and orthopaedic surgery, all of whom benefited from being exposed to high standards of clinical practice in India.

I wondered if the interest of the Apollo Group was due to the discovery of oil in Uganda, thus making it an attractive proposition for the development of high level medical services to take advantage of the predicted oil wealth.

For my part, I was not sure what would happen to the country when we began extracting the promised oil. Several companies had been drilling for oil in the Lake Albert Basin for a number of years. The first company, known as Heritage Oil, struck what they thought was a rich well (because the oil came out under great pressure), only to discover that the pressure was caused by a build up of carbon dioxide gas. It was like shaking a fizzy drink, and the strike proved to be useless; but before long another company, Tullow Oil, had struck oil, and from then on it was a matter of counting the productive strikes and calculating the barrels. The oil deposits appeared to be plentiful, and plans were advanced for a mini-refinery, plus a pipeline to export the oil. Uganda was set to be an oil producing state and the question was would this bring tangible benefits to the ordinary citizen? The figures for oil producing African economies showed that they generally grew faster than their non-oil producing neighbours, but that the discovery of oil or mineral wealth had actually caused certain countries to regress. Apparently the main factor was not the level of the oil, but the level of good governance.

In the case of Uganda the economy was growing steadily, even without oil revenues, but we could not yet make a definitive judgement as to whether the levels of good governance and checks against pilfering of the national resources were sufficient to ensure prosperity for the masses.

There was a case in which land was purchased by the National Social Security Fund, in which the manager claimed that he was pressurised by politicians. The minister involved was absolved by the President, though the Parliamentary inquiry was split on who was to blame, but the case illustrated the temptation for those in public office to use their influence to manipulate public resources, and if this happened with oil, we would be in trouble.

In Nigeria the temptation was such that almost all the oil wealth disappeared into the generals' personal bank accounts, leaving the ordinary Nigerian impoverished. The history of oil producing countries with poor governance was that, after an initial boost from the oil revenues, ordinary people were left more impoverished because of the upsurge of inflation and rampant corruption. Funds which were meant for the development of infrastructure were misspent, but since the example of corruption was set from the top, ordinary people felt justified in acting in the same way. Bribes and pilfering at every level of the society then became the norm, and it was difficult to carry out businesses in any cost effective manner. One only had to look across the border at Congo to realise that, although they had vast mineral wealth, the cost of doing business in Congo was so astronomical there was little development which benefited ordinary people. The promise of oil wealth also raised the stakes politically, and the argument that the end justified the means became more compelling. The President saw the revenues generated by oil as a means to develop long term infrastructure, such as a pipeline to the coast, a mini-refinery for the region, roads, power supply and railway lines, all of which were noble aspirations. But would it happen? Heritage Oil decided to cash in immediately and sold out to Tullow Oil for a price of $1.35 billion, which represented just under half of Uganda's national budget.

I was still interested in a more substantive collaboration with a centre of excellence in India or with specialists from other parts of the world, since I needed to fill the gaps in our expertise and build up the professionalism necessary to develop high-tech medicine. One specialised area was cardiac surgery which was not being carried out within Uganda, apart from inserting pacemakers. I had been approached by a Ugandan lady whose husband, Dr Clement Agyn, was a cardiac surgeon working in London. She told me that her husband was prepared to come to Uganda to carry out heart surgery; the question was did we have the facilities and equipment for such high level procedures? Although we had the theatres and the physical facilities, we were still building up our medical equipment for sophisticated procedures.

The equipment in the hospital was a mixture of second-hand and new equipment since we did not have sufficient resources to purchase everything new. We had bought some second-hand equipment from the UK, we had new equipment from Europe, and we had received donations of used equipment from Ireland and Australia. Some of the equipment from Ireland came through a retired anaesthetist who scoured the hospitals in Northern Ireland, filled up his garage, and then sent out a container with various types of hospital equipment. Some of it was very useful and continued to serve us for several years, but, unfortunately, many items had small faults, and we had difficulty getting these items fully functional. He sent six electric operating tables, but, no matter how we tried, we could only make one of them functional, not because they had major faults, but because we did not have the full technical manuals, and our biomedical engineers were limited in their capability. Donated medical equipment was a mixed blessing, and the more high-tech items were particularly apt to fail due to some relatively minor problem, or the lack of a part which we could not source. The low-tech stuff, such as hospital beds, stainless steel trolleys, theatre lights and drip stands, was relatively easy to fix, and small electrical instruments, like ECG machines, defibrillators and monitors, worked well, though there was a high attrition rate and we needed surplus machines for spare parts.

It was not easy to get the balance right; new equipment was the most desirable, but was exceedingly expensive, and when staff were not familiar with these new gadgets, they sometimes found unique ways to disable them. I was never sure if the abuse was intentional, but since there was a cultural mentality that the fault always lay with the machine and not the operator, no-one had any compunction about pressing all the wrong buttons and then reporting: 'It has refused', meaning that it was not my fault that I did not read the instructions.

Knowing that many members of staff were technophobic, we ensured that the instructions were attached to the machines and that if, for example, the equipment was 110 volts, we not only labelled 110 volts on the machine itself but had a different plug which would not fit into the 220 supply. Despite these precautions, someone still managed to incinerate the theatre diathermy machine itself. In order to do this, he had to overcome great obstacles, like finding an extension cable which could connect the different types of plug and ignoring the 110 volts sign and the transformer. But he overcame all the difficulties and succeeded in frying the machine.

Of course, I was not happy when I heard of such incidents and made my displeasure felt quite vociferously, but my modern management technique of shouting at people still did not stop equipment being destroyed. We bought a very expensive battery-driven orthopaedic drill which someone then immersed in strong disinfectant. This did the trick of ensuring the drill was decontaminated, but also corroded all the wiring on a £20,000 drill, and the bill for repair was $7,000. Since I could buy a new Chinese drill for $2,000, I opted for that choice instead because if they broke it again the replacement would only be $2,000. The challenges of keeping equipment in good working order were immense as we also had to cope with power outages, power fluctuations, lack of spare parts, technophobia, and lack of basic scientific skills.

We had a very generous donation of a CT scanner from our friends at the Mater Hospital in Perth, but for some reason they did not send the printer, so although we could do scans, we could not print the films. After some time they sent the printer, but there were no cables, and the hard drive appeared to be corrupted. The CT was Toshiba and the Toshiba sub-dealership was in Nairobi, so they sent their representative who looked at the machine, charged us a couple of thousand dollars, and returned to Nairobi, saying she would be back to finish the job – which was the last we heard of that company. There was also a company in South Africa representing Toshiba who made a proposal to train us in the use of the machine. But we did not need to be trained; we wanted it to print films. We were then contacted by an Indian company who claimed they were experts on Toshiba CT scanners. They sent over an engineer who worked on the machine with some success, so we thought that, at last, we were about to solve the problem, but he also left, saying that the machine needed a part which would cost another five thousand dollars, and when he received the money, he would come back to make the machine fully functional – and that was the last we saw of that company, or our five thousand dollars. The struggle to purchase medical equipment and keep it working was part of my everyday responsibility, and I learned as I went along – mostly that second-hand medical equipment meant hard work and sleepless nights, but, on the other hand, much of this used equipment served to get us started, and the value of the equipment which was sabotaged by staff was less than the new stuff.

Dr Clement was an experienced cardiothoracic surgeon with strong connections to Uganda in the form of his wife, and his children who were at school in Uganda. A London hospital had donated a heart-lung bypass machine and a set of cardiac instruments, all of which were shipped to IHK.

Cardiac surgery is one of the most complicated forms of surgery since it requires that the heart be stopped for certain procedures, such as the repair of a hole in the heart or the replacement of heart valves. The blood is then circulated through the heart lung by-pass machine in order that the brain and the other organs continue to receive oxygen, and the heart is cooled and paralysed. Clement worked with Dr Moses for several months to ensure that we had all the necessary equipment and were sufficiently prepared to carry out this complex surgery. It was also important that the Intensive Care Unit was up to par since this was not just a case of doing the surgery: the patients needed specialised intensive care in the post-operative period.

After nine months of preparations, we judged that we had everything in place, and open heart surgery was carried out on several destitute children who had congenital heart defects. This was made possible through the sponsorship of a local business Hwan Sung Industries. We did the first open heart surgery without fanfare and ensured that our patients were well on the way to recovery before we informed the press. But since

361

this was the first time that open heart surgery had been carried out in Uganda, there was intense interest, and the story made the headlines. The only people who were not happy were the surgeons at the cardiology department in the government hospital since they felt it was their mandate to carry out these pioneering procedures, and we had pipped them at the post. But the event eventually worked in their favour in that they were able to lobby for government funds to equip their own department.

Carrying out open heart surgery at International Hospital was a definite milestone for us and allowed us to see how far we had come, from the time we had first treated patients in Luweero under a tree and opened the first clinic in Kampala. The fact that we were able to carry out such a sophisticated procedure helped us to benchmark what was possible and where we still wanted to get to in the future.

Our journey was still not at an end, and perhaps this was just a beginning for the development of tertiary care at IHK.

# A sense of civic responsibility

Uganda is a beautiful country, and Kampala is said to be a city set on seven hills. Actually, it is set on many more than seven, but either someone could not count, or they liked the symmetry of seven. If one stands on top of one of the hills overlooking the city, it appears beautiful, with much greenery and with Lake Victoria shimmering in the background. It is only when one gets onto the streets themselves that Kampala is seen to be the filthy city it is – apart from a few areas of the central business district which are kept swept and clean for the benefit of visiting dignitaries. Otherwise, the rubbish, plastic bags and filth, washed down with the dirt eroded from the hills, block the storm drains which then overflow onto the streets. I always felt bad driving through the rubbish-strewn streets, but it was not my job to clean them, nor would I have known where to start. So, when I got a call from the Deputy Secretary to the Treasury that I had been summoned by higher powers to help clean up the city, I felt it was my civic responsibility to help.

I had heard that Britain was using cameras to catch people throwing litter out of their cars, but this would hardly be necessary in Uganda as one could follow any vehicle by the trail of plastic bottles and litter that spewed out from the windows. Otherwise well educated people saw no problem with chucking their litter on the road, and in most scenic locations the ground was covered with plastic bags and rubbish. In fact, if archaeologists were to carry out a dig in a thousand years time, they would be able to mark this generation of African civilisation by the layer of plastic bags. The sight of a plastic bag strewn landscape was so ubiquitous that the government finally decided to do something about it. Uganda and Rwanda therefore banned plastic bags, but while Rwanda banned all plastic bags, period, Uganda banned certain types of plastic bags so that there was no noticeable difference, and plastic bags continued to litter the landscape. We recognised the problem but managed to fudge the issue and then do nothing.

People in Uganda are generally very clean, in terms of personal hygiene and cleanliness of their own homes, but they have no compunction about throwing their garbage over the wall, and once it is in the public domain, they do not see it as their responsibility. This problem is particularly acute in the slums where there is no formal garbage collection, and rubbish decomposes where it is left. This, taken together with the lack of drainage, poses a public health hazard, and diseases, such as cholera and dysentery, are rife in the slums. Donors do not generally wish to make funding available for the provision of such basic utilities, but efficient garbage collections and education in civic responsibility for the environment would do wonders for most African countries.

My experience of trying to clean up the environment brought mixed results. It started with the message that the President wished me to get involved in a City clean-up because Uganda was about to host a large African Development Bank conference. For some reason my name came up in the planning meetings as someone who could help to clean up the city. Perhaps it was because the President felt that it was a public health issue, and, as a doctor, I should therefore fix it. I was flattered that I had been singled out – even though it was a rather menial task. It was pointed out by some mean-spirited people, that, while others had been given prestigious positions as senior presidential advisors on health etc, I had the job of 'Official Presidential Garbage Collector.' But I was happy to oblige since I thought that it would be a good way to demonstrate that an ordinary citizen could help to make a cleaner city.

I was asked to work with a Division of the City Council to clean up several roads, which included sweeping, removing piles of rubbish, grass cutting, and picking up litter. The Treasury allocated a budget of 15,000,000 shillings ($7,000) for the task, and I was put in charge of the project. I hired casual labourers, bought the necessary brooms and shovels, hired trucks, a tractor, and grass cutter and got on with the job. It was not a very complicated task, and with the combination of three city council trucks and two of my own, plus several pickups and fifty workers, we were able to make an impact fairly quickly. There was some resistance at first because I stopped the practice of the city council truck drivers taking their trucks home in the evenings, as I knew that they drove their trucks to a slum in Kampala where the fuel was siphoned off and sold. The drivers were not impressed that I had stopped this source of income, but it saved the project a significant amount of money. The conference took place, the roads looked clean and tidy, and I received a personal letter of thanks from the President for my trouble.

I had not been asked to keep any accounts for the money which I received, but since this was public money, I kept detailed accounts of all that was spent. We opened a spreadsheet, made workers sign for their wages, kept the records and, at the end of the exercise, I submitted the records to the Deputy Secretary of the Treasury. I also had a small amount of money left and asked what I should do with it.

'Should I return it?' I enquired.

I think that she was somewhat stumped by my question since no-one ever offered to give money back.

'Just keep it and continue what you are doing,' was her reply, which I did until the money was finished.

Several years later I was once again asked to partner with the Ministry of Works and the First Lady's office in cleaning up and beautifying the city when Uganda hosted the Commonwealth Heads of Government Conference (CHOGM). This biannual event, where the heads of fifty-three countries meet for a two day conference, is held in various commonwealth countries, and Uganda had been chosen to host the conference that particular year. There were immense implications in hosting such a conference in terms of developing the infrastructure, organising security, planting trees and cleaning up the city. Various sub-committees were formed, chaired by the Permanent Secretaries of the concerned ministries. I received a fax from the President appointing me to the committee for infrastructure and beautification. I think this was in my capacity as a doctor and public health physician once again, since there were various mandates contained in the fax: beautification of the city and green spaces, improving the infrastructure of roads and pavements, cleaning up garbage and, on the public health side, there was a line which read, '...and keep all these people from peeing all over the place.'

This was another interesting mandate from the President which stemmed from his observation that Ugandan men were constantly to be seen 'peeing' at the sides of the roads. Short of hiring a 'pee patrol' with a cattle prod to arrest those who were caught in the act, one could only address the problem by building more public conveniences and educating the male members of the community in their proper use. I was thinking of what title I could attach to this particular mandate and decided on 'Presidential Advisor on Proper Peeing Practice.'

I was co-opted to the committee with the Mayors of Kampala and Entebbe and a host of civil servants and politicians. These were from the level of Minister down: Ministers of State, Permanent Secretaries, Commissioners, Chief Engineers and bureaucrats; I was the only person from the private sector. By the time I was appointed, there was still about a year to run until the event, which was sufficient time for preparations, though it was getting late for tree planting.

One of the main players was the senior engineer from the Ministry of Works and Transport who had the advantage of being able to disburse finances from his normal budget in order to get some things done. The committee had been discussing issues, such as garbage collection, for several months and had prepared a budget which had been revised twenty-one times before I joined. Many of the meetings were spent revising the budget, but then nothing happened since no money was released by the Ministry of Finance. On the only occasion when there were actual funds released, I was not present, and various Ministries and Municipalities quickly allocated the funds among themselves. I kept singing a song about getting on with the work. We could start planting trees, even if we did not have a large budget, because certain organisations had already promised seedlings; we needed to fix the existing potholes because the roads were deteriorating before our eyes; we needed a comprehensive plan to collect the garbage in the city. The chief engineer assured me after one of the meetings, 'Yes, yes, Dr, we know your concerns – potholes and garbage.'

But still nothing happened. Despite all my years in Uganda, I was still at odds with the way the government system worked.

After some time I began to wonder what I was doing – since I had no authority, no budget and nothing was happening – so I mooted that I would start work, myself, on the beautification of a small park in the centre of the city. The suggestion was greeted with enthusiasm and applause, and the Mayor himself took me to the park and gave the project his blessing, even informing me that there was now a small budget for this particular project. No money materialised, but with the help of the Chief Engineer, some machinery was provided to grade the park, remove the old covering, and spread new topsoil. So I got on with the job and persuaded my old friend, Roger Wood, who had green fingers, to landscape the park free of charge. No sooner had we commenced work than I received a phone-call from the company, Uganda Telecom, asking me what I thought I was doing tearing up their land.

'There must be a mistake; this is a Kampala City Council Park.'

'It definitely is not,' I was told, 'our company purchased that land more than a year ago, and we intend to build our new headquarters there.'

I failed to understand how the Mayor of a city had mislaid a park, but, when I confronted him with this new information, he just shrugged his shoulders as if this were normal. State House still wished to have the park remodelled since the President drove past it every day, so the owners, wishing to keep on the right side of the powers that be, gave their permission to continue, but told me they intended to rip it up again after CHOGM. This was a bit disheartening since my objective had been to make a park for the city which people could enjoy for years to come. By this time, I had already spent my own money, but, since CHOGM funds were now being released, I was encouraged to requisition funds for the project. It was suggested that I lay paving stones for pathways, plant flowers etc.

'I will need money to cover the work that I have already carried out,' I suggested.

'But it is not in the budget. If you are carrying out work, you must first tender, then it has to be passed through the Public Procurement and Disposal of Assets body (the PPDA), and then you may be awarded the contract and paid in due course.'

'But I have already spent the money and carried out some of the work,' I pointed out.

As far as the Permanent Secretary was concerned, this was not his problem, and procedures were procedures. To the uninitiated, the purpose of the meetings appeared to be to ensure that money was allocated to contractors who could work hand in hand with the civil servants, but I was not an insider and did not really know what was going on.

It was later found that much of the funds could not be accounted for, and there was a public outcry about the shoddy work. The Inspectorate of Government was put under pressure to take action and prosecuted the chief engineer of the Ministry of Works for neglect of duty. He was picked up by the police on the way to the airport and spent a couple of nights in jail while he awaited bail; he did look a bit shocked when he was carted off – maybe he should have listened to my 'song' and just fixed the potholes.

Subsequently, it was shown that there had been misuse and theft of funds on a staggering scale, with contracts being awarded with little to show for the money. Hotels which were not ready received large advances, and civil servants were simply unable to account for where the money had disappeared. The procedures were obviously being manipulated; no procedure could substitute for integrity, and the introduction of ever more complex bureaucracy and procedures created more layers for people to hide behind. However, the chief Engineer did not fare well because he had awarded certain contracts without proper authorisation and was unable to prove that he had followed procedures. He was, therefore, imprisoned for two years for causing financial loss to the government, but he was again out on bail within a short time.

During the CHOGM initiative, I learned there was little I could do within the system, so I finished the park and never went back to any further time-wasting committee meetings. It was a definite improvement on the piece of waste ground it had previously been, and the Telecom Company finally decided not to build their headquarters on that site, so the park survived.

Two years after the first clean-up of Kampala, a Parliamentary public accounts committee was going through the Inspector General's report on the government's expenditure for that year. They came across an allocation of 50,000,000 shillings to Kampala City Council which had been designated 'for buying rubbish bins, fixing street lights and cleaning the city.' So they called the Town Clerk to account for the use of the money, and she told them that Dr Ian Clarke had been given 15,000,000 shillings for cleaning up the city, in collaboration with Kampala City Council, while the other 35,000,000 shillings had been given to an engineer to make rubbish bins. The members of the committee were immediately interested in this piece of information, since it was unusual that a doctor should be given money to clean the city, and they smelled a rat – so to speak.

'Where is the accountability?' they asked immediately.

The Town Clerk blustered that, since she had been called at short notice, she had not had time to contact me but promised to bring the necessary documents the following week.

The press were covering the proceedings and picked up on the interchange and the following day the headline ran:

'Clarke mentioned in the loss of 50,000,000 shillings.'

I was furious with the newspaper, which seemed to be misreporting, but then I realised that the committee itself had presumed guilt until I proved myself innocent, and the reporter had reflected the tone of the meeting. I called the chairman and told him that I had already given the accountability two years previously, even though no one seemed interested at the time. He was non-committal.

'I have the information in a spreadsheet; I can send it to you.'

'That is no use,' was his immediate response, 'you could simply have made that up. Where is the proof of deliverables?'

'The deliverable was that I did the work,' I responded. 'At the time everyone expressed their satisfaction in the job done, I even had a letter of thanks from the President.'

'That is not relevant,' he said. 'Look, you may have to pay this money back.'

I began to dig up all the receipts and proof of payments from the time. I found the books where the workers had signed for their wages, receipts of fuel and items purchased, placed them with the spread sheet to show the disbursement of the funds and a letter of explanation, and took it personally to the

370

chairman's office. I called him later that night and it was apparent that he had not even gone through the file.

'Is what I sent you sufficient?' I asked him

'No, it is not enough.'

'But you have the copies of the payments, receipts, and disbursements,' I objected, 'what more do you need?'

He then seemed to take a look at what he had been sent and told me that they would call me later, and that was the last I heard from him.

Although I was never easily put down, these incidents made me think twice about getting involved in any more civic works associated with the government. It was, therefore, not surprising that others did not feel any sense of civic responsibility, and rubbish piled up, the environment was destroyed, and the natural beauty of Africa continued to be defaced.

In contrast, visitors to Rwanda were impressed by how clean and orderly the country was. The difference was that if the Rwandan President decreed there was a general cleaning day once a month, everyone turned out and picked up the rubbish, including the President himself. If there was a fine for people throwing litter out of their cars, there would certainly be no trail of plastic bottles. The difference between the cleanliness of Rwanda and many other sub-Saharan countries was striking because the laws on the environment were actually enforced.

# How deep is this pothole?

Kampala had been cleaned up somewhat for the Commonwealth Heads of Government Conference – at least along the routes for the official delegates. There was no problem with traffic for anyone with a big CHOGM sticker on his vehicle since other ordinary mortals were run off the roads, or the roads were closed to non-CHOGM traffic. As a result, great inconvenience was caused to normal Ugandans trying to get to and from work or conduct business, but the conference delegates did not notice. They were, however, taken aback by the breakneck speeds at which they were whisked through Kampala as if they were a medical emergency. We were all used to VIP convoys, where cars with heavily tinted windows sped through the streets, with police escorts in front and motorcycle outriders following.

Actually, we were used to high speed vehicles ripping through Kampala on any pretext. The funniest emergency which I observed was an ambulance which had been converted into a hearse by painting it entirely black, but they had left the flashing lights and the siren in place. So when they had an urgent dead body to transport, they went whistling through Kampala with sirens and lights blazing. Understandably, there were many jokes about having an urgent appointment with death, or Ugandans always being in a hurry even to reach the grave.

CHOGM brought a new kind of convoy where security operatives, riding in unmarked cars, drove on the wrong side of the road to force oncoming traffic off the road. Naturally, since they were speeding down the wrong side, they tended to crash into oncoming vehicles which were not nimble enough to dodge out of their way. One of these overenthusiastic escort vehicles was going so fast the driver could not manage to negotiate his way round the roundabout and just ploughed straight across, mashing up the newly created flower beds.

One key figure who had been responsible for ensuring the success of CHOGM was a Ugandan who owned a large conference centre by the lake, and who committed himself to build another luxury hotel to accommodate the heads of government. Although, notionally, there had been four years to prepare for CHOGM, nothing much was done for the first three years, and the hotel then had to be built and fully operational in under one year. This was a fairly normal way for government to work, and some of the projects, such as the refurbishment of the airport, were actually completed about two years after the event.

Sudhir Ruperalia's family had lived in Uganda for many years, having emigrated from India in the last century during the construction of the railway line from Mombasa to Kampala. The family members were traders but were then expelled by Idi Amin, so as a boy he grew up in the UK, but returned to Uganda with his new bride in the mid eighties. Within two decades he had become a multi-millionaire, with many businesses within and outside of Uganda, including a bank, property development, insurance, radio station, a rose farm and schools. His business and property interests were so extensive that sometimes it was easier to point out what he did not own, and there were many who questioned how he had become so fabulously rich in such a short time. But no matter how people speculated, he had put a large part of his money back into developing Uganda, including the huge conference facility which was one of the only places in East Africa with the capacity to host large international conferences for thousands of delegates.

The success of CHOGM hinged largely on Sudhir being able to finish his luxury all-suite hotel on time, and people were getting edgy, but Sudhir was a hands-on kind of guy, even though he had so many businesses. So he moved into the

373

conference centre and supervised the work himself. He was his own Clerk of Works and contractor and was there on the job overseeing every detail, down to tasting the jams. His work methods may have been unorthodox, but he succeeded in getting the job done. A few days before the conference, the landscape gardeners were still moving palm trees and laying the turf, but by the time the heads of government arrived, the hotel was fully operational, and there was not a construction worker to be seen. Sudhir had pulled it off, much to the President's relief. He had managed to build a five star hotel in less than a year, in a country where nothing ever went according to plan and where Murphy's Law was the rule.

'Why did you do it?' I later asked him, since the whole project must have been highly stressful.

'Not many people can say they have hosted fifty-six Heads of State at their place,' was his response. I suppose there was that.

Although the country got new hotels, (though some were incomplete by the time the conference started), and roads and pavements were repaired, it was not long before the roads reverted to their normal state, and we were left to struggle through the potholes again.

Unfortunately, although a large amount of money was thrown at CHOGM, there was very little to show for it in terms of lasting infrastructure, such as improved roads. There are different ways in which countries can be graded in terms of development, such as the corruption index, ease of doing business, or the transparency index. Personally, I thought that if one wanted a quick indicator of the level of development of any country, all one had to do was to use the 'pothole index' since the first impression that any visitor has on arriving in a country is created by the state of the roads. The capital cities of Uganda, Kenya and Tanzania were affectionately known by nicknames which summed up their main characteristics:

Nairobi was Nai-robbery, Dar es Salaam was Dar is a slum, and Kampala was Kam-pothole.

In western countries, where potholes were a thing of the past, only referred to in bedtime stories, cars which had two millimetres ground clearance could be driven with impunity, and people had forgotten what it was like to drive on a road strewn with potholes. Those who were foolish enough to purchase such vehicles for Uganda had to use them very carefully, in the awareness that they could be swallowed up by any self-respecting pothole, never be seen again if they made a wrong judgment. Either that or they just drove them around a couple of kilometres of well tarmaced roads in the Central Business District to show them off.

On my pothole index, Sweden or Germany, with their autobahns, would score 0 out of 10, since they did not even remember what a pothole looked like, while Uganda would score 10 out of 10, since we had redefined roads: a series of potholes with intervening tarmac. There were certain roads in Kampala where one would not even venture in a normal car after it had rained because one could not be sure how deep the potholes were. Some of Kampala's roads had been built on a swamp, and when the potholes developed, the road had no foundation, so it was possible to lose a whole car in one of them. But mostly we did not lose entire vehicles; we just lost patience, time, and shock absorbers as we negotiated our way along the roads.

Personally, I felt that potholes were a symbol of the defeat of a whole society, since we had collectively allowed potholes to multiply rampantly without checks or balances. Fixing a pothole was not exactly rocket science, but we signally failed to deal with them at any level. Anyone who used mechanized transport to get to work in Kampala spent hours in traffic jams, due to vehicles being slowed down at various junctions by strategically placed potholes. We then complained loudly and bitterly about the state of the roads, and yet there was apparently no-one in the whole of Uganda who was clever enough to tackle the pothole problem. This national failure was possibly explained by the fact that potholes were tricky and unpredictable, and, like the Ugandan female population, they had a high fertility and multiplied at an alarming rate. If they were fixed, they then cleverly rearranged themselves in different positions, and drivers got confused as to their location, so perhaps it was a strategic decision just to leave them alone.

Uganda was a great place to live – if you knew your way around, both figuratively and literally. This applied to whether one was doing business, or just driving or walking round the streets. Those of us who lived in Kampala were familiar with the location of the potholes, the open drainage channels, the uncovered manholes, the places where thieves hung out and even when there was likely to be a bad traffic snarl-up. We just dodged the hazards as a matter of everyday existence, but sometimes visitors were not so lucky. A journalist from an Irish newspaper contacted me to arrange an interview on a medical issue, so I fixed a time to meet her, but, unfortunately, due to the nightly traffic jam, she was late and had to cancel the appointment. The next day she sent a sms saying that she would be late again as she had been robbed the previous evening.

Apparently, after she got stuck in the traffic, she got out of the taxi and went to a shopping centre to use the internet; then at around six-thirty, she decided to walk the short distance back to her hotel. One of the features of the pavement along which she was walking was the open manholes from which the concrete covers had been stolen long ago. All the locals automatically avoided them, but being new, she did not know where they were located and fell into one. Fortunately, she landed on her feet and the manhole was dry, so she ended up standing in the hole, with her head and arms sticking out, clutching her glasses in one hand and her rucksack in the other.

As people passed by, they said, 'Oh sorry,' in the usual sympathetic Ugandan manner, but left her standing there. Perhaps they thought it was normal behaviour for Irish women to stand around in manholes. Eventually, she was able to climb out and continued on her way back to the hotel, but by this time darkness was falling and a man swooped down on her, tugged the bag off her shoulder, and disappeared into the bushes in the adjoining golf course. She shouted for help, and a couple of passers-by came to her aid and helpfully warned that it was not safe to pass that way in the evenings because thieves hung around the golf course. At this point the advice was somewhat redundant.

She was told she should report the theft to the police, and, after making it back to the hotel, she was able to get in contact with some friends who accompanied her to the police post to make the report. She recounted her tale to the policeman who laboriously copied it down into a large book, all the while plying her with probing investigative queries such as 'What tribe are you?' and 'Are you a housewife?' This was after she had explained that she was a journalist. When this exercise had been completed, the policeman said she would have to return the following day to make a full report because the laborious recording in the large book was just a log and not the real report.

Meantime, another policeman said they could go down to the golf-course where they knew these gangs hung out and obtain information, or even retrieve the stolen goods – with the help of a soda. She was under the impression that the police were going to do some community policing where they would distribute sodas to the golf course communities and information would be forthcoming. She was, therefore, confused when the policeman explained that giving a 'soda' was a small facilitation for them to go down to the golf-course, find those who were hanging around, and give them a good beating. This was a trusted and tried method of questioning, analogous to helping the police with their inquiries. And giving a soda did not actually mean a literal soda like a coke, but 'something small.'

# Who would be a President?

Living in Uganda was in certain ways like living in Northern Ireland since people talked politics morning, noon and night. Politics was not something which I wished to become actively engaged in, but it is not possible to live in Africa without having some opinion about local politics, since its influence is pervasive in every sphere. My opinion about Ugandan politics was not as clear cut or judgmental as some international commentators, and I tried to keep an open mind. All African politicians had their constituency to please, and, although some may have gone into politics for the right reasons, they almost all ended up being held hostage to the game of politics itself. There were politicians who were there by conviction and those who were pragmatists, but the former mutated into the latter as time went by.

The image of the African President has been tarnished by dictators who became caricatures of African politicians, notably Idi Amin, Robert Mugabe and Mobutu, among many others. Unfortunately, such men not only ran their countries like personal fiefdoms, but created an image in the minds of western commentators as to how all African Presidents would inevitably turn out. When presidential term limits were abolished in Uganda, there was a tacit judgment by the western media that this was the beginning of the end. This may or may not be true, but for those of us who had made a commitment to Uganda, one could not build our future on the forecasts of the pundits, though the honeymoon which President Museveni had enjoyed in the media definitely came to an end when term limits were abolished. This reaction was understandable as he could have abided by the system, stuck to the original constitution and had an orderly transition of power. Such a course of action would have demonstrated that the system was stronger than the man, but Uganda was still a relatively young

379

democracy, and people had more faith in the person than the system, which could also be said of many other African countries. And when the constitution was changed, other amendments were also introduced such as multiparty democracy, which was considered progressive by western powers. The problem people had with the abolition of term limits was the suspicion that coercion or inducements had been involved and that the country was now at the mercy of another 'big man' rather than a statesman.

In the event, President Museveni had the support of a clear majority of the population, both for the abolition of term limits and for his re-election. If there had been a clear succession plan, the issue might not have arisen, but there was no heir apparent, and people felt Museveni was the best option. Not only that, the choice of the opposition gave people pause for concern since he appeared to have old scores to settle. The opposition candidate, Col Besigye, had been an insider who felt that the President had departed from the original ideals. Unfortunately, the good that Colonel Besigye encapsulated was swallowed up in people's minds by the fear of violence since many believed that the incumbent President would not allow a peaceful transition, and the country could degenerate into more bloodshed. Ugandans had seen this so often in the past that most were happy to take the safe option of the President they knew – warts and all. Better the devil you know than the devil you don't know.

When I examined all the factors which an African President must balance: the different groups to be kept happy, the tribes where support must be garnered, the armed factions to be neutralized, I felt that the President had to be an expert juggler. Uganda's politics were far from perfect, particularly on the issue of dealing with corruption, but broadly speaking, the courts, Parliament, and the practice of democratic politics worked, after a fashion. President Museveni was not elected against the will of the majority; he was there because he was trusted by the majority, but as time passed, there was a growing minority who felt that he should move on. The problem was that as the number supporting the president shrank and the strength of the opposition grew, there were those with vested interests who felt there was too much at stake to leave the results of elections to chance. It was just a question of time as to when the majority might want a change, but those surrounding the President might not, and which of the two would prevail?

When the National Resistance Movement took power, they decided to take an inclusive line, in which the ruling party absorbed their former enemies into positions in the army and the government. This was on the basis of that well known political ideology: keep your friends close and your enemies closer. Hence, rebel groups and factions were absorbed and their former leaders given places and ministerial posts in the government. While this was a non-divisive line to follow, it set a precedent that one way to gain advantage was to be a dissident and then sit back and see what was on offer.

I was in South Sudan when talks were being held with the Lord's Resistance Army, and I met some of the delegation representing the LRA. While I understood that most of the representatives were not fighters themselves, some of them had given active financial support to the LRA. But I was surprised to find among their ranks a lawyer from Kampala whom I had known for a number of years and would never have pegged as a supporter of this murderous group. The story was that he had developed a grudge against the government because he had not progressed politically and was prepared to switch sides to represent the LRA in the hope of gaining leverage. There was also the matter of money because the members of the delegation were being handsomely rewarded on a per diem basis by the international agencies. My 'friend' was a failed politician and saw this role as a way back into politics. The inclusive approach taken by the President had spawned a political gravy train, since there were rewards for those who were sycophants, and there were rewards for those who opposed the government but were open to offers. Either way, politics was just business and it was easy to be cynical.

Since we had a western electoral system, the government stood or fell according to the electoral process. One consequence of this was that elections were prone to manipulation, rigging, and dirty tricks, since everything hinged on the results. A western democratic system works well in mature societies with well developed systems, but how much does an election really mean when the electorate themselves are looking for some tangible benefit for their vote in terms of sugar, salt, school fees or a little cash?

After the introduction of a multiparty system, the ruling party undertook a systematic campaign to unbalance the opposition candidate, including bringing charges of treason and rape. At first he was held in prison, but when he was brought before the courts he was given bail. The government was not happy with this decision and wished to have him re-arrested on fresh charges, so the court was surrounded by paramilitary figures dressed in black, (who were immediately nick-named the Black Mambas by the local population). Besigye and his fellow accused saw what was happening and took refuge in the Judge's chambers, but the Black Mambas followed their quarry into their Lordships' chambers, and a scuffle broke out. Understandably, the judiciary and the legal fraternity strongly objected to the manner in which these re-arrests were carried out, and the whole episode generated many column inches in the press, provoked media debates, and inflamed tempers. The Judiciary expressed their displeasure by going on strike, and the Law Society suspended membership for prominent government officials who were also qualified lawyers.

The Chief of Police, who was himself a law graduate, when interviewed by the media, made a curt, and to the point, response to his suspension by the Law Society.

'They can go to hell!' he said.

At the time there were questions raised: were these events the beginning of the end of constitutional democracy in Uganda? Was the separation of powers between the Executive and the Judiciary being over-ridden? Was this the beginning of dictatorship, or the rule of a rogue regime, as Col Besigye was fond of referring to the ruling party? Or was it all a storm in a teacup? The response of one DJ on a popular radio programme summed up the feelings of many: 'In Uganda life is good and beer is cheap, so what is all the fuss about?'

But the questions were legitimate, and the organs of state security had definitely overstepped their boundaries by barging right into their Lordships' chambers, where there was a general undignified fracas. The operation was carried out with the finesse of a bull in a china shop, and if those acting as the security arm of government had been more informed as to where the boundaries existed, and less prepared to ride roughshod over the rights of the court, there would have been no issue. But it was often the case in Africa that subordinates were so keen to do the 'big man's' bidding that in the process normal civil liberties were trampled underfoot.

In Besigye's court case, there had been a charge of rape and another of treason to answer, similar to the rape charge against Jacob Zuma in South Africa, and both Besigye and Zuma were acquitted. The reason the Ugandan trial faltered, which was probably also reflected in the South African trial, was that the State appeared to have such an obvious hand in supporting the key witness that her testimony was less credible. In essence, the case rested on the young lady's contention that she was not a willing partner. There was also the issue of her becoming HIV positive which she claimed was the result of her relationship with the colonel. While there was a certain ring of truth in her story, there was also the timing of the prosecution, which was years after the event and happened to be very convenient for the government in the midst of an election campaign. If there was a case to answer, one wondered why it had not been brought many years earlier.

The story was that the girl was being sponsored through her education by Besigye, who was her 'uncle', but one day, when they were home alone, he grabbed her and raped her, which resulted in a pregnancy and a subsequent abortion. However, they then continued the relationship as an affair, and he continued her sponsorship at university. He certainly took advantage of the girl's position, but in Africa such stories were so common that they hardly raised an eyebrow – the uncle became the lover, the girl got continued support as a mistress and life went on. Such girls were damned if they did and damned if they didn't. If the girl refused sex she might be forcefully raped; if she complained to the man's wife, the wife would throw her out, and all support would end. If she acquiesced, the man would continue to take advantage, and she would probably become pregnant. Then she would have the choice of having an abortion or of the family knowing that she was having an affair with the 'uncle.'

Although it may be hard for someone from the western world to understand, in an African society the girl was the one who was treated with suspicion and judged to be in the wrong. If a rape case was brought, the shame for the family was such that they would rally around the man and not the girl, and the penalty under the law was so harsh (it could be the death sentence), that the onus of proof and trail of evidence must be watertight. Even if the girl were to go to a police station on the night of the rape and make a report, there would have to be evidence of forced sex and signs of injury, since, in the mind of many people, rape was not defined as sex where the girl was unwilling, but violent sex in which the girl was injured.

The President had not only to handle the opposition candidate but to ensure that his own supporters remained loyal, which meant that he must have support across the tribal boundaries. There were scores of tribes in Uganda, with about a dozen large tribal blocks and many small ones, and although there was some suspicion between the various tribes, Uganda, unlike Kenya, was unlikely to split on purely tribal lines. This was not to say that there were not serious differences or suspicions which surfaced from time to time, but these were not large enough for the society to fracture. The largest tribe was the *Baganda* and the restoration of the King, or the *Kabaka*, was very significant for the *Baganda*. Historically, the *Kabaka* had been the most powerful king of the region, ruling over the Kingdom of Buganda from which Uganda derived its name. Buganda was the kingdom and *Luganda* was the spoken language. Before Uganda became a British Protectorate, the *Kabaka* was an absolute monarch with powers of life and death, and the *Kabakaship* was revered.

With the restoration of his monarchy, there were also questions of land ownership to be settled since the *Kabaka* had owned thousands of hectares of land, plus buildings and palaces, before he was exiled by the Obote regime. Many of these properties had been taken over by the army, and much of the land had been settled by squatters. In theory, the *Kabaka* was a very rich man, but in practice he had little unless the government gave back his lands. The government and the army vacated many of the buildings they had occupied, but there was still the question of the ownership of other land which had now been heavily settled by squatters. A new land law was formulated which gave the squatters rights of tenure, and many people took the opportunity to grab land at the *Kabaka's* expense. The *Baganda* were aggrieved since most of the squatters were non-*Baganda*, and relations between the *Baganda* and the government soured until an apparently insignificant incident ignited the simmering discontent, and there was rioting in the streets.

The incident which sparked the riots was a proposed visit by the *Kabaka* to a sub-county in his Kingdom, but a local chief was laying claim to this small area, and the government decreed that it was not safe for the *Kabaka* to travel. This was taken as dictating to the King within the boundaries of his own kingdom, and there was uproar since it was perceived that what lay behind the government's strategy was a policy of divide and rule. People had been given rewards for loyalty to the President in the form of government posts and through the sub-division of districts to create more government positions, but the opportunities were dwindling, and some people were demanding restoration of tribal and cultural rights for personal gain. It had come to the point where certain people were no longer seeing their country as one to which they owed common loyalty, but as a spoil to be divided up for personal benefit.

The rioting, in which twenty-seven people died and property was destroyed, was a wake -up call as to just how perilously close the society had drifted towards anarchy. The differences between the government and the Buganda Kingdom were real, and there were grievances which needed to be aired, but the proper theatre of negotiation was not on the streets. There were still those who wanted to keep dividing up the cake of the country into smaller and smaller pieces, hence the process of decentralisation and the creation of new districts had gone to the extremes, where new districts were hardly viable. But government supporters saw the creation of their own district as a reward, and there was one notable case where a man ate a rat in front of the President to draw attention to his demand for a new district. Others got their reward through political posts, so that sixty-four cabinet posts, with all the trappings, were created, while some decided their reward would be to resurrect small Chiefdoms. It all bred a 'me too' attitude. The job of the President was to hold it all together, but some of his actions, and the signals he was sending, made the situation worse.

I did not envy the President his job since he had the task of balancing all the conflicting demands, though there were those who felt he had brought the situation on himself. There were times when a benign dictatorship or autocracy would have been preferable, and it would certainly have been simpler since it would allow the President to deal with the real issues, such as improving the infrastructure, dealing with the high infant mortality, the biting poverty and poor health services. Instead, he spent most of his time politicking in an effort to keep this or that faction on board. One could say that this was the direct result of staying in power too long, but as our neighbours in Kenya had demonstrated, it was possible to change power democratically and the last state to be worse than the first.

Democratic politics have a different connotation in many African countries than in mature democracies such as Britain. For the voter it simply means: what is in it for me if I support you? Not in terms of altruistic benefit to the society, but how much sugar or salt, or cash are you giving me for my vote?

So when it came time for the President to get tough on corruption, the issue of political considerations always had to be taken into account, and consequences were titrated accordingly. It was a chicken and egg situation, and there was no easy solution. Multiparty politics was forced on Uganda by western donors, but one wondered if it really was the best solution for fragile democracies. But what was the alternative?

# Developing scalability and Advocacy

Although politics was business for a large number of people in Uganda, my business was to grow and develop IMG into a sustainable long term organisation which would serve the medical needs of Ugandans for generations to come. Although I had a great management team, and well defined company structure, much still rested on my shoulders, until I was joined by Kevin who brought a wealth of new management experience to the organization.

I had known Kevin since he was a student, and when we bought our house in England it happened to be round the corner from his home. His wife, Pamela, and Robbie were good friends, and although I would have described Kevin as a 'good bloke', we had not known each other very well and had lost touch while I was working in Uganda. Kevin had been successful in the world of finance, insurance, and IT, using the combination of his knowledge of IT and insurance to help set up direct selling divisions for large insurance organizations in the UK, such as Scottish Widows and The Prudential. He then developed his own consulting company, but in his mid forties he also asked the question I had asked many years previously: is this it?

He had some notion of contacting one of the large aid organizations and offering his services, but on a whim, he 'googled' me and was surprised to find that we already had a large organization and were making an impact on development in a third world country, so he called me up and asked if he could come to visit. This was the start of a significant relationship since Kevin decided that he wished to be involved in International Medical Group and brought a whole new raft of management skills and experience (and introduced new terminology – words such as inflection point, steady state, reaching a position of non-displacement and bandwidth. I had obviously not been reading the right management books).

He bought into the vision and volunteered to set up a UK registered charitable foundation through which he could channel donations to our non-profit projects and which would also allow the foundation to claim refunds on taxpayers' donations. We called the new foundation Suubi Trust – *suubi* being the *Luganda* word for Hope. Since Kevin had corporate and financial experience, I invited him to become a non-executive board member. He travelled from the UK at least three times a year for board meetings and strategic planning sessions, and his input was invaluable.

During his time as non-executive director, International Medical Foundation (IMF) became fully registered as an NGO (Non Government Organization) and he was appointed Chairman. In the first year of Suubi Trust's existence he raised $120,000 in philanthropic donations, including a significant amount from his own company. As International Medical Group continued to grow, Kevin was no longer satisfied with his role in visiting several times a year and wished for greater involvement, but this appeared to be difficult since his wife and family were firmly rooted in the UK. Then he asked to see me one evening before he was due to return again to the UK and came straight to the point.

'I want to join you,' he said.

I was quite taken aback because I had already accepted that it was not practical for him to move to Uganda.

'I can commute,' he stated.

This was a novel idea, when one lived five thousand miles away from one's place of employment, but he was not actually meaning to commute every day; he felt that if he organized his diary, he could work in Uganda and return after several weeks to the UK, while at other times his wife could travel to Uganda to be with him. He was quite serious about the plan because, with present day technology of e-mail and Blackberry, he could continue working from a distance. For my part I was delighted to have him on board and invited him to join me as Managing Director. It was a somewhat unusual arrangement to have a home in the UK and commute to Uganda, and he had interesting reactions from a few friends and acquaintances, who got the idea that he and Pamela were splitting up. Also they could not understand what he was going to do in Uganda. He was not a missionary, he was neither an aid worker nor a technical expert, and he was not going to work for a charity or a church. So what exactly was he doing?

'I will be doing exactly what I have been doing here,' he would explain. 'I will be managing a business: an HR department, a finance department, a sales and marketing department and an IT department just like any large business here. I will get up in the mornings and go to the office, and the conversations I will have with people regarding the management of the business will be similar to the conversations which I would have in the UK. Except that they will be with Ugandans, and I will be running a hospital group and not a financial institution.'

This seemed too much for people to take in, especially since he also said that he was being paid a commercial rate for the job. This was not what one was supposed to do in Africa; one was supposed to go there to help the poor people, to build schools or churches, or dig wells, not to run hospitals as corporate organizations.

After Kevin had been in the position of Managing Director for a few months, while I was the Chief Executive Officer, I decided that we were simply splitting the workload, and I would prefer him to take over as full CEO, while I stepped into the role of Chairman. By doing this I was relinquishing control of day to day matters, but it freed me for strategic developments and more medical involvement. I had been building the organization for fourteen years, while prior to that I had worked in Kiwoko Hospital for six years. Now I wanted to prioritize my time and not allow myself to be driven by the next most pressing need – at least that was the theory.

They say that the good will always be done at the expense of the best, or the urgent will take precedence over the important, and I wanted to prioritize the important. Although I was an energetic person, I was aware of my own mortality, having had cancer twice. I believed passionately in what I was doing, but I did not wish to go to my grave chasing the details and wished to have more time for strategy and advocacy in the effective delivery of healthcare in developing countries

The arrival of Kevin was an inflection point (to use his terminology) for the organization, in that we had added significant managerial skills which had a multiplier effect on what we could do. Kevin and I seemed to spark each other, such that the possible scope of projects mushroomed. Perhaps this was because I was more confident in our ability to carry out ever more complex projects. Kevin commented that when he first got involved in IMG he made the assumption I was a big picture man and did not know the details of the organization, but as he became more involved, he realized this was not the case. For my part, it had not been from choice but necessity, and one of my mantras, which I continually repeated, was 'the difference is in the detail.' Kevin's arrival allowed him to fine tune the systems and structures and optimize what we had been putting in place. It was a tribute to the tenacity and skills of the managers such as Hannah, Judy, Jackie, Marianne, Patricia, Rose, Moses and Andrew, that we had grown a clinic with no systems to a respected corporate entity employing seven hundred people.

During this time we were visited by some consultants from McKinsey who were carrying out a survey on behalf of the World Bank to establish the degree to which healthcare was delivered by the private sector in sub-Saharan Africa. They travelled round various countries and came out with a report entitled 'The Business of Health in Africa,' in which they quantified the amount of healthcare delivered by the private sector in Africa as being 45 -60%. This included all healthcare providers outside the government sector. The figure was no surprise to those of us working in Africa, but it seemed to come as a great revelation to the large donors and multilateral organizations, and the talk was of support for private healthcare. The realization was finally dawning that healthcare was not the sole prerogative of government, and although donors were putting practically 100% of resources into supporting government programmes, up to 60% of healthcare provision was not coming from government. The evidence showed that there was a contradiction in the way that healthcare was being funded and the manner in which it was being delivered.

Even though the evidence was there, donors did not immediately change their method of funding, which basically involved throwing money at the Ministries of Health and hoping that some of it would stick. A large part of the reason for donors staying with what they knew was that they had already invested large amounts of money, but there was a growing restlessness. As a tentative experiment, some of the larger donors and foundations decided to support a private equity fund aimed at investing in the private healthcare sector. The usual suspects put money into this fund, including the Gates Foundation and International Finance Corporation, the private arm of the World Bank. The funds were assigned to a private equity company, known as Aureos Capital, which was tasked with the duty of finding small and medium sized companies in the private healthcare field which needed equity to grow their businesses.

This development was precisely at the time when IMG needed more capital since our planned programme of expansion was greater than the resources available. We never seemed to have any money, and I was tired of being under pressure. So the idea of having an equity partner, with the same goals as us, was appealing.

We met Chas and Shakir in the Aureos' Nairobi office. Chas was the jovial, hail-fellow-well-met type, while Shakir was the canny, numbers-crunching Kenyan Indian. We liked them both and, when we talked, we were excited about what a partnership between Aureos Capital and IMG might mean. They had in mind the usual pattern for a private equity investment: they would put in money to buy a certain share of the company, with the understanding that the extra cash and leverage would lead to a liquidity event within five years. This could be a share offering on the local stock market or a buy-out by a larger hospital group who wished to expand to Africa. Both of us were interested in promoting our model for development and the word 'scalability' was often mentioned in the conversation: could the model be grown regionally? Could it be transplanted elsewhere? Chas was interested in the bottom of the pyramid since they had an investment in a local bank which had targeted the grass-roots market and which had then become one of the biggest banks in Kenya. He felt that we could use International Medical Foundation as a vehicle to experiment with different methods of financing and delivering healthcare in rural areas – making healthcare accessible to as many people as possible.

Part of the reason why we needed more money was because we wished to move International Hospital to another level in terms of equipment. We were already a good secondary hospital, with some tertiary specialties such as Intensive Care and heart surgery, but if we were to reach the standards of our competitors in Nairobi, we had to improve the level of equipment which meant a significant investment of three to four million dollars. Although this is not a large amount for a medium sized business in the UK or America, it was large for Uganda and would be expensive to borrow. The option of raising the necessary funds through a private equity

393

partnership, particularly when our goals were aligned, therefore seemed attractive. We met several times with Chas and Shakir, and I got the idea that they were playing a game of good cop, bad cop, with Chas as the enthusiastic visionary talking up the possibilities, while Shakir was positioned as the numbers-driven pessimist. His job was to soften us up by telling us how little our business was worth and what a favour they would be doing by investing in our company. He had an interesting way of valuing the assets which was fairly simple: he completely discounted them, so the actual hospital building – which I had built with sweat and tears – had no value, according to him

'After all,' he quipped, 'a hotel in the desert doesn't have any value.'

Our negotiations and interchanges were good humoured, and during the discussions someone remarked that this potential partnership was like a marriage in which we needed to get to know each other, to which Clive, who was negotiating on our behalf, added that if we were the bride we would like to be kissed before we got screwed. Shakir who was feeling somewhat hurt because his initial overtures had been roundly rejected, immediately shot back, 'So if you are the bride, then why is my butt hurting!'

Despite the apparent alignment of our organizations and the fact that I liked the principle behind the health fund, the cash which Aureos was offering was very expensive, and we turned them down. I was left wondering how this Health Fund would pan out – they had $100,000,000 given on the conditionality that they invested in health related businesses in Sub-Saharan Africa which affected the bottom of the pyramid, but the cost of their money was so high; how were they going to get takers for their fund? It looked like a good plan, but like all these things, the difference was in the detail, and perhaps Shakir was just a bit too commercially geared since the business of healthcare in Africa, particularly if one wished to serve the bottom billion, could not be highly profitable. If one was able to make such a business viable at all, it should be considered a success.

We had turned down Aureos' offer because we were not desperate. While I didn't wish to continue to run the business on a wing and a prayer, we were generating funds internally and some of the local banks and the medical equipment companies themselves were offering us finance. Philips Equipment had set up an African financial arm whereby they could finance the acquisition of their equipment over a four year period with a six months grace period. Siemens could make finance available and even the Chinese equipment companies were providing short term finance. Our dealings with Aureos had been another learning curve and helped us to consolidate our ideas regarding our strategic development plan for the next five years.

There were different aspects to what we were doing. On the one hand, we were striving to attain tertiary level services in order that we could be competitive and become a regional referral centre. On the other hand, we wished our services to be affordable for the patients and found that the optimal means of paying for them was through our own IAA medical schemes. We also wished to expand the primary care centres up-country, so that we could make quality healthcare available at the grassroots, particularly through our International Medical Foundation projects, such as the cross subsidised clinic in Lira, and the various HIV testing and treatment projects which we ran throughout Uganda.

We had already carried out open heart surgery on a number of occasions, but in order to maintain the required standards of practice in cardiology and cardiac surgery, we needed to develop the facilities further. This would enable us to carry out cardiac surgery and interventional cardiology on a regular basis, but the required investment was high. We had to buy a cardiac catheterization unit – a sort of giant X-ray machine – which tracked the passage of dye through tubes passed into the vessels of the heart. The pictures allowed the cardiologists to fix the plumbing by introducing balloons to open up blockages and insert stents to keep the pipes open. This piece of kit cost around one million dollars and was only one of several other pieces of equipment necessary for such a service. Setting up an interventional cardiology unit would cost at least $2,000,000 for the equipment, and even if we did have the necessary equipment, we did not have the expertise within Uganda. We would therefore have to collaborate with an international centre of excellence outside Uganda.

Joan Kelly owned an Irish pub in Kampala. She had worked in Uganda for quite a number of years and had all manner of occupations, from working at the visa section of the British High Commission to running the Irish pub. I reckoned that these particular occupations had more in common than people imagined, one of the fundamental skills required being the ability to tell miscreants that they had been refused entry, or as Joan was fond of saying,' you're barred!' The Irish pub was good *craic,* but there was a burst of Irish pub investment in Kampala, and two other Irish pubs opened at the same time, proving the adage that there is nothing new under the sun. Sadly, the competition was too great and only one man was left standing: a pub, which had been physically transported from the west of Ireland, with the name Bubbles O'Leary. So Joan was out of a job. When I met her again she had overcome this setback and was setting up an electronic data management company, as one does if one has experience working in the British Visa section and running an Irish pub. This particular project was with the aid of a development grant from the Government of the Netherlands.

'How did you get the grant?' I immediately inquired.

'One has to put in a proposal which involves collaborating with a foreign partner,' she told me. 'The foreign partner

396

provides the technical expertise on some new technology, while you provide the local knowledge. You set up the company, your partners bring in the technical know-how and train local people, and that is it. It used to be only in partnership with a Dutch company, but they dropped that requirement, and now the foreign partner can be from any country.'

'How did you qualify?' I asked

'Well I am the local partner, having lived here for so long,' she answered, 'and I married a Dutchman who is the foreign partner.'

Sounded like the perfect arranged marriage to me, and it did demonstrate a lot of commitment to the project.

I wondered if we should make an application to this organization for the interventional cardiology centre since we fitted all the criteria – though I wasn't prepared to marry a Dutchman. The fact was that this grant fitted exactly with the way I had been thinking; we needed a foreign partner to bring the training and expertise, and I knew just who to ask.

The general manager of the Tilda Rice Estate, Venu, had introduced me to his brother-in-law, Mohan, who worked for a hospital group in Kerala, South India, which owned a six-hundred-bed hospital known as Malabar Institute of Medical Science (MIMS). Most middle class professional Indians appeared to believe that Africa was backward, and it was only after they had paid a visit to Uganda that they were convinced that we were not living in the forest and swinging through the trees, Tarzan and Jane like. Mohan paid a visit and thought that this was not such a bad place and then persuaded his medical colleagues to come and see for themselves. These were highly skilled cardiac surgeons and cardiologists who had pioneered developments such as beating heart surgery in their part of the world and got excited about the opportunities for development which Uganda presented. Uganda was twenty years behind India medically, which motivated them to get involved in developing the same sort of services for Uganda which India now enjoyed.

We set up a joint venture, in which IHK would provide the infrastructure, the local knowledge, and the capital, while MIMS would provide the training and expertise, and we applied to the Netherlands development agency, EVD, for funding. EVD had done very few development projects in the field of healthcare and were initially sceptical that it could work, but finally the project was approved. In such a pioneering development, which required a large amount of capital and the introduction of new technology and expertise, there were many elements which needed to come together to make the project successful. The EVD grant was a stepping stone, without which we would have been unable to embark on the project because the risks and the financial exposure were high. But the collaboration with MIMS and the support from EVD made the development of an interventional cardiology centre a viable proposition.

While all this was going on, some planners in the Ministry of Health were pushing ahead with a proposal for the development of a Social Health Insurance Fund. Variations of such schemes were being run in Tanzania, Rwanda and Kenya, and someone had managed to get the introduction of social health insurance into the NRM party manifesto. The idea was that a further 4% would be collected in taxes, which would be matched with 4% from the employer. This money would be put in a pool, which would be managed as a health insurance fund from which extra health benefits would be provided to the population. Such a fund was supposed to act as a stimulus to the private sector to develop sophisticated medical facilities since there would be more cash available.

The principle was fine, but there were several major obstacles. The first was that most of the income for the fund would be coming from the formal private sector, which was already being heavily taxed, and Social Health Insurance would add a further 8% tax burden to that narrow tax base. The second problem was that the scheme would be a semi-autonomous government scheme, and Uganda had a terrible record in the stewardship of such bodies, including the NSSF, or any other fund controlled by the public sector. Another basic flaw was that those behind the proposal spent so much time lobbying for the legislation to pass that they forgot about the practicalities of how such a scheme would work. Very little in the way of accurate actuarial analysis had been carried out, and the method of payments for services and scope of the service were particularly sketchy. There was talk of 'fee for service payments' and great promises made about the benefits, but since no-one had any figures there was no substance behind the promises.

While I was not against such a scheme in principle, I did not agree that payment could be made on a fee for service basis since this was a recipe for over-treatment and fraud by the clinics. I had been in Uganda long enough to know that such a fund could not be entrusted to the public sector which had signally failed to manage any other public fund. I was also sceptical that the ordinary worker or his employer could be burdened with more taxation. The argument waxed and waned, and I found myself in public debates on television or the radio, debating the proposal with the proponents from the Ministry of Health. At around this time there was also a health sector review, and there was general consensus that something radical must be done to improve the delivery of health services within Uganda. As there had been a signal failure of delivery of basic services through the present system of budget support, the donors were at last wakening up, and there was a new willingness to look at different paradigms for funding and delivery of services.

The Ministry of Health planners invited the organisation Providing for Health (P4H), funded by the World Bank among others, to carry out a study on methods of healthcare financing. This group did a comprehensive study and advanced a number of different models for the financing and delivery of healthcare using several funds, including social health insurance. Surprisingly, the proposal, which gained acceptance, incorporated all the principles which I had been advocating, such as payment for delivery of service, separation of audit, payment and provision of service (the purchaser provider split), payment for primary healthcare through capitation schemes, and acceptance of the principles of transparency and international audit. At a meeting of the employers association where the proposals were discussed, I commented to the Commissioner working in the Ministry of Health, 'Do you realise that you are making proposals which basically put the Ministry of Health out of a job? What do your colleagues think of that?'

'It has been endorsed by the Ministry,' was his reply. Perhaps the combination of the failure of budget support and the poor delivery of services by government had finally registered.

When I first set foot in Uganda I was personally driven by the need to have a purposeful life. I had not been satisfied with my work as a GP in Northern Ireland and wished to use my professional skills where they were most needed. Thus began our journey which was summed up by the strap line of our organisation IMG: Making a difference to Healthcare in Uganda. When we lived in Luweero, carrying out community health and setting up Kiwoko Hospital, we were working at the coalface. We were at the cutting edge, where we saw the needs of the people in the raw and did what we could to meet them, often with limited resources. We were there as the AIDS epidemic unfolded; we witnessed the hopelessness and

400

experienced the gut wrenching despair of telling patients and close friends that they were going to die. We saw and experienced the devastation, destruction and hopelessness that resulted from Uganda's years of terrorism under Idi Amin and civil war under Milton Obote.

We had cried for ourselves, we had cried for those we lost, and in the midst of the hopelessness, we knew that our purpose was to bring new hope through what we were building. Now, over twenty years later, we had not only established a mission hospital but a private hospital and clinics that employed over seven hundred people, providing a livelihood for at least three thousand Ugandans. We had fifteen clinics throughout Uganda; a University, designed to improve standards in healthcare; a non profit foundation, with twelve projects providing charitable and community treatment; and we were embarking on a programme to make IHK a regional referral hospital.

Much of what we had done was not only in an effort to make our own system sustainable, but to develop a model and principles which could be used in the wider context of healthcare delivery. We had three bottom lines which drove us: we had to be viable and pay our way; we should have social impact, not just for a few wealthy Ugandans but for the society in which we worked; and we should have an advocacy role in the wider context of development and delivery of healthcare. We were now being taken seriously because of the work we had established and, as a result, I was invited to be part of a committee advising the President through an organisation known as the 'Presidential Investors Round Table.' This was a meeting which took place twice a year and where the President met with local and foreign investors to hear their suggestions as to how to improve the investment climate in Uganda. My role was to make proposals regarding the delivery of healthcare.

Sometimes, as I sat in those high-level meetings, I thought back to the time when I had come to Luweero and treated

401

patients under a tree, or when I had started the first private International Medical Centre and wondered if any patients would turn up. There were those who admired what we had done, but thought it was a one off and was not scalable. Every journey starts with the first step and we had been prepared to start right at the grass roots, but over the years we had developed a model for sustainable, accessible and scalable healthcare.

# Seasons

While Robbie and I were busy building up a medical organisation in Uganda, our family had grown and gone their separate ways in far flung corners of the world. Both my biological sons bore a striking resemblance to me, but Michael was so like me that he was a virtual clone. In Michael's case, he not only looked like me, he had similar mannerisms, gestures and even walked and stood like me. Michael was also the first of our children to come back to work in Africa, though not to Uganda.

Robbie and I had escaped between Christmas and the New Year to Zanzibar, with the operative word being escape, since if we stayed in Uganda my phone kept ringing. The coast was a favourite destination for us since Uganda was landlocked, and we missed the sound of the waves to which we had grown accustomed when we lived beside the sea in Ireland. While we were in Zanzibar we took lunch every day at a little beach restaurant run by a South African lady called Deena and got into conversation about how she had started her hotel in Zanzibar. She introduced us to her local partner, Issa, who had been a Rastafarian – dreadlocks and all – but decided to cut the dreads and go into business. I had never met a Moslem Rastafarian until I went to Zanzibar.

'Can one still buy property along the coast?' I asked Issa

'Sure, why not?' was Issa's laidback reply. 'I can organise for you to see some sites if you like.'

'What do you think Robbie?' I asked half jokingly. 'Would you like to get a piece of property on a tropical island?'

Normally, I am the one with the mad ideas; if we were a car, I would be the accelerator and she would be the brakes, but on this occasion she also had her foot on the accelerator and wanted to pursue the idea.

'I have some money put aside for my old age, and it is not doing so well on the stock market these days,' she volunteered. 'Maybe we should put it to good use.'

'Like buying a bit of an island?' I suggested.

So the next day we set off on a tour of the island, with Issa showing us round Zanzibar, made up of prehistoric coral, sand and scrub. He took us to several sites, and before the end of the day, we had agreed a deal to buy a piece of land on the east coast. The transaction took some months, with much bureaucracy to complete, but at the end we had purchased the lease on a one hundred and eighty metre stretch of coastline and had permission to build a small hotel.

We chose the name 'Seasons' since I believe that my life has been in seasons. There was the season when I was a GP in Ireland, followed by the season of working in Kiwoko, and those were very nearly my only seasons when life almost came to an end due to the cancer, but it continued into a whole new season for developing International Hospital and International Medical Group. Perhaps this new venture heralded another season where I would be able to spend more time with the family, more time prioritising, and perhaps not being so driven. And it might mean that I would finally get time to write the book I had always promised myself. To do so sitting on a tropical island would not be so onerous.

Every dream has to start somewhere, and, as I looked back, each of my seasons had started with small and difficult beginnings when I had to get out of my comfort zone, but they had been worth it. I didn't mind starting small again and building up from scratch.

The land we had purchased was covered with kasarina trees and little else, none of the beautiful tropical vegetation that can be seen in such resorts, and there was very sparse soil covering the long dead coral. We had purchased a piece of a tropical island, but unless we were going to sling our hammocks under the trees, there was a huge amount of work to do, and we did not have much in the way of spare cash. But I had never let such basic necessities stand in the way of a dream, and I was too old to change. I had a clever plan as to how to get things going, since I was still far too engaged in the field of healthcare in Uganda to spend much time in Zanzibar. At that time Michael was living in a caravan on a beach in southern Spain, working for an events management company, and I thought I would ask him to change beaches and come to supervise the project in Zanzibar. He came with his dog, and Michael adjusted to Zanzibari ways and loved the work he was doing.

Zanzibar has one of the oldest civilisations in Africa, with a fort which is four hundred years old and palaces dating from the time of the Sultans. It is packed with interesting history and architecture, but the way of life is slow, and modern civilisation appears to have passed Zanzibar by. As Michael embarked on the project, it was sometimes a struggle just to get an e-mail or a photocopy machine which was working. Petrol was not always available, and power was erratic, until someone accidentally severed the electricity cable from the mainland, and then there was no power at all. Zanzibar reminded me of Uganda twenty years earlier, yet it was a civilisation which had existed for hundreds of years.

We visited Michael regularly, and since he was driving a pick-up, there were times when there was no room for me in the front, and I had to ride on the back. He laughed at me, sitting in the back of a pick-up, because our roles had been reversed. As we drove around town, stopping here and there to buy tools and supplies for the project, I watched my son conducting his daily life, moving from shop to shop, haggling for the best prices and doing what I used to do. It was at that moment that I saw that my own love for Africa had been passed on to the next generation. I did not see my children all that much over the years since we were often in different countries, but when I did get the opportunity to stand back and observe, they were a tremendous source of satisfaction.

We met an American hotelier who had lived in Zanzibar for twenty years, and had run the renowned hotel Emerson and Green in Stonetown. Emerson had great ideas as to how we could develop the site, and we put together a plan which used local materials and depended on the Swahili, Arabic and Indian styles which were the hallmarks of Zanzibari design. We wished to be eco friendly and, since we were building on dead coral, we used coral itself for the walls, using the local method of building with *choka*, made by kilning the coral powder to form a traditional lime mix. It was slow drying, but dried out white, which, when used with the natural coral, made a beautiful textured finish. The island did not have much wood, except the kasarina trees which were used for scaffolding, but it had hundreds of thousands of coconut palm trees. Some of the older trees were being culled from the plantations, and we did not see any reason why we should not use this coconut wood. It was hard on the outside, while the inside was soft, so it had to be machined and managed properly, but it made good furniture, supports and beams. We also purchased solar panels and solar water heaters since there were few places on earth which got more sun.

While Michael was getting on with island life in Zanzibar, my oldest son, Sean, had married and settled in Bristol. Sean and Linzi were teachers and had spent several years in Lebanon, teaching Druze kids in the Shuf Mountains. This was a rewarding, though somewhat cold, experience, since their school was located high in the mountains. They then returned to Bristol, where Sean started a coffee shop and Linzi started a baby, so I became a grandfather, or to use the Ugandan word – a *Jjaja*. I had mixed feelings about this event since I was not yet adjusted to the role. The new grandmother travelled back for the arrival, but I thought that I would wait until the offspring was of an age when we could sit down, have a conversation, and do a bit of bonding.

Later Sean and Linzi also moved back to Uganda and I was able to do that bonding. But at first I had to admit that I was not wildly keen on the idea that I was now third generation and had become superfluous since the genealogy had been assured. Genetically, my use was over and the cycle of life would move on without me. There is a bible verse about living to see your children's children and there was a time in my life when I did not think I would see those children, but now that season had come.

It was also the World Cup season, played on the African continent for the first time. I had just made a short trip to Zanzibar to check on how the project was progressing and travelled back to Uganda on the day of the World Cup finals. Robbie was in England for the birth of our second granddaughter, so I went with some friends to a sports bar on the other side of town to see the match. It was a lack lustre affair, and I decided to drive home at half time. As I was nearing home, I noticed an unusual amount of activity round the Ethiopian Restaurant, but just thought it was part of World Cup fever. However, on reaching home I got a call from the operations manager of the hospital to say that a bomb had gone off at the same Ethiopian restaurant, and the casualties were being taken to International Hospital. I immediately went to the hospital, meanwhile calling in more doctors.

Emergencies often come in waves, and at first half a dozen casualties arrived, but then there was the next lot and the next, and if we had not been well prepared, the hospital would have been swamped. Moses, the general surgeon, had already arrived by the time I got there and was preparing to take two patients to theatre. I took charge of overall co-ordination and called in more doctors and heads of departments. Eventually, I had brought in four general surgeons, two neurosurgeons, one orthopaedic surgeon, the Director of Nursing Services, more theatre nurses and ICU nurses, the head of operations, more ambulance drivers and security personnel, the Director of Clinical Services, the whole radiology team and more medical officers, four anaesthetists and ICU physicians.

All the staff came in readily, and the team functioned well. After the first wave of casualties, we began to receive patients with serious head injuries from another location and realised that another bomb had gone off. Suicide bombers had detonated themselves at two locations: the Ethiopian Restaurant and a rugby ground where a big screen had been set up to watch the match. The bombs were packed with ball-bearings and designed to cause maximum death.

Over seventy people died that night, most of them young people. As we carried on our work, more casualties kept coming, and we had to separate those who were either dead, or past hope, from the living. One young American was brought in dead; he had signs of only one small puncture wound, but it was directly above the large vessels in his chest. Two other men were carried on tarpaulins, both covered in blood; one was dead while the other had a serious head injury. A young man and a young woman were carried in together, both with serious head injuries; the girl died within an hour, the man survived. She was just a young girl who had gone out with her friends to watch the match. We treated forty casualties, most of them seriously injured. Nine patients were taken to ICU, many of whom had serious head injuries. The CT scans showed they had fractured skulls, bleeding into the brain tissue and the ventricles of the brain, and swelling of the brain. There were also bits of shrapnel embedded in the brain matter. By the following day four people had died of their head injuries, three survived, while most of those who had penetrating abdominal wounds and broken bones were stable.

We had been able to respond to this national emergency because we had been building up our facilities and capacity at the hospital for years, and in the event, we were better co-ordinated and able to cope than the public hospital. When we carried out a debriefing several days later, I pointed out that if we did the routine things well and the systems worked, then we could cope with an emergency.

The attacks were the work of Al Shabaab, a Somalian Al Qaeda type group who were opposed to Uganda's role in supporting the African Union peacekeepers in Mogadishu. It was a sad day for Uganda. It was also a sad commentary on Africa, that while we celebrated the holding of the World Cup on African soil as a portent of hope for the continent, there were those who took the opportunity to wreak death and destruction. For my part it made it somewhat easier that we were able to be meaningfully involved in mitigating the effects of these bombs – it is easier to be engaged than to stand by.

Michael had met a beautiful Tanzanian girl called Maria, and they had a traditional marriage ceremony in Dar es Salaam, where Maria's family lived. Maria was now pregnant, and one reason I had travelled to Zanzibar was to make arrangements for the birth of their baby. We decided it was safest for her to come back to Uganda to deliver at International Hospital, and the week after the bomb I got a call from Michael to tell me she had passed a 'show' which indicated that she would soon deliver. Within days of arrival, Maria went into labour and delivered a healthy baby girl at IHK. This was definitely a VIP delivery, since two obstetricians, a paediatrician and two midwives were present – I suppose in deference to the fact that this was the grandchild of the boss. As I reflected on what had taken place at the hospital during the past few weeks, it was easy to see why we were there; we were doing what any hospital does, dealing with life and death. In the bombs which had rained death on Kampala, we were able to save some, but we also lost some. But as lives were lost, new life was also being born. This time there was a difference because the new life was my own granddaughter, being born at the hospital which I had founded.

As I look back over the past twenty-three years of living in Africa, I would not claim to be an African, though I am a Ugandan citizen. I am still an Irishman in Africa, and I brought my background and Irish cultural heritage with me. But I have learned much about Ugandan culture and been accepted by Ugandans in a way that I could never have expected. Now, when I jog round the roads and dirt tracks of Kampala, the children still call '*Mzungu Mzungu*', but some of them call 'Ianee' while others chant 'Docta Ian, Docta Ian.' The truth is that I am more at home in this green and fertile land on the equator than I could be in the other green island in the northern hemisphere. There are many expert opinions aired about Africa, development, and the problems of Africa. I have aired many opinions myself; I have never been reticent to say what I think, but that has been the amazing thing about living in Uganda: people have allowed me to say what I think. They have not expected me to be politically correct, they have not rejected me because of the colour of my skin; quite the contrary, they have accepted me for who I am. I sometimes feel that I am more at home in Uganda than Ireland, though I do the splits, standing astride the culture of Uganda and my own roots. Perhaps this is what gives me a unique view of my adopted homeland.

I started this book by saying that I am no longer a missionary, I am not an aid worker and I don't work for the diplomatic community, I am just a private citizen. Much of the reason for putting this book on record is the hope that people will open their minds to a different perception and paradigm of Africa. The other reason is so that we will not forget because so much of the culture of Africa is oral and is already being lost.

In terms of development, there are many vested interests in the status quo, therefore much aid continues to feed the system in ways which are ineffective, distort the economy, and prop up the system of lack of accountability and corruption. Africa is not all about poverty and certainly not about despair; there is a zest for life, and there is hope, and a large part of our purpose here has been to be facilitators of that hope.

Living in Uganda has been like watching a movie in 3D: the place is alive and vibrant. Yes, there is much that I can take issue with, but only because I see the unrealised potential and how good this country could be if we were getting things right. I am a doctor and an entrepreneur, and Uganda has given me unique opportunities for development. I hope that this book has been a window into understanding life in Uganda. In some ways my life here is not all that different from someone living in a developed country: I get up in the mornings and go to work, I struggle with everyday things, and I still worry about paying the bills. There is no magic in it; I am earning a living like everyone else. Perhaps the surprise was that I found that as an individual I could also make a difference. I did not need to be part of an aid agency; I didn't need to be part of the U.N.; I did not have to be part of some government's foreign affairs programme; I just had to make some commonsense decisions and do what I thought was right.

But I wonder why commonsense is so rarely applied to Africa? Why do people lose the power of reasoning when it comes to African development, the use of our resources and aid? Why do we apply completely different standards and paradigms when it comes to Africa? I don't believe that there is a single answer to poverty or the development of countries such as Uganda. I do believe that the private sector is the way forwards and that too many governments and aid agencies ignore this. Until we are prepared to change, until we are prepared to look at different options, particularly in the private

411

sector, aid will continue to be part of the problem and not part
of the solution.

# Glossary

**Kiwoko Hospital**  The mission hospital established in Luweero in 1991.

**IMG**  International Medical Group, the umbrella organisation for the hospital, clinics and HMO.

**IHK**  International Hospital Kampala, a one hundred bed hospital, first phase established 2005.

**IMCs**  International Medical Centres, first clinic established in Kampala 1995, followed by other clinics in Kampala and upcountry.

**IAA**  International Air Ambulance, sometimes involved in air ambulance evacuation, but somewhat of a misnomer since its core business is as an HMO providing prepaid medical schemes, with the service provision being from IMCs and IHK.

**IMG Construction**  A division of IMG which built the hospital and clinics for the group.

**IHSU**  International Health Science University, first registered by the Uganda National Higher Education Council as a University in 2008 with 600 students by 2010.

**IMF**  International Medical Foundation, a registered NGO carrying out the charitable, community and research activities of IMG.

**Suubi Trust** The registered UK charity supporting the work of International Medical Foundation.